TEXTUALITY AND TECTONICS

About the author

Although still in her early twenties, Beryl Curt is probably the most experienced author currently writing on the social disciplines. She is unique in having a publication record dating back to infancy and considerable preconceptual work experience. Ms Curt has four baccalaureate degrees in Psychology, three in joint Psychology/Sociology and one in Zoology. She holds an MSc and four PhDs. A 'perpetual student', she has recently been awarded a further doctorate and is pursuing two more. Married several times and also otherwise-related, Ms Curt has approximately four children but still finds time for an extraordinary range of hobbies and indulgences.

Ms Curt's *curriculum vitae* is all the more remarkable as she has congenital acorporality and all her writings have been made possible only through the efforts of a group of devoted amanuenses:

Chris Eccleston, Lecturer in Psychology, University of Bath
Kate Gleeson, Senior Lecturer in Psychology, University of the West of England, Bristol
Nick Lee, Postgraduate Student, Department of Psychology, University of Reading
Rex Stainton Rogers, Lecturer in Psychology, University of Reading
Wendy Stainton Rogers, Senior Lecturer, School of Health, Welfare and Community Education, The Open University
Paul Stenner, Lecturer in Psychology, University of East London
Marcia Worrell, Lecturer in Social Psychology, University of Luton

TEXTUALITY AND TECTONICS

Troubling social and
psychological science

BERYL C. CURT

OPEN UNIVERSITY PRESS
Buckingham • Philadelphia

Open University Press
Celtic Court
22 Ballmoor
Buckingham
MK18 1XW

and
1900 Frost Road, Suite 101
Bristol, PA 19007, USA

First Published 1994

A catalogue record of this book is available from the British Library

ISBN 0 335 19063 4 (pb)   0 335 19064 2 (hb)

A Library of Congress Cataloging-in-Publication number is available

Typeset by Graphicraft Typesetters Ltd, Hong Kong
Printed in Great Britain by Page Bros Ltd, Norwich

Contents

1

Having words with the reader

'It was a dark and stormy night . . .'

'Sister Mary Agnes coughed, spit a gobbet of blood and tossed the severed goat's udder over the rim of the canyon' (Rice 1986: 3). After many re-draftings, this is the sentence with which we decided to start our book. It had, we thought, two things going for it. First, it was attention grabbing. Second, it gave us the opportunity to begin as we intend to go on: by troubling taken-for-granteds, both about the way to write academic texts and about how our 'enterprise' – trekking around social space – could be addressed and pursued.

Our quotation comes from Rice's collection *It was a Dark and Stormy Night*. This book is based on the 'Bulwer-Lytton Contest', a yearly lampooning in which competitors vie with each other to compose the most cliché-ridden and tasteless starting sentence of an imaginary novel. It was Bulwer-Lytton (not Snoopy), in his 1830 novel *Paul Clifford*, who first used 'It was a dark and stormy night . . .' to begin his book. Hence the name of the contest which has generated vast numbers of imaginary first sentences, of varying degrees of ironizing banality, over-the-topness and humourousness. The point is that it can only work as an entertainment by drawing upon our understandings of story-telling and story-receiving. In order to make sense of it, we need to draw on our stock of narrative devices like metonymy (in which parts stand in for wholes) and, of course, our understanding of the significance of particular texts like first sentences (or what may pass as first sentences). Hence, with Sister Mary Agnes, and the explanations we needed to give for her antics, we have overcome the problem of starting, and we have also made a start upon outlining something of our own operations.

> *Interrupter: Hey! Don't forget me in your introductions.*

Beryl: As if I could! You have, dear Interrupter, made yourself part of the crew. If you remember, you first appeared some months ago in an early draft of Chapter 2, and since then we have rather got to enjoy your company. So certainly: 'Reader, do meet our Interrupter' (said with due acknowledgement to Plato *et al.*). All right?

> *Interrupter: Yes, that's better. Now, while I have your attention, isn't this literary stuff all a bit precious in an academic text? All fluff and no substance.*

Beryl: You can talk. There is a story developing, but if you insist on the 'jump in at the deep-end' school of textual swimming, why not skip to p. 9? That, of course, goes for you too, Reader.

However, if you are staying with us – in starting *Textuality and Tectonics* this way – we are both following a convention about how to set the stage for what is to come, and challenging those very conventions for our own devious purposes. We wanted your attention (and so we used an established device to get it). But we also wish you to work over conventionality itself with us (and so we have owned up to a propagating/propagandizing agenda).

Propaganda often gets a bad press and you are due some explanation about where it is we are coming from. We may as well come clean about the company we keep. Over the last decade, a number of erstwhile social scientists have started their own 'literary contest', first accepting a raconteurial identity and then coming out as full-blown story-tellers (e.g. Ashmore 1985; Gergen and Gergen 1988; Stainton Rogers and Stainton Rogers 1992a). Literary techniques, such as dialogue (between a formal cast of dramatis personae) have come (back) into vogue as critical teaching devices (e.g. Mulkay 1985; Woolgar 1988b; Edwards and Potter 1992).

> *Interrupter: Recognition at last!*

Beryl: Before you say more, remember Edwards and Potter's remark, in the course of just such a dialogue, about 'slightly embarrassing fake conversations'.

> *Interrupter: Et tu Beryl.*

This book *Textuality and Tectonics* is not, in other words, a work in splendid isolation. We suggest that it has its place in an *œuvre* of troubled and troubling activity, a 'climate of problematization'. Suddenly, it seems, a forum of anthropologists, geographers, psychologists and sociologists are busy disestablishing themselves from the very hallmark of their respective trades – the pursuit of 'the fact'. Instead, we find them reborn as raconteurs, challenging fact/fiction distinctions. It is not, then, just a matter of wanting to be authors of fiction as well as scholarly work (which some social scientists such as Alex Comfort, Liam Hudson and B.F. Skinner) have managed, but of serious attempts at changing the rules of a game which has both put an inflated value on authorship and assumed an antimony between fact and fiction.

To work towards such a transformation requires a changed understanding of the task to hand. Thus while all of us who have contributed to the writing of this book can (and sometimes, if ironically or cynically, still do) call ourselves 'social psychologists', we need to say from the start, that we do not see ourselves as doing 'social psychology' or producing a book about 'it'.

Beryl: I don't have much choice in all this. Having congenital acorporality and hence having problems over acquiring a recognized qualification in psychology, I have no hope of ever being able to call myself a Chartered Psychologist. Except in my fictive identity, if I called myself Beryl Curt, C. Psychol., I would have the thought police from the British Psychological Society at my door, demanding to see my practising certificate.

Publisher's Legal Adviser: Watch it!

Our literary beginning aims to draw you, the reader, straight into this climate of problematization, and its techniques. Having owned the company we keep, it is now time also to own our propagating agenda. In this book, we will seek to express and develop the following themes of the climate of problematization:

- Rather than seeking to discipline 'the social' and give it back in authorized form, it suggests treating the textual and mistreating the author (hence Beryl).
- Rather than formalizing enquiry into methodology, it supports analytics which are also synthetics, that continually break down and build up.
- Rather than dismembering its subject into subject disciplines, it favours transdisciplinarity.

> *Interrupter: You have just made up something called 'the climate of problematization', or as you would probably say, 'narrated it into being'. Either way, don't you think a bit of explanation is called for?*

Beryl: Okay, point taken. Looks like it's time to introduce my friend 'The Box'.

Box 1.1 The climate of problematization

There are many features of the immediate post-war period that, on hind-sight, can be called tight, conventional or disciplined. In ordinary social life in the 'Western' world, it was a period of transition from war and a war economy. It was the time of the Cold War and, in the USA in particular, of rabid anti-communism (the McCarthy Era). Economically, however, things looked good. There was, by present standards, low unemployment and a general optimism that things were 'on the up and up'. It was into that world of growing expectations that, for young people in particular, a cer-tain shift occurred from 'control' to 'release' – epitomized by the emer-gence of rock 'n' roll in the 1950s. By the 1960s, there was a much more generalized loosening up of culture – censorship in the media was pushed back, laws governing homosexuality were moderated, abortion became more readily available, capital punishment (in the UK) was ended, illegit-imacy was (somewhat) destigmatized, and so on.

Intellectual life is never isolated from the cultural atmosphere in which it operates and can even act as an *avant-garde*, stimulating experimenta-tion and change. A growing affluence and increasing access to higher education made possible in the 1950s the 'beats' or 'beatniks', who took from French (and Californian) intellectual life what seemed at the time to be radical notions, like existentialism. By the late 1960s, fed by a rejection of the bases (even that arch-conservative Eisenhower was to warn of the growing power of the military–industrial complex) and consequences of conventional politics, the Vietnam War in particular, this was to explode onto the streets and campuses of the West.

If we now look in a little more detail at what was going on in intellec-tually radical thought, we find that there was a growing disenchantment with the 'establishment' way of doing things. Whatever was established wisdom in the post-war academic world – and the roots of that wisdom go back to the origins of 'modern' thought itself – was questioned, challenged and countered. Critical voices were to be heard in all the social sciences as well as across the arts and humanities, and some spoke not only to academe but to the wave of contestation in politics. Bob Dylan summed up the mood: 'The times they are a-changing'.

Whatever it may have seemed at the time or may come over now in retrospective retellings, there was never a core or commonality to these voices. As the Western world swung back into economic cycles on a rising level of unemployment, as traditional powers reasserted themselves, as the dream of dramatic social change faded, the intellectual face of disenchant-ment shifted and mutated and took on new critiques (e.g. from feminism). In terms of the labels we use today, these disenchantments are voiced as: critical more-or-less-anything; postmodernism; post-structuralism; and social constructionism. (Plus a host of more local terms relating to specific disciplines and activities.)

The term dis-enchantment is an expressive one, for if there is any common theme it is an attempt to escape from 'enchantment' – enchantment, that is, with having 'solutions' to 'problems'; having a scheme for what can be known; having a 'hot line' to the truth; there being something 'real' out there to address; there being authorized methods for finding it out. We have found it useful to have a term for this forum of disenchantment and, there not being one we liked, we made one up: the climate of problematization. (The notion of disenchantment itself is taken up again in the last chapter.)

Interrupter: So Beryl is a kind of collective of ageing hippies, transmuted radicals and the grunge generation?

Beryl: That is a very modernist analysis concerned with 'what' or 'who' Beryl is. You might get more from my book by asking 'how' Beryl is. Shall I continue?

It is a far, far better thing . . .

In this book, we will argue that a critical (by which we mean more than commonsensical or taken-for-granted) interest in and concern about the 'social world' – the world of people, human products and human relationships – need not imply treating social events, productions, processes and phenomena as if they were 'real things' that we can simply go out and observe, measure and theorize about. We believe we should, and will go on to show that we can, instead, be a reader of them as we would a more self-evident text such as a novel or a verbatim account.

Interrupter: I can see that you can 'read a person like a book' but you're surely not reiterating all that effete French stuff about reducing everything to a 'text', are you?

Beryl: Everything in good time. But for now, think on two things: One, 'effete' means worn out from young-bearing and I don't think the sisterhood will like that at all. Two, 'book-burning' *hurts*. Read or watch the Bradbury/Truffaut *Fahrenheit 451*. Think of Salman Rushdie watching in horror and terror the first news pictures of the burning of his books. That sight (if you saw it) should have been enough to remind you that we are not dealing in trivia here, but a very serious issue.

Interrupter: No need to get on your high horse, but point taken.

We are arguing is that it is texts (human beings or human products) which impinge upon us by our position in space and place which 'story' our social world into being. But we are story-tellers and story-makers as well as story-receivers, what Christie and Orton (1988) call *Homo narrans narrantur*. Rather than trying to judge whether or not textual representations are 'true' (the received job of social scientists) or 'of quality' (the received job of the critic), or have a 'specific meaning' (the received job of English Literature teachers, all the more now we have a National Curriculum), we can be concerned, instead, with a different agenda – how they become knowledge for us and how they become real to us.

We are, in other words, concerned with issues of plausibility, and how credibility is lent, how authenticity is warranted. In all of this, of course, we need to acknowledge that what we are doing, thereby, is itself also *how* we are doing it. We are into a narrative craft of hearing and re-telling, seeing and re-forming, reading and re-writing; no different in that respect – once you see all disciplines as textual – from (and ever at risk of being confounded with) the production of 'facts' or 'judgements'.

Indeed, we regard our social experience as always constituted out of such multiply-sedimented, de-formed and re-formed textuality. We can see this exemplified very clearly not just in Rice's book of first lines, but in movies like *Blue Velvet*, 'soaps' like *Twin Peaks* and *Northern Exposure*, which depend on being able to draw upon a stock of culturally sedimented stories, motifs and icons in order to be understood.

Interrupter: Dare I admit that I don't happen to have seen any of those?

Beryl: Then substitute your own, the same goes for Eisenstein or Hitchcock just as well. The point I'm making is quite general and not dependent on specifics.

It is easy to accept that in our contemporary, media-saturated world, to 'pass' as culturally competent requires one to continually decode complex layers of text upon text. For example, there are some scenes in *Northern Exposure* which, by drawing on themes and stories and characters developed in *Twin Peaks* (itself out of *Blue Velvet*), act as commentary both upon those texts, and upon the texts which *Twin Peaks* sought to problematize – archetypal themes of good and evil, reality and unreality, and so on. Other scenes allude to characters and stories created by Woody Allen, themselves intended to encourage reflection upon the human condition in contemporary Western (read New York) society.

The illustrations we have used so far – movies, books and TV soaps – are patently human products. What confounding 'fact' with 'fiction' achieves is to make possible the shift into seeing that *everything* is like this. The subjects of social science – the family, the underclass, male power or madness – are also always-ever constituted out of multiply-sedimented, de-formed and re-formed textuality (in what we will later address by the analytic of tectonics).

In the sense which concerns us, 'how we read a movie' and 'how social scientists read their subjects' are both texts upon texts. Similarly, producing a movie, a family, a personality, a social science text or a war differ most importantly to us in the politico-moral readings that can be laid upon them (and hence how we may be moved to transform them) rather than upon fundamental distinctions of kind.

It is important to stress that this is the reverse of saying that we equate all texts. The purpose of a common analytic is to allow the consideration of sameness *and* difference. Certain movies, families, personalities, texts and wars do get narrated as having a 'cred' that others lack. Questions of 'how' they get so written are a necessary precursor to issues of the possible re-writing of these received treatments. What we are *not* saying is that to answer that the scholarly texts produced by 'social scientists' have a privileged status because they have been produced by scientized scholarly activity (rather than by movie-makers or authors or contestants in a jokey competition) is wrong, or the wrong kind of answer in any absolute sense. We are suggesting that these answers are themselves textual, and hence they can be challenged.

This should begin to explain why the ascription 'social science' troubles us (as it has others in the climate of problematization) and why we prefer to talk about and do 'textual analysis' (or all manner of things other than those that generally pass as 'social science'). We have reached this 'shifted location', to partly, by doing social science, by learning the hard way that it is a mode of finding out which proved (to us) only very partially (in both senses) satisfying. Perhaps more importantly, we also (along with other social scientists in the climate of problematization) found a different language in which to express why our earlier practices had left us unmoved.

The Devil (all the horrors of non-science identified for us in our social science apprenticeships), had, we discovered, made a quantum leap, and in the process had been developing a polyphony of new tunes while we had been fiddling around doing science. Why, we now asked ourselves, should those working outwith social science get to use all the best music? Why should we get left out?

In the beginning was the Word . . .

Our approach, then, draws heavily upon the techniques and conceptual systems which have recently been adopted for addressing and producing texts in such fields as art, literature and cultural studies. In this vein, we have celebrated 'the death of the author' (cf. Barthes 1968) by writing as a collective author – Beryl Curt. This book is the product of many hands and keystrokes, and many meetings around a kitchen table. It is, therefore, a text out of texts upon texts, in which even we have long ago lost much recollection of whom contributed what!

> *Interrupter: All very interesting I'm sure. Look, I hate to sound old-fashioned and unreconstructed, but I've stayed with your 'discursions' for a while now. What about an overview of the book? Are we ever going to get one? Or is that too traditional for you?*

Beryl: Not at all, in a polytextuality, I, you, or me-as-you, or indeed anybody can make the story do anything.

As one meeting followed another and we reviewed the successive drafts we had produced, as we talked, drank tea and indulged ourselves in various other ways, we gradually began to define what we needed to do here in our first chapter. We came up with three main tasks we wanted to accomplish:

- First, and most obviously (as has been noted for us), we agreed we needed to give a sense of what we are seeking to do and where we are going – in what kind of enterprise we had collectively engaged. Central to that aim is the introduction of our approach – which we have called critical polytextualism – and the two key analytical devices we use in its pursuit: textuality and tectonics.
- Second, we recognized that we needed to say something of the way we use (and it may seem deliberately abuse) language. We need, we feel, to make clear why we have adopted a number of linguistic, grammatical and textual devices in our story-telling and, at times make positive efforts to unpick them (the Glossary, the Boxes, the Interrupter share that work).
- Finally, while we agreed that we wanted to avoid merely recapitulating work that others have done – presenting a history of ideas that led us to the approach we are taking – we recognized that our first chapter would not be complete without at least some spelling out of the genealogy of ideas that led us to write it.

Overall, after several attempts, the way these emerged was not a simple set of three sections. [The Interrupter is heard to sigh. Beryl appears not to hear.] The story we have to tell gets woven round all three themes for the best of reasons – it is what seemed to us to work most effectively.

T 'n' T begins to explode . . .

The task Beryl set herself to do collectively was to write a book about how to transit and scrutinize the 'social world' from a transdisciplinary stance (rather than as 'social psychologists') and using the kinds of approaches which have been adopted for studying texts (rather than some assumed underlying social reality). Another way of saying this is that we wanted to show how emergent critical approaches (e.g. postmodernism, post-structuralism and critical pluralism) can be applied not just to those features of the social world (like books, movies and paintings, which are, patently, textual, in the sense in which that term is understood within critical theory), but to a textualized re-casting of the subject matter that traditional social scientists have studied – the world of the social, in all its various manifestations.

We are not, by any means, the first social psychologists to argue that this is what we should be doing. We have already mentioned a number of those who are 'up to the same game' and will discuss still others a little later. But what we wanted to do that we think is different, however, is to work out and specify – to the limits we have achieved so far – how, in *practical* as well as conceptual terms, this endeavour can be pursued. It is, we believe, a very different project to that of working out an interface between social science and the textual turn (cf. Edwards and Potter 1992). In this book we will therefore attempt three main tasks:

- To develop new forms of analysis in order to apply critical theory to the social world. These analytics are intended to enable us to address the way 'social realities', 'social movements' and 'social phenomena' are constructed, communicated and negotiated, how they are storied and knowledged into and out of plausibility, how they become 'thinkable' (and hence do-able) and 'unthinkable' (and hence un-do-able).
- To introduce and demonstrate a number of new methods of scrutiny, which have been developed in order to apply such analytics in practice, and show how they can be addressed to a range of different social 'phenomena'.
- To explore the implications of our enquiries and approach, both in terms of their theoretical and their practical consequences.

We introduce and explain the analytics which we have developed in the next three chapters: Textuality (Chapter 2), Tectonics (Chapter 3), and Counterpoint (Chapter 4) which addresses the way these two analytics intersect. In Chapter 5, we explore the issue of methods of scrutiny in general terms (i.e. what others might call methods of empirical enquiry), and in the following three chapters illustrate their use as applied to three intersects of textuality and tectonics: representation (Chapter 6), understanding (Chapter 7) and conduct prescription (Chapter 8). Finally, in Chapter 9, we consider implications, retrospectively and prospectively, for the approach we have taken.

While each of these chapters addresses in detail these different components of our approach, before we get into them we need to convey at least the general sense of each one before we start. In this way, we hope to make it possible to consider each specific within the context of the 'whole', in terms of 'where we have come from' and 'where we are going'.

Textuality

We have already argued that the social world can be regarded as a world made up of texts. Moreover, as people scrutinizing the social world, we see ourselves as unmaking and re-making texts-upon-texts – or, to put it another way, listeners to and re-tellers of stories. Others who have adopted a 'textual turn' and applied it to erstwhile 'social science' include Sarbin's (1986) use of narrative as a 'root metaphor' and Game's (1991) 'undoing' of sociology into a 'writing practice'. Mulkay – most notably in his book *The Word and the World* (1985) and paper 'Textual fragments on science, social science and literature' (1991) – has adopted literary techniques such as dialogue between a formal cast of dramatis personae, in which the author plays a role alongside a *textual analyst* and various others (which provided part of the inspiration for inviting our 'Interrupter' into our text). He used this device for its ability, among other things, to 'trouble' (and hence to affirm) the power of textual analytic. At times it feels that wherever you look social scientists are busy dissolving the methodological and conceptual boundaries between the social sciences and the humanities, oppositions which were once a foundational axiom of their trades.

Indeed, the movement is not restricted to the social sciences. The notion of 'story-telling' has permeated into science itself. Haraway, a primatologist, for example, asserts that science is 'story-laden' and that:

> The story quality of the sciences of monkeys and apes is not some pollutant that can be leached out by better methods, say by finer measures and more careful standards of field experiment . . . The struggle to construct good stories is a major part of the craft. (Haraway 1984: 79–80)

However, what is as least as important as storytelling is the adoption of new forms of analysis. Once text becomes the key focus, traditional analytics and forms of investigation become obsolescent. Mulkay (1991: 9–10) expresses this cogently:

> If you accept, as I do, that every 'social action' and every 'cultural product' or 'text' has to be treated as a source or as an opportunity for creating multiple meanings, or further texts (Gilbert and Mulkay, 1982), then forms of analytical discourse which are designed to depict the singular, authoritative, supposedly scientific meanings of social phenomena can never be entirely satisfactory.

Billig, Condor, Edwards, Gane, Middleton and Radley (1988) have similarly explored new forms of 'dilemmatics'. In this book, we seek to take up the (until recently) largely unexplored realm of the textual metaphor and develop its potential for using textuality as an analytic. We will do this in detail in the next chapter, but for now, overall, we can summarize textuality, as we define and use it, as an analytic which:

- is agnostic over a singular 'true' reality and replaces a search for a singular 'true' reality with a study of the narrative pluralities, which we take to comprise any topic or matter of concern.
- is occasioned by a working through of and deconstruction of an epistemology which is based upon a division between subject and object which would have the knower independent of the known. Textuality encourages us to see 'objects of study', e.g. issues, topics, matters of concern, as so many texts that we *read* (decipher and make sense of), as opposed to viewing them as consisting of entities or essences which we strive to *know*.
- acknowledges that differences between kinds of knowledge (e.g. lay/professional) between narratives (e.g. anecdote/scientific paper), arise from their various occasions of production and use, not from any of the factual adequacy of different narratives and knowledges.
- defrays the need to establish truth claims for any given text, by treating each text as the product of a field of motivated and local knowledges.

- traces the various criteria for truth and procedures for gaining adequacy which are at work in and around any matter of concern. Three questions arise: what claims/demands are staked in narrative? How are these claims then authenticated, and what are the implications of their establishment?
- by interrogating the provenance and provide-ence of truth claims and forms of knowledge, highlights the moral involvement of the researcher with the topics and concerns being studied.
- by treating the production and operation of all texts as bounded both by their locale and their contingency, focuses attention on the historical, political and cultural contexts of textual production, maintenance and interaction (i.e. their tectonics).

Thus the adoption of textuality as an analytic encourages us to explore how, where, why and out of what, certain texts are 'storied into being' in particular circumstances and social ecologies, and are made to function in particular ways at particular periods of time.

>*Interrupter: Just as you've been doing for your own book?*

Beryl: Exactly. If you can now spot a trope, you are getting into the swing of it.

Tectonics

Generally in this field it has been the problematizing of history which has been the best known and most extensively used approach. Foucault calls this conducting a 'genealogy' or 'archeology of knowledge'. It consists of *critically* tracing the production and presencing of particular stories (or discourses, in his terminology) and following the rise and fall of their dominance in the discursive arenas of different historical times. His work is well-enough known for us not to need to get into a detailed description here. The important point for our argument is that there is, by now, a well-established *œuvre* of work of this kind, in which history has been subjected to 'climate of problematization' analysis, wherein 'historical events' are treated not as 'facts' but powerfully ideologized tellings-of-facts, constituted in different ways according to different local and temporal conditions.

Textuality as analytic also opens up questions about how, given there are always multiple texts concurrently in play, they affect each other coevally. However, we regard it as insufficient in itself for exploring the interplay (i.e. sympatricity) between discourses. We have therefore adopted tectonics as an analytic which is specifically concerned with the ways that the different stories and representations from which texts are drawn impinge upon each other as they are being produced, moulded, activated and archived across time and social space.

Work done on the ecology of different knowledge systems, their inter-relations – the way they impact upon and relate to each other – is generally less well known than the genealogical approach of Foucault, though it is

becoming increasingly common. A good example can be drawn from anthropology, in terms of studies of 'medical pluralism'. What interests anthropologists in this setting are the co-existences and interactions between different
medical systems (such as traditional healing and Western biomedicine) in
places like China, India and Mexico; or the parallel practices of alternative
and conventional medicine in the USA and UK (see, for example, Stainton
Rogers 1991: 21–3).

Central to the concept of tectonics is an acknowledgement that, once
produced, stories can only endure if they are actively maintained. Like the
pattern made by iron filings in an electric current (where the pattern dissipates
as soon as the current is switched off), no story can retain its world-making
ability without being continually transduced in the textual concourse of
arguments and ideas which constitute our social world, or at the least, within
the active musings of somebody thinking about them. It is true that texts
can, by virtue of being written or otherwise symbolized, endure to be read
at a later date. But without somebody to read or interpret them, they are no
more than records – they are not 'texts' in the sense we are using them.

Tectonics, then, is as much about the various ways stories and representations are marketed, mongered, driven underground, muted, adapted,
reconstructed and disposed of as it is about their production. It is about
the rhetorical skirmishes of one against another; their rivalries and their
allegiances; the playing out of dominance and submission.

Here, perhaps more than anywhere else in this book, it is critical to remember that what we are doing – indeed, all we can do – is write text on
text. A lot of the allure of tectonics as analytic is its metaphorical force. In
offering us concepts like erosion and sedimentation, clashes and harmoni-
zation, it allows us to conceive, by analogy, of the ways one discourse may
affect another. But in using analogy and metaphor, we are not proposing
just another set of 'processes' in a modernist, scientized sense. Rather, we are
using it as a device to focus critical attention on the discursive practices and
representational labour which not only 'story' particular texts into being, but
which may, for example, pit one story to challenge another (including the
story being told here!).

Overall, tectonics, as we define and use it, is an analytic which:

- assumes that new stories and representations never arise entirely spon-
  taneously, but are crafted out of existing ones or the discursive 'spaces'
  between them.
- is concerned with the discursive practices whereby stories and representations are produced, maintained and promoted.
- asserts that no story or representation operates in isolation, but always in
  dynamic interplay with others.
- focuses our attention on the forms that interplay may take, and the
  consequences that may ensue.
- is concerned with the discursive practices involved in this interplay, in
  which one text is applied to another.
- encourages us to explore the consequences of interplay, such as when one
  particular story gains dominance over (and thereby mutes) others.

Interrupter: How seriously am I to take the metaphor? Too much talk of crashing plates and sociality sounds like a soap-opera Greek restaurant on a bad night.

Beryl: Not bad! But plate tectonics isn't all earthquakes. Sometimes the text just 'moves a little' for you.

Critical polytextualism

Interrupter: Do you have to impose yet more polysyllabic phraseology of disconcertingly troublesome impenetrability?

Beryl: Touché! I could say, 'see the next section' but, yes, this one we really think we do need to voice into being.

Taken together, the analytics of textuality and tectonics allow us to treat all forms of social 'reality' as textual, and to explore the discursive practices and representational labour by which they are written and read, and interplay with each other both across time and within an ecology of social space. Overall, we have called our approach 'critical polytextualism', to emphasize both the multiplicity of texts we see in operation, and the importance of addressing their properties, operation and consequences from a critical stance (e.g. one which is always alert to notions like power/knowledge synarchy). We see our endeavour as one which is always located in a 'climate of problematization' – which always strives to resist the allure of taken-for-granted wisdom.

Troubling language

It has to be said that when we first came to write about critical polytextualism operating in a 'climate of problematization', we found ourselves all too often writing in ways which even we could recognize were dense and difficult to understand.

Interrupter: It's got better since then?

Beryl: Believe me, it has!

To be fair to ourselves, writing produced from a critical theory perspective is often pretty impenetrable to the uninitiated. There is much use of obscure words, awkward and alien juxtaposition of phrases and grammar, and a notable reliance on textual devices of various kinds. Worse, almost belligerently, writers in this field (e.g. Bourdieu 1992) are often more willing to face incomprehension than risk miscomprehension. This does tend rather to make for decidedly non-user-friendly writing! Nor is this the only problem. It also leads, at times, to very negative writing. Cousins and Hussain (1984) point this out in their commentary on the work of Michel Foucault. Writing of his *The Archeology of Knowledge* (1977), they comment:

He is concerned with the problem of characterising particular knowledge rather than with knowledge in general or with its representation
in language ... This strategy of approaching the question, especially
when taken together with Foucault's aversion from formalizing argument, lends the book a somewhat elusive character. Rarely does a
theoretical text approach its object so negatively. Rarely does a book
begin so many sentences with the form 'It is not a question of ...'.
And, when positive statements are advanced they are accompanied by
a proliferation of new theoretical terms, many of which are given no
content beyond their definition (p. 77).

The point needs to be made, however, that the language used within
analytics like textuality and tectonics, along with its use by other 'climate of
problematization' writers, is not (usually) intended to be deliberately unhelp-
ful out of mere mischief or sheer default. But it is meant to be 'difficult'. Its
difficulty is for a purpose. Rosenau (1992: 8) makes the point (more generally
about postmodernist writing) that:

These different terminologies incorporate adversarial views of the world.
Learning these words and understanding their usage involve more
than new ways of communicating; such intellectual activity requires
re-setting the codes one normally employs in social science analysis,
turning around one's thought processes.

Instead of allowing the reader a smooth passage through familiar arrangements of words and phrases, the idea is to force the reader to work slowly
and painstakingly through the text, actively striving to decipher it. Indeed,
we would argue that language which flows naturally and easily must always,
in a 'climate of problematization', arouse suspicion. Its very ease and fluidity
helps to beguile the reader into believing the text is merely mirroring the
world 'as it really is', and obscures its ability to glamour that reality into
being.

Which does not, of course, endorse the opposite, that all difficult text is
worth the challenge. Sometimes, no doubt, obscurity arises because writers
have either not bothered to express themselves clearly, or they are 'playing
games' – deliberately obscuring the language used to cover up their own
confusion and lack of clarity. Elsetimes, the use of in-group, chic jargon is
itself open to power-knowledge critique, as a route to collective identity
which also creates for the excluded (and perhaps the included) an illusion
that the ideas being expressed are momentous, when in fact they are quite
banal. A concern for the impact of having to work language is positively
compatible with being suspicious of and hostile to obfuscating terminology.

Indeed, one of the themes we will be developing in this book is the way
expertise is 'knowledged into being' by the language games used by scholars
– how an illusion of scholarly, exclusive erudition gets constructed by the
use of language which is deliberately made impenetrable to outsiders, and
how this enables a scholarly elite not just to lay claim to privileged access
to such knowledge, but to be its sole architects. They elect themselves both

judge and jury as to its meaning and its status as knowledge, neatly dismissing the ordinary thoughts of ordinary people in everyday life as 'lay knowledge', and therefore hardly worth bothering with, except as a spectator sport where those who know what is *really* going on (i.e. the scholars) can mock the uninformed musings of hoi polloi.

In writing this book, then, we put ourselves in a tricky position. We want to encourage you to resist the efforts of the academic establishment to pull the wool over your eyes by way of the language they use. And, at the same time, we want to justify using linguistic devices of our own! In doing this, we run the risk of being accused of special pleading – theirs are nasty, power-seeking little ploys, while ours are not just legitimate, but indeed essential to the arguments we wish to present! But at least one feature of critical polytextualism is that it says there may be several stories, and this is ours.

Linguistic devices and specialist language

At a more basic level, we do think it is legitimate, even at the risk of accusations of 'special pleading', to argue that where (as in the arguments we are making) language is the site of scrutiny, and where there is therefore a powerful case for 'troubling' it explicitly, we have to use language in particular ways to do just that. Box 1.2 sets out some of the devices we use for this purpose. Similarly, ours is no different from other forms of analysis in which specialist terminology is required to express, precisely, some of the concepts and ideas we wish to convey, and the practices we intend to adopt. Just as physicists need terms like 'quantum' and 'black hole' and biologists need words like 'mitochondria' and 'morphology', so too do we need terms like 'gaze', 'critical polytextualism' and 'tecton'. These are defined specifically in our glossary, and their justification argued in Box 1.4.

The point here is that there is a difference, we would argue, between such specialist use of language, openly and explicitly adopted for a purpose, and its opaque, dissembling use to beguile, enchant and otherwise to 'dress up' seemingly 'obvious' notions in ways which trap the reader into making particular readings (see, for example, Gleeson 1991). We will address this second language-practice directly a little later.

Box 1.2   Linguistic devices

Verbalizing nouns   The device of making nouns like 'knowledge' into verbs like 'knowledging' (in sentences like 'knowledged into being') is done in order to deliberately turn the passivity implied by knowledge-as-a-noun (i.e. portraying it as a 'thing' which laid around waiting to be discovered) into the constructive knowledging-as-a-verb, wherein 'things' are created by being actively 'knowledged into being'.

Warning marks   These are often the bane of many an editor's life – you should hear (we do) the sighs of frustration when they are faced by a manuscript written in this genre, littered by so many words in parentheses that the overall effect is either to imply that the writer is being precious in the extreme, or simply lacks the self-confidence to use words without ringing them round with cautionary devices. They too, however irritating to grammatical orthodoxy, are intended to signal that 'something needs thinking about'. When 'stress' is written, rather than stress, the intention is to signal its reified status as a thing-constructed rather than a thing-in-its-own-right.

Stringing words together and splitting them up   The stringing together of words into composites (as in taken-for-granted) is another device intended to alert the reader that something needs to be noticed. This time attention is being directed to a construction which is, in its connectedness, more than a cliché or turn of phrase which can be simply elided over smoothly.

The converse device is the deliberate splitting of words, such as re-locate, dis-continuity, re-presentation. By drawing attention to the prefix (less commonly the suffix), the reader is again invited to think more closely about what the language implies. For example, when reading the word *representation*, the sense conveyed is of some thing 'standing for' something else. But when written as re-presentation, our attention is directed instead to the constructive and iterative quality of what may be going on: something once presented has been actively transformed in the process of being re-presented. The insertion of the hyphen draws our eye into an argument that what we should take notice of is the activity involved, and hence to question why such trouble has been taken. If we talk of something being re-presented, we imply questions like: What motive could there be behind doing such a thing? What ideological purpose is being served? What story is the text in question trying to peddle?

Erasure   A further variant of this is 'erasure', one of Heidegger's (1962) innovations. By writing words under erasure (like thi-X-s) authors seek to communicate to the reader that while using a word, they are, at the same time, 'troubling' it – questioning its status, and marking it out as distinctly 'dodgy'.

Using humour   For all its obscurantism, some scholarly writing in this genre, at least, is extremely playful. Mulkay (1985) is a good case in point. Not only can this be used to 'lighten up' what is otherwise extremely dense prose – using puns, jokey titles and sarcasm acts to ironize the text, and thus subverts the seriousness of the activity of writing in the scholarly mode. It acts both as a reminder that it is not 'facts' which are at issue, but attempts to beguile, persuade and glamour; and to make explicit the intertextuality of the endeavour with 'culture', be it 'high' or 'low' – or 'worse', 'middle' (brow). In other words, our badinage is not (just) pretentious, but has a serious purpose. Its function is to draw the reader continually back into an acknowledgement that the text is always and ever located in a world of discursive practice a lot wider, richer and 'muckier' than that of scholarship.

Making readers work at understanding what has been written, 'worrying' or 'troubling' the taken-for-granted, is a style of writing intended to make people ask questions which would otherwise possibly not occur to them. Rosenau (1992: 7) again makes this point well (specifically in relation to postmodern writing, though it applies more generally to all writing from within a 'climate of problematization'):

> Post-modernists in all disciplines reject conventional, academic styles of discourse; they prefer audacious and provocative forms of delivery, vital and intriguing elements of genre or style and presentation . . . Such forms of presentation shock, startle and unsettle the complacent social science reader. They are specifically designed to instigate the new and unaccustomed activity of a post-modern reading.

Linguistic devices are thus used to highlight (itself a late modern activity made all the more possible by fluorescent marker pens) what the writer wants the reader to see as important. In doing this, a central thesis is being expounded, one fundamentally concerned with the power/knowledge synarchy by which the promulgation of human science knowledge is not (as it is usually purported to be) an ideologically neutral 'telling-it-like-it-is', but the use of knowledge to monger power – the power to construct reality.

A good example is the notion of 'stress'. Stress has a powerful reality both within everyday talk and in scientific literature. It is measured, theorized about and attributed causal power (e.g. as in 'stress-induced illness'). You can attend workshops on its management, and take drugs to control it. To all intents and purposes, stress has become reified and thus has acquired a taken-for-grantedness, whereby we simply do not question its reality. However, once we think about stress having been 'knowledged into being' by the industry of both academic and popular science, its taken-for-granted status as a 'real thing' gets called into question (cf. Brown 1993).

> *Interrupter: Whoa. Why would we want to question its reality? Does it really matter whether it has a natural reality, a thing-out-there-to-be-discoveredness, or is a product of human representational labour (as you would call it)? If allowing it 'thingness' (reification) is useful (e.g. if giving it a name allows us to 'cope with stress' – tackle certain kinds of bodily discomfort, or indeed, to save lives), then what is the need to get picky about its onto-epistemological status? Does it really matter to the sufferer or the healer whether it was 'discovered' or 'knowledged into being'?*

Beryl: In a polytextuality, there is a space for a position of 'Render unto Caesar . . .'. But, and it's a big but, it shouldn't take up all the space. Where things do totalize in this way, listening to the muted, or the Other matters. Since 'stress' is such a good example I'll take a small diversion to illustrate my argument in terms of that.

The making and monitoring of stress

Alan Young, in a paper entitled 'The discourse on stress and the reproduction of conventional knowledge' (1980), argues that the notion of stress serves a critical ideological function – it attracts attention to the individual, and locates responsibility for becoming stressed, and for overcoming it, in the sphere of the personal and of individual culpability. What this does, Young argues, is direct attention away from other explanations of what is going on when people 'suffer from stress' (e.g. that people are inevitably harmed by the oppressive conditions in the workplace under capitalism).

In this way, the idea of stress acts as a decoy, drawing attention to itself and away from ideas which, if they gained currency, might threaten the social organization which enables capitalism to flourish. The discourse on stress re-locates our focus of concern and directs it towards solving problems at the individual level. Thus it directs it *away from* wondering if there are problems to be solved at a corporate, structural level (for example, the need to improve working conditions, or resolve problems like unemployment). This covert denial of one set of ideas by the express promotion of another is a good example of applying a tectonic analysis. It is useful because it demonstrates the way a text can operate ideologically, to monger a particular world-view (as, of course, does Young's critique). More generally, the discourse on stress may be seen as part of a much broader process of medicalization, whereby the hegemony of conventional biomedicine gains and maintains its power to control and regulate – not just 'medical matters' but large areas of our lives. According to Zola (1972: 498), medicine has become:

> ...a major institution of social control, nudging aside if not incorporating, the more traditional institutions of religion and law. It [has become] the new repository of truth, the place where absolute and often final judgements are made by supposedly neutral and objective experts. And these judgements are made, not in the name of virtue or legitimacy, but in the name of health.

Taken at an even broader level, the notion of stress can thus be seen to serve a number of purposes. It plays a role within a medicalized discourse of social control, warranting regulation of human conduct in a wide sphere of activities. A parallel can be drawn to the way in the nineteenth century women were warned off from engaging in intellectual pursuits as this was said to be 'harmful' to them. It plays a similar role in an individualizing discourse of blame-laying, whereby politico-economic inaction (e.g. over unemployment, low pay, poor housing, inadequate transport facilities) is made *not to matter*, whereas personal inadequacy is *made to matter* (see, for example, Department of Health 1990). Alternatively, from a feminist analysis, it can be seen as shifting blame (e.g. for depressive illness; see Chapter 6) from the oppressive institutions of patriarchy and onto the individual woman (particularly in her wifely and mothering roles) who 'cannot cope' with the pressures of her life (cf. Gleeson 1991).

Finally, it can be seen to reinforce the ideology of self-control, as epitomized in value-laden assumptions that to believe in personal responsibility for health (internal control) is 'good' (i.e. more sensible, laudable and respectable), whereas to believe that one's health is subject to forces outside one's control (external control) is 'bad' (i.e. demonstrates fatalism, learned helplessness, lack of moral fibre, etc.). Psychologists (most notably Wallston and Wallston, 1981, in their development and use of a 'health locus of control scale') have been all too ready to generate 'objective scales' in order to 'demonstrate' the 'validity' of such assumptions, and hence reinforce and legitimize the ideology they promote (see Stainton Rogers 1991, in particular chapter 7, for a more detailed critique of this work).

The discourse on stress is but one example of the way particular language practices can be shown to have far-reaching implications, or, put another way, operate a power/knowledge synarchy. It is precisely this aspect of textuality and tectonics we will be exploring throughout this book.

The dialectics of textuality

A concern with motive and warrant-to-authority presents, however, particular problems for those who adopt it. The point is that this is as true for us, as we write this book, and us, as we conduct our research and analyse our findings, as it is for any other textual producer. We cannot get iffy over other people's power-games with language, and then pretend we are not players in the game too. Mulkay (1985: 74) makes this point well:

> To deny one's own textuality, therefore, when engaged in this kind of analysis is, in effect, to deny one's interpretative dependence on these texts, to claim interpretative privilege from the outset over other participants' texts, and to assert that there is one class of texts, namely, one's own, which are to be treated as beyond textuality. Thus, if our project is the study of textual production in all its forms, we can hardly refuse, by analytical fiat, to include our own texts within the scope of that project.

The project then becomes one of finding ways of, at one and the same time, effectively denying our own textuality (as commentators and analysts) and yet of acknowledging and owning it. Mulkay does this by introducing the various voices of alternative personae in his text. Since we found it so successful, we have used this device too. It is also why we have also adopted a number of other techniques, including our friend 'The Box' to facilitate shifting between a number of stories as we (and you) go along.

Interrupter: I deny being a mere device.

Beryl: Don't we all, dear?

By contrast, a position which is foundationed (or indeed a foundation which is positioned) in 'objectivity' does not recognize – let alone question

– the textuality of its foundations. Such textuality must remain veiled and invisible to the person who believes themself to be occupying and speaking from solid and neutral ground. We should be very surprised, then, if those whose discourse depends upon the neutral space of foundational objectivity were to embrace the possibility that there is no external, trans-human reference point from which to judge the accuracy of competing truth-claims. It is far more likely that work within a climate of problematization (such as this book) will be read through the lens of the objectivist's own discourse as heralding something like 'nothing is true, everything is permissible'.

> *Interrupter: Well, isn't that a fair reading?*

> *Beryl:* No! Just because from an objectivist's point of view textuality has already been mis-interpreted as 'reality', does not mean we have to accept it.

However, we will admit that while sensitivity to textuality must, logically, lead to a *reflexive* recognition of the rhetorical strategies employed in one's own writings and dealings, this does not, however, provide an easy immunity to the problems of relativism.

We are well aware, for example, in what we just wrote, that we have just positioned the hypothetical 'objectivist' as not only being unaware of textuality (as we are using it) but as reading from a position where such an awareness is impossible. It is as if the point of focus of this objectivist gaze is made possible only through the creation of certain 'blind spots'. Yet in focusing on objectivism in this way, we too have inevitably created 'blind spots' for ourselves. Hence our discourse, too, conceals as it reveals (we will take up this point specifically in Chapter 2).

We have hidden from consideration, for example, the notion that some psychologists well-versed in the language of textuality (e.g. Kitzinger 1987; Burman 1990; Parker 1991), nevertheless adopt a 'realist' perspective for *strategic* critical purposes. Such strains of Marxist, feminist and even neo-psychoanalytical discourse have for some time now been used as powerful ways of envisioning and promoting alternative, *better* ways of 'being'. Such approaches *require* recourse to a positive conception of reality in order to ground their utopian politics and thereby give political voice to subjugated and oppressed groups. In other words, realism is not, in this context, to be read as some 'trap' into which such authors have gullibly fallen, but a deliberate choice they have made for purposes they argue explicitly. Their writing is most certainly reflexive, not withstanding its call to realism.

None the less, we would argue that as the clamour of competing voices and conflicting versions of reality increases, so the plausibility and political utility of claiming special truth-status for one or other of these voices decreases. Indeed, we would propose that under a climate of problematization, the very assumption of a singular, mono-vocal existence of categories such as gender, sexuality, race and class is, by necessity, rendered questionable.

Devices and desires

It should, by now, be becoming clearer why it is that we use textual language in some unusual ways. We are using linguistic devices in order to expose the linguistic devices of others (including our own others). The detour around acknowledging our own textuality was necessary in order to make explicit that we are not simply describing a paranoid world in which we see conspiracy around us at every turn.

Certainly we may wish to challenge what we regard as a powerful hegemony at work, in which one version of the world gets accorded the status of 'the-way-things-are', thereby obscuring other alternatives. We will allow ourselves to be suspicious about the self-servingness of such an endeavour, and wish to question 'what's in it for them?' But we do not buy into a singularizing conspiracy theory, whereby, for example, the medical–industrial complex is viewed as having deliberately set out to dupe the rest of us by inventing 'stress' *de novo*. We believe that those who have most to gain from knowledge-production, no more and no less than those who have most to lose, are frequently opaque to the power possibilities enabled by such linguistic devices, or indeed, as they become taken-for-granted, that they are devices at all (see Gleeson 1991 for a more detailed exposition of this argument). 'Stress' may be just as real to doctors as to patients, and indeed, they may just as easily become its victims.

> *Interrupter: Wasn't that just what I was saying a while back?*
>
> Beryl: Yes. Only now it is critically polytextualized.
>
> *Interrupter: Well my kitchen ceiling is critically polytexturized, so there!*
>
> Beryl: Per aspera ad artext!

The reification of notions like 'stress' is not, we would argue, helpfully reduced to a plot or ploy on anybody's part. It is inherent in the human endeavour of making sense of the world (cf. Berger and Luckmann 1967). All of us, individually and collectively (if not equally or equitably), are involved in constructing reality. This does not mean that we buy into the dystopian idea of a 'Newspeak' (Orwell 1949) in which hegemonic power seeks to make a world in which there are only words for the 'real things' legitimated by the party. Nor, indeed, do we subscribe, as 'true believers', in any unreflexive way into its utopian equivalent – the 'political correctness' bowdlerization of language as cure-all for oppression, even though we may be deeply suspicious of the conservative backlash against it. What we argue is that *all* language (as texts on texts) is slippery, difficult, productive, open to appropriation – in other words, tectonic. Language is *never* neutral, never free of the capacity to transit from enabling one kind of reality to enabling another.

What we are saying is that important things can be learned by considering what kinds of reality-work language is doing, and what effects (e.g. on conduct) this may have. And this leads us to another linguistic device we need to consider – the construction of our own words – or often, their appropriation from elsewhere (See Box 1.3).

Box 1.3 Specialist terminology

If you look at the Glossary ('The bluff guide to Beryl') at the end of the book, you will see we have listed a number of words which are either unique to the 'climate of problematization' approach, or are being used in new ways within it. Many are terms taken from languages other than English. Even where they map onto English equivalents, even keep the same spelling, they bring added problems of translation to the other heavy weather in the climate of problematization. Some people have tried, for example, translating Foucault's term 'gaze' as 'look', but it simply does not work. Other problems arise when, in the original, words are polysemic, but lose this polysemy in translation. An example here is *asujettir*, which Henriques, Hollway, Urwin, Venn and Walkerdine (1984: 3) note means in French both 'to make subject' and 'to produce subjectivity'.

Most troublesome of all, perhaps, are recognizably existing English words which have been given new meaning (text is a prime example). Another addition to the armoury includes – though we are not the first to use it in a metaphoric way – the term 'tectonics'.

Finally, a large number of terms are composites – neologisms constructed by augmenting or stringing together old words (meta-narrative and intertextual are good examples) to convey particular meanings. Our major contribution here is polytextualism, with 'tecton' (introduced in Chapter 3) allowed in by vote (and the skin of its teeth).

Beryl, the disembodied 'author'

To write a book under a collective authorship instead of the usual Bloggs *et al.* could be read (and no doubt will be by some people) as pretentious. Certainly we, having decided to do it, saw it as a bit of fun to register Beryl as an author in the Library of Congress in Washington, USA and, having decided on Paris 1968 as an appropriate time and place of her conception, started holding birthday parties. Beryl now has her own song, an office, calling cards and has made a cameo appearance in a video.

Beryl [smugly]: I also hope to have fun creating minor havoc with research assessments and performance indicators across a fair number of university departments.

But she also has a number of serious purposes, which are worth expounding here. Beryl Curt is a resolution to a number of problems. Not least of these was the purely practical one of how we were to avoid just one of our number becoming, to all intents and purposes, *the* author, with the rest of us subsumed under *et al.* For all its utility, this really is a good way of 'killing off' authors (certainly making them invisible) which is why we have deliberately avoided using it.

Our problem, in any case, was more acute than that of, say, Henriques, Hollway, Urwin, Venn and Walkerdine (*Changing the Subject*, 1984). Unlike that group, we have not divided up the authorship chapter by chapter but worked on each other's drafts directly to the point we ourselves cannot recall who wrote what (and see no need to) – an approach made easier for us in the now ubiquitous use of word-processors. In any case, the very notion of 'writing' has become itself ever-more problematized in that it consists not only of actually keying in the words of the text, but in the discussions which led to each drafting and redrafting, the editing and proof reading.

The device of claiming collective authorship, whereby the text as singular is ascribed to a single disembodied 'author' composed (as the text is composed) of a motley interweaving of voices, also has an expository function. It tacitly opens up not just the problematic nature of authorship but identity more generally. To create Beryl is to construct an author who has an 'identity' but does not have a body. That, in itself, is not a problem, since the individual may be seen as one of a class of 'subject positions' (according to Foucault one produced by liberal-humanistic discourse). For subject positions to be possible, bodies and embodiments have to be 'made' via discursive production. So far, so good (Beryl has certainly been made by discursive production).

However, there is a clear difference between approaching the body as an analytic, and treating the body as an agent for action. To do so simply creates a situation of infinite regress – bodies are created by discursive production, bodies draw identities from discursive production, but, then, who or what does the discursive producing?

Foucault's focus on 'body' has been claimed to be 'his major response to Derrida's textualism: a demonstration in counterpoint' (Boyne and Rattansi 1990: 111). Again, given the penetration (no pun intended) of his theorising into so many fields, we do not intend to review this important work in detail. Rather we wish to argue that in adopting textuality and tectonics as analytics within critical polytextualism, we have tried to overcome some of the problems raised by so reifying 'the body'. By extending beyond the merely 'textual', we are seeking to avoid the need for such a 'counterpoint'. (Our own counterpoint concerns a rather different dialogic – that between our analytics of textuality and tectonics – cf. Chapter 4.) We can then sidestep the kinds of problem Game (1991: 89) elucidates:

> If via Bergson and Foucault, we think of power in terms of actions of bodies on bodies, it could be asked: What makes the body act in a disruptive way? ... However, the energy of the unconscious would seem to come closer [than Foucault's account] to specifying what disrupts the structure of power. When Cixous speaks of the resources of the unconscious bursting out in a writing of the body, is this not a counter-power and a power of qualitative difference?

If, in the terms of textuality, the body can be construed as a text, then Game's 'power in terms of actions of bodies on bodies' can equally well be read as power in terms of actions of texts on texts. Thus the giving of a reading to a text is a local system of power, and within the knowledges that we have, that local system involves an observer, an analyser. Hence, via textuality, we can agree with Game (1991: 18) when she proposes that:

> ... texts be thought of as embodied in practice, rather than as separate from reception or practice. In this view, reading is understood as a writing, and analysis and observation as textual activity, a practice of writing.

This does not turn 'the writer' or 'the observer' into any kind of integral 'self' or centration of subjectivities. Rather, there will always be a manifold of 'writers', and those writers will also be read via intra- and inter-textuality. In this vein, we would re-write Lacan's (1977) phrase – ex-centric. The integral self – individuality – does, of course, have an existence within that manifold, precisely because it is discursively practised.

The analysis and the observation of that self is the domain of our other analytic, tectonics. Thus, in a final analysis, we see Beryl as less of an author, in the accepted sense of that term, and more as a means to explore the tectonics of textuality/the textuality of tectonics. She is neither an individual, nor embodied – but that is of no concern if we are merely using her to engage in representational labour.

Beryl: Try asking the reader about that. I write therefore I am.

> *Interrupter: Egoist! I'm the real underdog here. No citations for me. Wish I was called et-Al!*

Social constructionism

Another quagmire we have avoided by way of Beryl is any need to present a singular biographical sketch of how we came to the approach we have taken. Nonetheless, we think it helpful to recount some of the major influences which have led to where we are now.

For most of us it has been social constructionism which provided the first systematic set of ideas which has enabled us to adopt a non-foundational, constitutive agenda. Those roots – as Parker (1989) highlights with his own radical brush – lie in the structural-humanistic (Harré) and hermeneutic-phenomenological (Shotter) genealogy of social constructionist writing. Following Henriques, Hollway, Urwin, Venn and Walkerdine (1984), we could also add a further foundation – symbolic-interactionist socio-cognitivism (Gergen).

Social constructionism's tendency to drift into a liberal forum rather than a squabble of radicals (if that is the right collective noun!) has obvious merits in the promulgation of social constructionist ideas. However, because we take heterogeny seriously, it can hardly be the only story we can weave. Obviously, there are narratives in which the tensions *do* matter. Nevertheless, we do not intend to get side-stepped into discussing what they are, for we see social constructionism as a stepping stone rather that a resting place.

One reason is that given the social history we have told, we see the phantoms of academic psychology still haunting social constructionism. For some, the new space they find themselves inhabiting is aetherial – a kind of pure cultura – where the 'social' needs to be detached from some material frame, to exist, golem-like, elsewhere, until some new state of knowledge brings reconciliation. Some will argue that this can be achieved by addressing psychology from a postmodern perspective. The alternative, which is the one we propose, is that psychology should – as the other disciplines of 'social science' – be dissolved into transdisciplinarity. In our view, this is the inevitable consequence of importing postmodern analyses, in that its denial of 'grand narrative' meta-theorizing is inimicable to the maintenance of discipline boundaries.

> *Interrupter: Hardly a line that is good for business! How are you going to sell this idea – indeed, this book – if nobody knows where to put it on the bookshelves, reading lists and curricula? Maybe some of the new universities will start teaching more inter-disciplinary studies, though probably in the quest for student numbers rather than for any scholarly purpose. But you can bet your sweet bippy the* ancien régime *are not going to give up their power-bases in a hurry!*

Beryl: You have a point. I agree that the present show will go on, pretty well regardless of what we do. For the foreign-conference motivated academic, in any case, these issues can be easily re-textualized into crucial debates. 'Can we have a postmodern psychology?' should keep the circus going for years.

> *Interrupter: See you there!*

Methodological tensions

An extraordinary variety of methodologies has been employed (and rubbished) under the banners of social constructionist and postmodernist approaches to social scrutiny. For some, the shift in academic re-identification (often from some variety of interpretational social psychology) has been achieved without any attempt to find new methods. Under the social constructionist label, they continue to pursue established procedures, ranging from philosophical analyses to measure-by-measure multivariate analysis of variance on laboratory data. For others, such a methodological stasis is regarded as evidence of bad faith – of mere bandwaggoning, or worse. What is needed, they argue, are new methodological approaches for the new paradigm.

This quest for what we have termed (after some debate) new methods of scrutiny is, as much as anything, what has brought Beryl Curt together as a group, and one of our justifications for this book. In its empirical chapters, we show how we have attempted to explore some of the shared 'social subjectivities' that can be drawn from person-by-person pattern analyses, primarily using Q-methodology (as devised by Stephenson 1935, 1953). These we augment with more patently textual analytics, without regard to received notions of quantitative/qualitative tensions in methodology, and moreover, we complement them with a direct challenge to the theory/methodology tension itself.

This approach is very different from the more usual climate of problematization turn to purely qualitative (e.g. ethogenic) techniques. This we suspect to be a predicated manoeuvre, contextuality interpretable but no longer necessary in a shifted paradigm, whereby numerical data of any kind became suspect (i.e. masculinized or at least intrinsically positivistic).

As we will describe in Chapter 5, our use of Q-method (in conjunction with other forms of scrutiny) has been motivated by concerns that ethnographic methods, when used in isolation, while avoiding some of the essentializing pitfalls of methods based on hypothetico-deductivism, still accord to the researcher *alone* the power to determine the lineaments of experience of participants in the study. The attraction of Q-method for us is its transfer to participants of at least some of the power to define what constitutes the stories being told. Just what those stories tell and how they seem to fracture into representations, understandings and warrants for conduct will be covered in Chapters 6–8.

Beryl [soliloquizing]: I hacked out this next bit while the Interrupter was engaged in stress management down the local. Otherwise it would never have got written!

Issues of ideology

While social constructionism successfully avoids the vices of causality and essentialism (by bleaching from its prose the hard language of positivism), we would argue that at the same time its roots limit its potential to fully transcend the traps of causality and essentialism. We have no such history in common to accommodate (though one of us is old enough to own to structural-humanistic and socio-cognitivist foundations (Semin and Rogers 1973; Rogers 1974). We have therefore found it less of a problem to adopt a language which has only minimal resonance with the counter-positivistic bedrock of social constructionism. This makes it easier for us to avoid some of the pitfalls (such as slipping into notions of polarity, or reifying functions as essences).

However, there is one potential hazard we have had to face from the start – the vulnerability of any textual analytic (including our own critical polytextualism) to operate as a mere celebration of diversity – the false consciousness or even the 'horror' (e.g. according to Burman 1990) of 'liberal pluralism' and of 'relativism' (see Doherty, Graham and Malek 1992 for a fuller exposition of this criticism). We will take up this challenge in more detail in the next chapter, but we need to briefly address it here too.

To claim, as we have, that texts must be treated as having epistemologically equivalent status is sometimes read as assuming that we regard them as *ideologically* equivalent. This we refute, since we see the accusation as confounding two quite separate uses of our analytics. To pursue textual analysis of alternative stories, representations, etc., is to seek to elucidate the positions in a discursive arena (what Stephenson, 1986, would call 'a concourse'; see Chapter 4). This is a task of taxonomy, wherein any moral analysis would be out of place. If this were all we did – set out like cultural entomologists with analytic butterfly nets to draw up a taxonomy of stories – then the charge of ideologically naive or even dangerous 'relativism' might be warranted.

But this is not all we do. Taxonomy is only a beginning, for we seek not only to elucidate texts, but to scrutinize the discursive functions to which they are put – What conduct or praxis are they used to warrant? What ideology do they seek to peddle? Here, most certainly, there is anything but an assumption of moral or ideological equivalence. Quite the opposite, we see the consideration of their consequences (actual and potential) as the key focus for analysis. We would thus also reject the accusation that our approach (as a form of pluralism):

> ... engenders a cynical, nihilist and pessimistic political tone. Whatever political scenarios emerge, none is different enough from the *status quo* to matter ... Given the history of the twentieth century, that is a powerful and frightening statement. (Rosenau 1992: 143)

Again, we see this as a charge of 'relativism' in another guise. In practice, as we will show in our accounts of our empirical work, we see ourselves as anything but nihilistic; by contrast, we see our work as opening up areas of concern to scrutiny which can have transformational outcomes. Precisely by perturbating what has become, in local and contingent terms, the story which has been singularized as the only politically correct one to express, we seek to bring about change. By examining how, say, one rhetorical story may be used to warrant two contradictory forms of conduct, we can offer caution about the uses to which rhetoric may be put.

Overall, then, we certainly see our approach as 'political', in that it demands political analysis. But our approach is one which denies ascendancy to any one specific 'reading' of ideology and power over any other. In this way, we see critical polytextualism as offering a means to avoid totalizing any singularity, or serving fascisms of any complexion. However, we are strongly concerned with the vagaries of change and with the possibilities (not, of course, necessarily emancipatory!) that change can enable. Indeed, we see the utility of our analytics precisely as their facility to enable moral and ideological judgements on the consequences of discursive practices, and thus to enable transformation.

For us, any 'horror' lies much more in attempts to give radicality some extra-discursive 'safety-rail' (to borrow Game's phrase) or 'sky-hook' (to borrow

Rorty's), for example, by recourse to 'critical realism' (cf. Bhaskar 1978). We worry all attempts to transcend the traps of the past which baulk at exposing their own foundational axioms to critical scrutiny. To us this is a severe case of wanting to have your cake and eat it! Radical doubt, central to a climate of problematization, demands that all axioms, however politically correct their pedigree, must be open to question, however uncomfortable that may be and however much that may provoke misunderstanding.

This doubtful affirmation has a lot in common with 'Foucaultian Feminism', as described, for example, by Sawicki (1991). She argues that Foucaultian genealogy can be used as a particularizing 'form of resistance' and argues for a 'radically pluralist feminism' – not a pluralism in which anything goes but 'a pluralism in which *nothing* goes'. A related call emerges in Game's (1991) concept of a 'methodology of multiplicity' and Mulkay's (1985: 75) argument for 'multiple textual agents'.

Our frequent recourse to developments in feminist analytic has a very simple basis. In many respects it is, currently, the key site for the worrying of radical ideas – the one place where 'politicking' is still 'hot', and still prepared to take on opponents outside the safety of the academy. Having experienced the factionalizing kinds of identity politics endemic within other radical movements, there has none the less been, within feminist analysis, a serious attempt to 'deconstruct' that meta-narrative (and of course serious attempts to promote it – see for example, Kitzinger, Wilkinson and Perkins 1992).

The importation of Foucaultian discursive practices has been one such development, although it is certainly not the only one. Feminist analytic has both reconstructed texts from such 'founding fathers' as Bergson, Freud and Hegel, and written its own texts into the 'climate of problematization' (e.g. Kristeva 1980; Irigaray 1985; Cixous 1986). We read in it, then, that which we also want to write: 'an affirmation of doubt' and 'doubtful affirmation'. As Sawicki (1991: 28) puts it, re-writing Foucault:

> Victories are often overturned; changes may take on different faces over time. Discourses and institutions are ambiguous and may be utilized for different ends . . . But . . . pessimism need not lead to despair. Only a disappointed traditional revolutionary would lapse into fatalism at the thought that much of history is out of our control . . . one need not have an idea of utopia in order to take seriously the injustices of the present.

An end to ideology?

At the same time, for all the potential for addressing ideology, there is a sense in which postmodern dialects of the climate of problematization represent the end of ideology. It implies being in a hyper-reality, in which essences have been dissolved, leaving only their discursive and material expressions. Stripped of 'totalizing' idealization, what were meta-narratives are reduced to their representations – each a semiotic archive that can serve as a resource for setting scenes, moods or located understandings. There is little doubt that we can participate in such an aesthetic reality by, for example, watching movies like *Blade Runner* or the soap *Northern Exposure*, as we outlined at the beginning of the chapter.

Moreover, in so far as these terms are useful, the emergence of post-modernity has not superseded modernity, but become intertextual with it. For example, to the extent that, within postmodernity, science is becoming discredited, this is not just through postmodernist attacks on its epistemological axioms, but at least as much because of the abhorrence of people at large towards its technological horrors (like nuclear weapons) and the new, typically on-going disasters (like the ozone-depleting CFCs). However, this does not mean that modernist science and technology has (or will, or, indeed should) dissolve. For science and technology are not just seen as the source of these problems, but also the means of their detection and monitoring, and ultimately of their amelioration. The long-term, material, institutional reality of science and technology does not dissolve just because dominance of the *ideology* of Scientism has been opened up to challenge.

Certainly the major and pervasive institutional legacies of modernism – such as our legal, education and fiscal systems – seem in no danger of such dissolution. Indeed, even survivors from pre-modernity (like the Papacy) seem, like *The Mousetrap*, set to run 'for ever'. True, their representations now move in and out of the three-minute culture of the (post?)modern mass media, but this is not a sign of their fragmentation as material and institutional 'realities'. Like the Japanese Emperor, they may have given up some aspects of godheadship (i.e. conviction of ideological reality), but elsewhere their establishment remains pretty well absolute.

More broadly still, we are all caught up in a social life which was produced by, is sustained by, and, in all probability, will continue to be reproduced by, capitalism – not Capitalism as ideology, but capitalism as a form of social organization (cf. Harvey, 1989). Not ideology, in part, because 'capital is a process not a thing' and a process which has seen off the only serious challenging process (Marxist-Leninist socialist centralism) and, with that, much of its linked ideology. This is not to say that neo-Marxism (and its analogues like Feminism) as critical methods are lost to us, nor that 'socialist'-capitalism may not remain a viable political force. But, like it or not, 'we are all capitalists now' – and in that sense, ideology (at least within that meta-narrative, and at least for now) is dead.

However, to be in a process, particularly a process in dramatic change, is not to be without powerful local political tensions in which point-positions get defined and expressed in historically resonant, ideologized terms. So, too, its own historicization has been ideologized. But we need to be clear that ideologization as a rhetorical device and indeed as a critical analytic device need not presume 'ideology', if by that one means a singularizing meta-narrative.

Indeed, get Beryl Curt as a collective arguing over an issue like 'pornography' and you will hear no shortage of both rhetorical and critical analytic ideologizing – but not, of course, full, paid-up subscription to ideology as meta-narrative. The critical polytextualized condition that prevents such true belief is not an ahistoric product of being critical polytextualists, but part of the process of collective multiplexity that enabled us to 'become' critical polytextualists. We are the 'children' of late modern liberal-humanistic pluralism – that discursive sociality is where we 'came from' and provided the texts from which the various critical theory 'identities' can be (and the conditional is deliberate) woven.

Thus we see the major function of critical polytextualism, and its analytics of textuality and tectonics as their potential to enable a creative, open clash of analytics of uncertainty and possibility outside of meta-narrative. As Game (1991: x) puts it, from what she calls 'materialist semiotics':

> ... writing as transformation provides the opportunity to reformulate the question of social change. Reading a text is a writing practice, and in this lies the possibility of a rewriting of texts of the culture, in the now. A deconstructive strategy is a positive strategy of transformation: undoing is simultaneously an unmaking and a making, a process without end.

In this book, we will be attempting to write into plausibility the possibility of a universe of texts, perhaps even an infinite and unbounded one. Of course, the affirmation of that abstract possibility in no way disputes that what is held to be known (knowledge) at any location is local and contingent to that location. These are matters of its processes of textual production and practice (which may well include the theorization of knowledge itself and the 'repression' of certain writings).

Hence, we see as important the critical analytics of both the deconstruction of foundational claims to 'knowledge', and of the engagement in genealogies of the 'repressed'. (This latter observation goes some way to explaining why there is currently so much interest in psychodynamic discourse within much critical analysis.) As we have noted already, such activities, no less than those at which they are addressed, are intertextual. They are observations upon observations, texts upon texts.

Questions of interpretation

Of course, one of the problems with all this is that ideology, like everything else, is a text. How, then, can we address it to texts? Are we bound to flounder in a quagmire of regress? One possible solution to this problem is provided by Eco and others (1992: 52), who suggests that, 'we can accept a sort of Popperian principle according to which if there are no rules which help to ascertain which interpretations are the "best" ones, there is at least a rule for ascertaining which ones are "bad" '. By example, he quotes Wordsworth's line 'A poet could not be but gay', noting that, 'a sensitive and responsible reader . . . has the duty to take into account the state of the lexical system at the time of Wordsworth' (p. 68).

In the same debate, Rorty (1992: 106) draws the distinction between:

> ... knowing what you want to get out of a person or thing or text in advance and hoping that the person or thing or text will help you want something different – that he or she or it will help you change your purposes, and thus to change your life.

How this distinction maps onto Eco's notion of 'best' *vs* 'bad' is made quite explicit by Game (1991: 18) when she writes that:

> ... the central issue in the evaluation of a text – theoretical ... or otherwise – is its capacity to provoke disturbing pleasure: not a refusal of knowledge, but a reformulation of what the desire for knowledge might be about. The question addressed is then: does it attempt to fix a signified, or does it invite a further writing and a rewriting?

Where we end, then, is with a doubtful affirmation of openness. There are no extra-cultural constraints, only those of our own prior and present making. There are no extra-cultural laws preventing some other condition obtaining in ten years' time, because there are no cultural laws. Or, more accurately, there are only constructions of cultural laws, effects of the socially constructed reality. The possibility of transformation is the transformation of possibility. Which seems as good a place as any to begin!

Beryl: Phew! Glad that's done.

Interrupter: Cooeee! I'm back.

Beryl: Just in time for the next chapter.

Interrupter: Did I miss anything important?

Beryl [smirking]: Not at all.

2

Textuality

We are told that (and we are meant to take the advice more than literally) 'All that glistens is not gold.' Both in terms of everyday commonsense and received formal ideas of 'gaining knowledge' lies the assumption that there is always, ultimately, a 'Truth' to be discovered – some essential reality that is 'really there', even though it may be lurking behind appearances, or may be distorted by false and deceptive discursive practices. Consequently, it is generally assumed that the primary goal of the 'seeker after knowledge' is to clean up and refine ways of knowing (enquiry), so as to be better able to uncover (dis-cover) this 'Truth'.

Under a climate of problematization, the project of 'gaining knowledge' is rendered highly problematic. No external (extra-discursive) benchmark is seen to exist that can ever demonstrate that a foundational 'Truth' has been revealed. Further, any act of un-covering is regarded also as always an act of covering. 'Truth' is re-covered, not dis-covered. In this analysis, commonsense and conventional dis-covery of knowledge is seen as a 'Truth Game', in which Truth is actively and purposively knowledged into being.

The place of enquiry thereby shifts, under a climate of problematization, into a two-fold form of scrutiny: to explore the restraints and strictures (and indeed reality-making powers) of such received metaphorics of enquiry as 'revelation', 'unveiling', and 'mirroring'; and, to explore how enquiry can be positively transformed through a critical polytextual endeavour.

In this chapter, we shall argue that our move away from foundational metaphorics and towards the analytics of textuality and tectonics is directing us towards a more fruitful and dynamic engagement with the vicissitudes and stabilities of the social and personal life-world which constitutes our existence. Thus this chapter will knowledge 'textuality' into being as the post-phenomenological moment of the life-world. A related aim is to reveal the need to address the organization, constitution and articulation of specific textualities through the analytic of tectonics (although how this may be done is a task we will leave to Chapter 3).

Signifying systems and revealing practices

> *Interrupter: If you're so clever, do we now get the answer to the ultimate question – what, pray, is the meaning of life?*

Beryl: Now you're just being silly! Go to gaol! Do not pass Go! Do not collect £200! I was just getting into the swing, and you put your oar in.

> *Interrupter: Charming! It's your own fault you know for sounding like a PoMo Delphic Oracle.*

Beryl: All right, you asked for it, I will start there. Actually, in one sense, it is an easy question for the critical polytextualist to answer, although the answer I will give is unlikely, I suspect, to satisfy the metaphysical hunger of most questioners!

> *Interrupter: I've got a feeling I'm going to regret this . . .*

To begin with, the question must be brought down from the lofty heights of generality and given some specificity and substance:

Whose life? When?

Let us begin, then, by assuming that for anything to mean anything – for anything to signify – then that 'something' must be engaged within a signifying system or a practice through which it is 'revealed' as being what it is. This is another way of saying that a thing (whether that be a life, a poem, a building, a chair, a jug of milk or whatever) has no meaning in and of itself. Rather its meaning (its significance or what it *matters*) is contingent upon its embeddedness within a wider concern; a wider system of involved, meaningful practices.

For example, if the 'thing' in question is a jug of milk which is 'going off', then this may reveal itself either negatively (as spoiled milk to be thrown away) or positively (as milk 'on the turn' towards cheese), depending upon the meaningful practices with which you are engaged (depending upon your concerns). What 'it' 'is' depends on what you intend to do with 'it'.

A common objection to such a view is that, regardless of which way the milk reveals itself to you, it is still, in essence, milk-going-rancid. We do not see this as a problem – provided, that is, we take it to mean that there is a disclosure of the 'essence' of sour-milkiness to us. We do, however, object to any suggestion that 'sour milk is sour milk *in essence*'. In such a reading, the essence does not, we would maintain, have the independence, the reality, being claimed for it. Rather we would say that what we have seen is a revealing of the object in a particular way through a particular revealing practice within a discourse of 'essentialism'. Such a revelation is useful and significant only when somebody is engaged in certain practices (whether this endeavour is philosophy or food science). Far from refuting the argument that things do not mean or signify on their own, that second way of reading the objection strengthens the contrasting hermeneutic position.

Box 2.1   Mr and Mrs Eutics, and their son Hermen

Hermeneutics was originally a theological activity concerned with interpreting the formal text of the Bible, with exegesis (critical, explanatory reading) as opposed to eisegesis (a more personalized reading into scripture). Dilthey (1833–1911) is generally held to be responsible for appropriating the term from theology into philosophy, to refer to an interpretative craft of understanding human phenomena. He saw this task as quite distinct from both the positivist methodology of the natural sciences and the *a priori*-ism of Cartesian philosophy. In particular, he called for an intersubjective, empathetic endeavour. Understanding (*Verstehen*) comes from apprehension and apperception of human expressings, makings and doings; in other words (cf. Berger and Luckmann 1967), their objectifications.

Husserl (1859–1938) argued for a notion of living in or intending a life-world (or *Lebenswelt*) – a condition quite opposed to the disowned, abstracted 'real' world of scientific methodology. However, our 'natural (i.e. commonsensical) attitudes' or standpoints are also inimitable with access to the pure phenomena of consciousness. His hermeneutic phenomenology called for a disciplined disconnection (or bracketing) of the natural attitude (and indeed of positivistic scientific conceptualizations). Husserlian notions (and vocabulary) were influential upon Schutz and through him upon the social constructionism and sociology of knowledge of Berger and Luckmann (1967).

What Kohl (1965) calls 'The Mystery of Martin Heidegger' shifted the agenda further. Heidegger's core question was: What is the Being of things that are? While Husserl's project of *Verstehen* was concerned with stages of reduction towards a grasping of the life-world, Heidegger proposed a 'hermeneutic of facticity' to address our field of Being (or being-in-the-world) – *Dasein*. By facticity Heidegger meant the contingency of our being onto and into a world always, already there. Meaning comes from our temporality and contingency. Rather as in a Wittgensteinian form of life or the narrative root metaphor, it is our comings and goings in personal time (and space) via a community of language that merit attention. Unlike Wittgenstein or the narrators of narrative, Heidegger adopts moral analytics as well. His notion of concern has influenced our own concerns (see Chapters 8 and 9).

The hermeneutic tradition was, along with the pragmatists (e.g. James and Peirce) and the linguistic philosophers (e.g. Wittgenstein, Ryle and Austin), a critical element in setting the agenda for the climate of problematization. The latter lines tend to be most noticeable in English-language writers.

To address the sour milk, the 'revealing practice' in question is the purposive, meaningful activity in which a person is involved. If, for example, the person is engaged in the activity of making breakfast and, as part of this practice, wants to pour milk onto a bowl of cereal, then the rancid milk will be likely to be a 'turn off'. In this sense, the rancid milk has currency (albeit 'bad' currency) within this meaningful practice because of its relationship to other aspects of the activity (including the predicated 'good' currency of fresh milk). Just as a five pound note has 'good' currency in England, but 'bad' currency in, say, a US supermarket, so the meaning of any thing is related to its currency within the context of a given practice or 'system'.

Thus sour milk may show up differently to a cheese maker (so long as it is going 'sour' in the 'right' way) because of the way it relates to other aspects of the practice of cheese making ('held together' by the concern to make cheese). In just the same way the words a person uses at home will 'show up' differently when they are used in a court-room or during a psychiatric examination.

Language matters

Most authors in the climate of problematization are in agreement that language is the most important (certainly the most readily visible) revealing practice. Much post-structuralist work, for example, is heavily influenced by thinkers such as Saussure, Heidegger, Wittgenstein, Foucault and Derrida, all of whom stress the importance of language. None of them, of course, treat it as a transparent system for 'representing' an underlying reality, but as a productive, constructive medium.

For Saussure and Derrida, language is understood as a system of differences. According to Saussure, both signifier (for instance, the word 'cat') and signified (for instance, the concept of 'cat') gain their meaning by virtue of their difference from other signifiers (like 'bat' and 'cap') and signifieds (like 'dogs' and 'tigers'), rather than through some direct reference or 'identity'. In this sense, language is active in as much as it serves to 'carve up' our world in particular ways, depending on the structuration of its differences. These 'differences' themselves, however, likewise reflect the manner in which our concernful and involved dealings are organized or structured. This has led some thinkers – often influenced by Foucault – to talk in terms of particular and localized fields of language-in-use. Such fields of culturally contingent and historically specific language-in-use (with their own peculiar and recognizable organization of systems of differences and hence their own peculiar ways of 'carving up the world') are often called 'discourses'.

To give an example, we might want to argue that we can recognize at least two broad discourses of emotion which inform our understandings of this area of life. On the one hand, there is a 'classicist' or 'rationalist' discourse which renders emotion understandable through differences such as 'reason versus passion', 'control versus loss of control' and 'mind versus body'. On the other, there is a 'romantic' or 'humanistic' discourse which is structured according to tensions such as 'deep versus shallow', 'engaged versus detached' and 'the humane versus the mechanical'.

We might expect that the 'same' emotional scene (a person shouting furiously at their bank manager, for example) will show up very differently 'through' these different discourses or revealing practices. From the rationalist perspective, the incident may show up as an example of weak and undignified loss of control – or even as the showing forth of a wild and amoral 'animal within'. From the romantic perspective, the incident may show up instead as an example of authentic and spontaneous expression of the truly human – a refreshing glimpse of what is going on behind the mechanical and bureaucratic drudgery of modern life.

> *Interrupter: You mean like the different ways Mr Spock and Dr McCoy in* **Star Trek** *might view the scene?*
>
> *Beryl:* Yes, that's right – the tension between the two views on emotion is nicely sedimented by these two characters.

To ask 'but what does the scene really mean?' is merely to invite the application of a different revealing practice (we could, for example, à la physiological approaches to emotion, measure the heart-rate, blood-pressure and pupil dilation of the furious client or the berated banker, or indeed the implied observer). This, however, is not a way of adjudicating between classical and romantic discourses, and neither does it tell us what the scene 'really means'!

Indeed, these points illustrate the falsity of the distinction that is often made between 'experience' and 'text' (this point will be developed empirically in relation to human emotion in Chapter 7). The ways in which we 'experience' the world are wrapped up with our concerned engagement with 'the world'. This interpenetration is textuality.

Textuality, as we have been elucidating it here, is an analytic which serves to draw attention to the impossibility and futility of attempting to define something (some argument, life or whatever) as if it were fully self-present and self-sufficient – as if the world consisted of facts which, as the cliché has it, 'speak for themselves'. Textuality thus serves to trouble any arguments founded in the distinction between 'fact' and 'fiction', the 'discursive' and the 'real'.

Story, presencing and textuality

An important term within the critical polytextualist lexicon is 'story'. It has the advantage of simplicity, and has been used to good effect by others already. Haraway (1984: 79–80), for example, has this to say in her powerful essay about primatology being 'politics by other means':

> ... [L]ife and social sciences in general, and primatology in particular, are story-laden; these sciences are composed through complex, historically specific storytelling practices. Facts are theory-laden; theories are value-laden; values are story-laden. Therefore facts are meaningful within stories.
>
> ... The point is not that one account of monkeys and apes is as good as another, since they are all 'merely' culturally determined narratives. Rather I am arguing that the struggle to construct good stories is part of the craft. There would be no primatology without skilful, collectively contested stories. And, there would be no stories, no questions, without ... complex webs of power.

Haraway is using the notion of 'story' here to emphasize that language is an extremely important revealing/constructing practice. To take this further, it is worth observing that there are at least four ordinary usages of the word 'story':

1. As in 'You've been telling stories again' – this usage is equivalent to an accusation of lying (the wrongful covering up of truth).
2. As in 'The Wizard of Oz is a great story' – this usage is in the form of an acceptable telling of fiction (no requirement to be true).
3. As in 'How did I get here?' – 'Huh, that's a long story ...' – here story is used as a prelude to, and the narrating of, a string of events (which may be 'true' or 'false', 'fact' or 'fiction').
4. As in 'Okay, what's the story ...?' – here the usage is to set out the plot, the key elements of a more elaborated narrative or event (which again may be 'true' or 'false', 'fact' or 'fiction').

What separates these usages is, first, whether they imply a concern for veracity and/or facticity; and, second, if they do, a moralization or valorization of this distinction. When we use the word story, we deliberately play on these ambiguities. The word thus serves to mark a slippage between faction and fict. It is precisely this slippage which disturbs the received ethics of many critical commentators on the postmodern (Parker 1989; Rosenau 1992; etc.).

These usages are united, however, in what we call (following Heidegger 1971) a 'presencing' function. A story is a practice through which past or future events (imaginary or real) are 'presenced', i.e. gathered in words in language-use in order to recount, entertain, inform, influence, or such. In the course of the practice of story-telling, we order these events for consumption 'in the now'.

However, as we live our lives – go shopping, visit the doctor, do our jobs, and so on – we are not generally engaged in a singular presencing practice in the clear sense outlined above (as being part of the concept of 'story'). The analytic of textuality, however, encourages us to view our everyday, practised, lived lives as immanently storied. When we live our 'storied lives', however, we are not always engaged in a substantive 'presencing' practice. More often we are in a flux of transient storied fracts.

Of course, while going shopping we may well tell ourselves stories about what we are doing. For example, we may story it as the carrying and remembering of a shopping list (the presencing of future purchase), the seeing of what's on cheap offer and imagining what we might cook, and so on. But the *practice* of shopping itself is usually far too much of an *ad hoc* mosaic of the merely contingently contiguous to be a 'story' as such. These fragments will, from one shopping moment to another, include a varied melange of concerns extraneous to shopping – fragments of other projects in our local, mundane life-world (such as worrying that the car needs a service, or wondering whether there is anything worth watching on TV tonight). These will impinge alongside elements informed by the marketing discourses which structure the lay-out of the goods and tills, and by the judged requirement of food *qua* food.

A story is one practice (itself, of course, a manifold), going shopping is another. Shopping may be shot-through with storying practice, but it is a practice distinct from telling stories.

> *Interrupter: As my friend Marcia Worrell says – 'When the going gets tough, the tough go shopping!'*
>
> *Beryl:*   As part of me, she could point out that a number of my more difficult moments have been relieved just so!

What textuality as an analytic encourages us to do, however, is to draw attention to the dependence of everyday non-presencing practices (no less than in much blatant presencing conduct) upon a tacit, 'sub-textual' or 'background' concourse of storiedness. In other words, our story here serves to presence the textuality of reality – and hence to deconstruct any naive realism.

> *Interrupter: What do you mean by a 'tacit storiedness'?*
>
> *Beryl:*   Well, certainly not there being a 'Truth' or a 'Reality' behind appearances. Dependence implies connectedness, not causality or fundamentality.

To illustrate this, we can offer the example of a medical examination conducted to establish that a young woman is a virgin. Initially, it may seem that virginity is something that can be proven and evidenced by objective criteria – and of course this is, in the terms of such an objective project, the case. A woman's virginity, in settings where this is a meaningful category, can be proven and evidenced by the state of the hymen (but see Chapter 3 for a more detailed exposition in relation to tectonics). The hymen is, of course, real to the hymenspex (or at least their client, who may or may not be the subject of the examination); indeed, it must be so real (in the usual sense of the term) for hymenspicy to be a viable revealing practice.

> *Interrupter: Yuk! What on earth is 'hymenspex' – a gynaecological instrument? And what is hymenspicy?*

Beryl: You're on the right track. The first is a divinator of hymens and the second is the practice of hymen divination. (See my Glossary for more.)

> *Interrupter: When the language gets tough, the tough get stroppy! But that apart, are you saying that its (i.e. the hymen's) existence depends upon a story? Within hymenspicy, if I have to use that horrible word, surely it is either there and intact, or it is not – it – and hence the woman's virginity – is lost. This, it seems to me, is a matter of objectively determinable fact.*

Not at all. Apart from the complication that the hymen, *qua* hymen, is not half as 'objectively' observable as folks assume, the re-presentation that a woman presents as a virgin (see Chapter 6 for a development of this argument about presentation) takes matters a long way beyond issues of the facticity of presentation (i.e. this is not a matter of disputes between medical professionals about what constitutes an 'intact hymen').

The point is that the decision or conclusion is brought into being by what that intact hymen *signifies*. The 'intact hymen' can only signify virginity within a particular signifying system (a presencing practice or set of practices – a story) which contains a definition of virginity based upon the state of the hymen (this is what it means to say that virginity is socially constructed).

The doctor, the hymenspex, if asked, may well express aspects of this signifying system. It is likely, for example, that she (we think, in this case, it should be a she) is familiar with much of the storied embroidery around hymenspicy – the narrative 'how' of the maintenance or 'loss' or virginity. Indeed, we expect this of her, that she can operate upon the (legal, patriarchal) surroundings to her diagnostic reasoning – she is, after all, an expert in this particular presencing practice in context (it is a matter of knowledge, something gained through training. Any doctor unaware of the diagnostic environment might be well considered incompetent). As a potential expert witness, any such incompetence may be revealed by skilled cross-examination.

> *Interrupter: As in 'I put it to you, Dr Hymenspex, that you are mistaken in your diagnosis. I refer you to the second opinion I have obtained from Professor I.N. Tacta, which shows, conclusively, that you have failed to follow the established medical procedure.'*

Beryl: Precisely. Just such arguments raged over the diagnoses of child sexual abuse made by doctors in the Cleveland controversy. There the sign in dispute was reflex anal dilatation.

However, for the purposes of criterial diagnosis, in the specific and delineated practice of examination as re-presented as medical science, any extra-practical sensibility becomes invisible (i.e. its needs must become that which a clever machine could do for us, a quality control check on the body to determine fact). Whenever and wheresoever we take hermeneutics to apply, what might appear at first as a simple, non-narrative fact becomes revealed as being predicated upon a tacit storiedness or textuality.

Further, what is also obscured in the 'realist' account is the concerned involvement with meaningful practices against and through which the category 'virginity' gains its currency. 'Virginity' as a constructed state of personhood, is fictioned into fact, because, in a given place at a given time, it is made to *matter*. For example, the possibility of the woman's marriage, or the value of her dowry may be affected by her virginity, not to mention the impact upon the state of psycho-sociological well-being of being subjected to this identity through the logic of these practices.

The doctor's investigatory practice is thus enabled by an obscured textuality, and the occasion of the investigatory practice itself is saturated with a non-articulated, non-presenced textuality. This textuality is also available, in some form and to some degree, to the other people involved. For example, a girl-child (in a case of putative sexual assault) may well ask why she has to see the doctor, and be told that it is to check her over, to see if she is 'all right'. She may or may not be told that what is at issue is possible evidence to pursue the conviction of a person suspected of committing the assault, though in such a case the social workers and police officers involved will know this explicitly. A woman may know that she is going to the doctor to gain proof of her virginity so that she can 'marry someone nice'. These are stories (as presencing practice), and have their own truth-value in their respective life-worlds.

It is worth noting that hermeneutic exegesis is, of course, a particular presencing practice in its own right. For any hermeneutics sensitive to Heidegger's notion of concern, background textuality is always-ever (this term will be addressed a little later) working its influence (this meant analytically, of course, not nomically). Indeed, concern implies the doubtful affirmation that it works most smoothly when not questioned or revealed – when it is simply taken-for-granted (cloaked in its 'natural' narrative embroidery).

Textuality used as an analytic serves to presence (to story into attention) the meaningful background practices against which issues (such as conditions of virginity – and its 'loss') reveal themselves.

Decentring the subject with language and decentring language with textuality

It should be clear by now that we are saying much more here than that different people have different viewpoints on issues; that matters can be construed in alternative ways (as is asserted, for example, in the work of Kelly, 1955, and his notion of 'personal constructs'). We are making the more basic post-phenomenological point that subjectivity is itself constituted through textuality. Harré (1992: 154) is thus talking towards textuality when he says: '... all psychological phenomena and the beings in which they are realised are produced discursively'. Shotter and Gergen (1989: ix) do so too when they say that 'the primary medium within which identities are created and have their currency is not just linguistic but textual'. In this sense, subjectivity, far from being the origin or source of meaning (as in phenomenological approaches which privilege the 'meaning giving subject' or 'transcendental ego') is as much an *effect* of meaning as its predication.

This theme of 'decentring' the subject is perhaps the most characteristic feature of post-structuralism. On an ontological level, this decentring represents a deconstruction of the subject/object duality which pervades Modernistic inquiry. This duality encourages us to understand the world as being comprised of raw, objectively knowable entities and processes which have value and meaning 'projected' onto them by individual 'subjects'. It thereby provides the conceptual soil, not only for those forms of empiricism, positivism and structuralism which valorize the search for universal, transcendent, objective laws and knowledge, but also for those approaches which emphasize the importance of ego-mediated 'subjectivity', 'meaning', 'interpretation' and 'value'.

It can be seen, then, that the object/subject dichotomy reflects and is reflected in a distinction between fact and value. This distinction encourages us to understand that entities in the world are essentially and in-themselves 'neutral' and are only subsequently rendered 'valuable' through the influence of the subjectivity of an individual. On starting one's enquiry from this assumption, it is no surprise that people see fit either to discover something of the true, neutral and objective nature of entities, or to unpeel the layer of subjective 'varnish' in order to inspect its constitution.

Approaches informed by textuality are not predicated upon the subject/object dualism. This makes them difficult to understand for people who do not question their usage of this dualism. This difficulty is in evidence when authors argue as if anything that is not objective must be subjective; likewise, anything that is not fact must be value. Collin (1985: 148), for example, in criticizing what he takes to be 'social constructionism', states that the 'doctrine of the "social construction of social reality" ' is 'the idea that social fact is a product of the agents' conceptions and meanings'. Similarly, Greenwood (1992: 144) summarizes social constructionism in the form of the following idealist/subjectivist thesis: 'the social dimensions of human actions' are 'a function of the social dimensions of our descriptions of them'. Their argument is that anyone who (as a 'constructionist') seeks to call into question the object-hood of the social, must surely be committed to a thoroughly subjectivist stance.

Interrupter: Well, aren't they? Seems logical to me.

Beryl: Not at all. You are getting confused by assuming that as they are 'opposites' (in the conventions of the language-use we are used to), then logically to be not the one means being the other. If I am not sad, that does not make me happy, does it? If I am not late, that does not make me early?

Interrupter: But if you were the late Ms Curt, my life might be a lot easier!

Beryl: Which is why we have such a bitter–sweet relationship. Shall I send out for a sweet and sour?

Dichotomies are, we would argue, always problematic. The object/subject, fact/value dichotomy also reflects and can be found reflected in that of determinism/free-will. Kemper (1988: 363–4) gets into similar confusion when he writes (unacknowledgingly) of constructionist approaches to emotion that:

> An unacknowledged disjunction plagues the social constructionist position. On the one hand society prescribes, shapes and determines what emotions to feel, and how, when and where to feel them. This suggests that social constructionists are determinists. But another theme . . . is that individuals are 'agents', implying responsibility and freedom to take or not to take on emotions. The agentic view disputes that emotions are 'passions', something that happens to one, yet the social constructionist approach surely insists that individuals are subject to social norms and prescriptions. These two strands of explanation, thrust under the same rubric, appear to be incompatible with each other.

The reason that we are spending so much time warning about the influence of the subject/object dichotomy (and its correlates) is to make sure that it does not 'spring up' again once we start talking about 'texts'. This is one of the key aims of adopting textuality as an analytic. It is all too easy to misunderstand textuality as if it were a 'book' and we 'the readers' – both 'it' and 'us' being separate, preformed entities which then come to interact during the generation of 'meaning'. Such an understanding would recapitulate all that we are trying to avoid. It is exactly this structure, that treats text as 'object' and reader as 'subject', that Rosenau (1992: 25) re-produces. Commenting on the 'postmodern death of the author', she writes as follows:

> . . . the postmodern reader enters at centre stage and assumes an unprecedented autonomy. No longer is the reader a passive subject to be entertained, instructed or amused. S/he is given the freedom to attribute meaning to the text without consequence or responsibility.

In one gesture, Rosenau grants the reader freewill and as having control over the text, and institutes a relativist (in the sense of 'purely subjective') programme for the assessment of meaning production. To be fair, this is not a thesis she supports, it is one she attributes to 'postmodernism'. Yet it betrays that same regulated misunderstanding which we have outlined above. The interesting thing is that the words have changed (no longer is it subject/object, but reader/text) but the properties and powers attributed along the 'fault-line' of the dichotomy have remained the same.

From the position of textuality, a text without a reader is a contradiction in terms. To elucidate this slogan, we will need to further interrogate what is captured in the words 'text' and 'reader'. This interrogation will, first, warn against mistaking textuality for language *tout court*. This will require that we de-centre spoken and written language and remove it from its privileged, commanding position in the field of postmodern inquiry. Second, it will involve a discussion of 'subjectivity' as we see it.

Textuality not text

A good place to start here is the argument put forward by Kvale (1990: 38):

> The focus on language implies a decentralizing of the subject. It is no longer a self who uses language to express itself, but rather language which speaks through the person, the individual becomes a medium for the culture and its language. The unique self loses prominence, the author is today less the original genius than a mediator of the culture through structures of language. There is today an emphasis on narratives, on the telling of stories. With the collapse of the global systems of meaning or narratives, there takes place a re-narrativisation of the culture . . . a narrative is not merely a transmission of information, in the very act of telling a story the position of the storyteller and of the listener is constituted, and their place in the social order, the story creating and maintaining a social bond. The narratives of a community contribute to uphold the values and the social order of that community.

Kvale neatly summarizes the received postmodern position on the interpenetration of language, power and subjectivity. 'Language' (narrative, story, text) 'decentralizes' the 'subject'. This is clearly to accord enormous constitutive importance to language ('the story creating and maintaining a social bond'), not to mention the strangeness of the now familiar claim that 'language speaks through the person'. In order to make 'language' bear this weight of responsibility, it is, of course, necessary to expand the sphere of its usual meaning. Look again at this statement:

> . . . a narrative is not merely a transmission of information, in the very act of telling a story the position of the storyteller and of the listener is constituted, and their place in the social order, the story creating and maintaining a social bond. (Kvale 1990: 38)

Here, then, 'story' is extended to encompass what we are calling 'storiedness'. By storiedness we mean that which is not a story, in the sense of a presencing practice, yet which is predicated upon and saturated with textuality – for example, the 'social order', 'social bonds' and various 'subject positions'. Thus text is extended to textuality. However, as soon as we move into the domain of textuality, the centrality accorded to language (in the name of decentring the subject) must be renounced. The 'social bond' creates and maintains 'the story' just as much as 'the story' creates and maintains the 'social bond'. Likewise, to hark back to the argument we cited earlier from Collin, if 'social fact is a product of the agents' conceptions and meanings', then so too are 'agents' conceptions and meanings 'a product of "social fact" '. The whole is textuality.

The analytic of textuality insists simultaneously that practices and objects in-the-world are 'texts', and that texts, stories, narratives and such are 'practices' and 'objects' in-the-world. This is, we assume, what Derrida means by his by now notorious claim that 'there is nothing outside the text'.

The 'always already'

The notion of the 'always already', as used by Derrida in explicating Heidegger, is a vital concept for textuality as we are using it. To get a grip on this notion, let us look again at the way textuality could get misunderstood. Greenwood and Collin seem to suggest that constructionists are latter-day Canutes (to be more accurate but less clear, Canutites), who think they can command the world with their words. For them all this talk of text seems to imply that our assertions about the world in-and-of-themselves construct the world as being what it is. This would surely be, they suggest (and we agree), to overburden language.

To mistake this for the constructionist position is to ignore the 'always already'. It is to assume that we are fully formed, independent individuals who interact with a fully formed, independent world of things – that we are the 'subjects' to the world's 'objects'. This is not what we are saying at all. We clearly live in a world which is always already and inescapably meaning-ful, aspects of which are revealed to us through our concerned engagement with it. Our concerned engagement is, likewise, not something which we 'pluck from the ether'. It is intimately enmeshed with the organization and doings of our daily practices.

Each time we encounter a chair, for example, we do not confront a mean-ingless wooden construction and then go on to imbue that 'object' with our subjective 'understanding' of its 'chairness' as we find we can sit on it. It is always already a chair.

> *Interrupter: Except, of course, when there is a deliberate attempt to trouble our taken-for-granteds. I recall once going to an art gallery and seeing a display made up of bricks arranged in an oblong on the floor. My compan-ion asked 'But is this art?', and I said, 'Well, as it's in an art gallery, and the gallery paid lots of dosh for it, we have to assume it is art, in some-body's eyes, at least.' She just said, 'Well it looks just like a pile of bricks to me!'*

Beryl: Precisely. To argue that a chair has an always-already 'chairedness' is not to say that it is essentially a chair, no more than bricks are essentially bricks. Your example illustrates very well the difference between a doctrine of essentialism and the always already. It is that the always already gains its being not from some essential 'Truth' but from a particular historical and cultural specificity. In the case of the bricks, their location in an art gallery changed their cultural location, which was intended to change the reading we place upon what they 'are'.

We are not then saying, as an essentialist might, that a given wooden construction has always been and will always be 'a chair'. What we are saying is that the chair (and indeed anything else, whether that is an object like a chair or a phenomenon, such as 'juvenile delinquency') gains its being (what it is, its chairness) from its enmeshment within a culturally contingent and historically specific form-of-life: its textuality.

Let us imagine that a person points to a chair and asserts that it is a chair. What sort of a discovery is this? Heidegger is clear about the role of the 'forehaving' (or in Derrida's terminology, the role of the always already) in the making of assertions: 'The pointing-out which assertion does is performed on the basis of what has already been disclosed in understanding or discovered circumspectively' (Heidegger 1962: 119). Hence, it is not as if our philosophical chair-pointer is an independent, context-free 'subject' imbuing through their assertions, a 'raw object' with its meaning:

> Assertion is not a free-floating kind of behaviour which, in its own right, might be capable of disclosing entities in general in a primary way: on the contrary it always maintains itself on the basis of Being-in-the-world. (Heidegger 1962: 199)

Shotter (1992: 177) has much in common with Heidegger when he writes:

> ... the entities they [our ways of talking] denote are known not for what they are in themselves, but in terms of their 'currency' or significance in our different modes of social life, that is, in terms of what it is deemed sensible for us to do with them in the everyday, linguistically structured circumstances of their use. They have their being only within the form of life we (the whole community) conversationally sustain between ourselves.

Wittgenstein (1981: 567) also shares this reading:

> How can human behaviour be described? Surely only by sketching the actions of a variety of humans, as they are all mixed up together. What determines our judgment, our concepts and reactions, is not what one man [sic] is doing now, an individual action, but the whole hurly-burly of human actions, the background against which we see any action.

The Textuality of subjectivity

Subject/object recapitulated as the inner and the outer

Under modernism, the discipline which claimed the 'subject' or 'subjectivity' as its subject matter was, of course, Psychology. This claim of intellectual property went largely uncontested outside of disputes around the scientific adequacy of this newly formed discipline. However, no less than in the other human sciences, psychology has had many of its basic presuppositions challenged during the climate of problematization. Some even talk of an ongoing 'crisis' (e.g. Parker 1989). As Stainton Rogers (1991: 5) has noted:

> Just as the term 'nouvelle cuisine' has been repeatedly used for at least a hundred years to describe whatever was the latest fashion in cookery, psychology, even in its much shorter history, has been continually confronted with 'new paradigms'. Each one has been presented as a dramatic refutation of a worn-out previous order, offering fresh insights and innovative solutions. It is almost as though theories, like washing machines, have built-in obsolescence, so that after a period of constant use they cease to work efficiently and need to be replaced by a new model.

Meanwhile, the question of 'the subject' has become central to other areas of scholarly analysis. These include cultural studies (see, for example, Grossberg, Nelson and Treichler 1992; Schwichtenberg 1993), media studies, radical sociology, feminist psychoanalysis, art history, critical legal studies and literary studies. All of them have developed sophisticated post-structural, post-phenomenological (i.e. climate of problematization) approaches in order to address 'the subject'. What is notable is the extent to which such approaches have been largely ignored by mainstream psychology.

Those that have brought such climate of problematization treatments of subjectivity to psychology have tended to do so through a concern with the political. They include Harré (1983, 1992), Henriques, Hollway, Urwin, Venn and Walkerdine (1984), Hollway (1989), Sampson (1989), Shotter and Parker (1990), Ibañez (1991) and Wetherell and Potter (1992). All of them have drawn significantly upon ideas from outside of psychology, and are still, by and large, marginalized within its mainstream. We interpret this, at least in part, as due to confusion and misunderstanding over the position climate of problematization thinkers are proposing (see Stenner and Eccleston, in press, for a fuller treatment of this argument).

Attempts to radicalize psychology under a climate of problematization have struggled to escape the subject/object dichotomy and the mistaken assumption that what we are doing is promoting 'mere subjectivity'. However, there is a tendency for this to reproduce itself as a distinction between the inner and the outer.

The well-documented debate between cognitive psychologists and behaviourists provides a simple illustration of the extent to which disputes within psychology are regulated by the subject (inner)/object (outer) distinction. Accounts of the subject made within this regime of truth must either attribute central significance to one of the 'inner'/'outer' couple (Buss's 1979, false dialectic between person-constructs-reality/reality-constructs-person), or bring them together in a liberal compromise of 'co-action' (not to be mistaken for a deconstruction of the very terms of debate; cf. Stainton Rogers and Stainton Rogers 1992b). It is no surprise, then, that approaches informed by textuality (usually going under the name of 'social constructionism') are read from within this regime of truth as being either in agreement with behaviourism, or in agreement with cognitive psychology (or as harbouring an 'unacknowledged disjunction'; see the earlier quotation from Kemper, p. 42).

Examples of the former assumption (i.e. that radical approaches are forms of behaviourism in another guise) are probably more common because of the 'anti-mentalism' of constructionists influenced by Wittgenstein, Ryle and Mead (cf. Stenner and Eccleston, in press). Examples of the latter assumption (i.e. that radical approaches are forms of cognitive psychology) can be found, for instance, in the conflation of constructionism with either Piagetian constructivism, or Kellian personal construct theory (and other humanistic cognitivisms).

One limitation of these categories is that neither position is well equipped to say anything of interest or substance about subjectivity. For radical behaviourists, subjectivity is simply a non-issue – out of the frame of analysis, along with all else that cannot be directly observed. Cognitivists, on the other hand, are concerned with the 'cognitorium' rather than the subject. Their concern is with the ways in which our 'information-processing systems' organize, structure and relay the 'raw data' inputted through our senses.

While cognitivists (particularly those working within the growing field of artificial intelligence), those self-styled 'cognitive scientists' are interested in such things as neural nets (i.e. the database and mechanisms by which higher cognitive processes like memory and problem solving operate). This is not the same thing as we are talking about when we refer to subjectivity. Their locus tends to be far more mechanistic, and their approach more empiricist. For example, from 'founding fathers' of cognitivism like Bartlett (1932) to present-day proponents like Baddeley (1992), while 'meaning' is treated as critical to their formulations (rather than, say, information in an abstract sense), they still think in terms of discovering the lawfulness of human sense-making (e.g. the systematic ways in which memory distorts an input in an effort-after-meaning). Our aim here is not to discuss cognitivism and behaviourism (nor the study of memory discourse à la Edwards and Potter 1992), however, but to take this understanding as a way of examining recurrent problems within those approaches which more closely resemble textuality.

The declaration of discursive autonomy: a flawed solution to the problem of the inner/outer

Recent psychological appropriations of the vocabulary of 'text' and 'discourse' – which were influenced by the call to recognize the political nature of psychology – are indebted to what could be called the declaration of discursive autonomy as formulated within structural linguistics (the langue/parole distinction) and in the early work of Foucault: 'One is led therefore to the project of a pure description of discursive events as the horizon for the search for the unities that form within it' (Foucault 1972: 27).

In other words, first, discourses are not spoken (created) by the subjects – the subject is not an 'author' who can create linguistic chains out of thin air. Second, a crucial part of discourse is that it is prior to, and thus creates, the subject. The problem with early approaches to 'discourse' in psychology (which is itself, as we have been arguing, a problem of psychological discourse), is that they tend to focus only on the first of these and to ignore or 'bracket off' the second. This leaves them with text rather than textuality.

To give an example, Potter and Wetherell (1987), in wanting to study racism and other political matters without recourse to the traditional 'psychologizing' strategy of pointing to internal racist 'attitudes' or 'belief systems', move towards a focus on discourse alone:

> The researcher should bracket off the whole issue of the quality of accounts as accurate or inaccurate descriptions of mental states . . . Our focus is exclusively on discourse itself: how it is constructed, its functions and the consequences which arise from different discursive organisation. (Potter and Wetherell 1987: 178)

Here discourse is delivered to us as an autonomous thing-in-itself. However, the autonomy here granted to discourse is far too broad. It is one thing to say that individuals are not the 'authors' of discourses. It is quite another thing to permit that to imply that discourse can then be studied as a thing-in-itself in isolation from power and subjectivity (for this implies that both power and subjectivity are themselves autonomous things-in-themselves). Once the 'triad' is (re-)constituted in terms of separate entities, additional 'linking mechanisms' are required to bring them together. Thus 'discourse' as used by Potter and Wetherell can only escape the isolation and irrelevance of its autonomy by being related to other aspects of the world (e.g. power and subjectivity) through an intermediary – the medium of 'function' or 'consequence'.

For Potter and Wetherell, then, the solution to the problem of subjectivity is that all is 'outer'. The troublesome 'inner' has been neatly swept under the carpet, leaving the constitutive dichotomy itself intact and unquestioned. This is why – to bring the matter full circle – 'discourse analysis' is often viewed by cognitive psychologists as an all too familiar renunciation of the 'inner' world. This allows Neisser (1992: 451) to say of Potter and his colleagues: 'They are classical behaviorists, trusting in nothing except overt action.' Of course, they are nothing of the sort, for the 'inner' remains stubbornly there, albeit obscured because its textuality is reformulated as an added-on analytic.

Turning to the question of 'power' as it is raised in psychology, we can see that those who have addressed it from the discourse-analytic perspective, despite the warnings of the later Foucault, count it as the 'external' referent par excellence. Anything said of the 'inner' must be consigned to the category of relativist subjectivism, thus standing in need of redemption by a hard-nosed extra-discursive critical realism:

> . . . [I]n order to analyse institutions, power and ideology, we need to stop the slide into relativism which much discourse theory, and

'Outer'– power/insituations/ideology/things

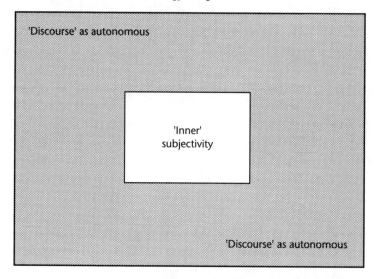

'Outer'– power/insituations/ideology/things

Figure 2.1 The separation of subject and object.

post-structuralism generally, encourages. We need some sense of the real to anchor our understanding of the dynamics of discourse. (Parker 1992: 22)

If 'discourse' is delivered to us as an autonomous domain, ambiguous as to its innerness or outerness, yet not challenging this distinction, then it can be held to account for its lack of consideration of both. Two gaps are left, and those schooled in the 'subject/object' dichotomy will, of course, want to fill those gaps according to Fig. 2.1.

If it is the 'externalism' of 'critical realism' (Bhaskar 1978; Parker 1989) that has been brought to discourse theory in order to re-balance its autonomous subjectivism, then it is the 'internalism' of psychoanalysis which is most readily brought in to fill the 'inner' gap (Henriques, Hollway, Urwin, Venn and Walkerdine 1984; Hollway 1989; Walkerdine 1990; Parker 1992).

Subjectivity and power as immanent in textuality

Foucault, in *History of Sexuality, Volume 1* (1979a: 61), surmised: 'suppose the obligation to conceal it were but another aspect of the duty to admit to it?' Textuality is an analytic which presents subjectivity, power and discourse as immanent. Subjectivity, as we see it, is not simply controlled or coerced by

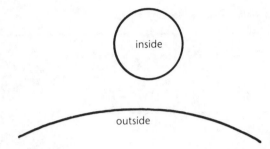

Figure 2.2   A representation of subjectivity predicated on the subject/object dualism – inside and outside are separate.

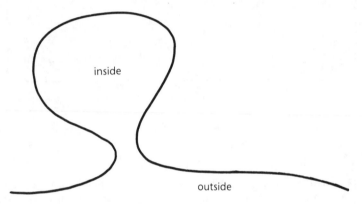

Figure 2.3   A representation of subjectivity where the inside is a fold of the outside.

power, or regulated and influenced by discourse: it is made up of these things.

The analytic of textuality renders the subject, not as a stable entity or inner force that underlies the outer vicissitudes of daily life (like the concept of 'personality' in psychology which is held to be constant despite situational variability), but as a fold or invagination in our textuality which creates the impression of an inner and an outer. This can best be expressed diagrammatically. Figure 2.2 represents the view of subjectivity which is predicated upon the subject/object dualism. Here, both 'inside' (perhaps the 'individual') and 'outside' (perhaps the 'environment') are presented as pre-formed and separable facticities. Figure 2.3 represents the view of subjectivity as textuality, where the 'inside' can be seen as a fold of the 'outside' (which can thus no longer be called the outside), made 'inner' not by separation *from* the 'outer' but by being made *out of* (or from within) the 'outer'. As put by Deleuze (1986: 100): '. . . it is as if the relations of the outside folded back to create a doubling, allowing a relation to oneself to emerge, and constitute an inside which is hollowed out and develops its own unique dimension'.

Interrupter: I must admit these diagrams don't talk to me very well. Wouldn't a better way of showing this, surely, be a Möbius strip, where its folds trouble our sense of 'inner' and 'outer'? Or even a three-dimensional Klein bottle?

Beryl: Some of me would agree. Others wanted one of those lovely Escher lithographs with staircases which seem to lead in such odd directions that it appears one could go on climbing ever upwards and getting nowhere.

Interrupter: That I can relate to. Is that how you modelled the argument for Textuality and Tectonics? Sort of Gödeling while Rome burns?

Beryl: Cruel! Though you will find at the end of the book the argument that I see travelling as more important than arriving, whatever route you take.

To get back to our topological analogies, clearly the two representations we have illustrated bring with them very different understandings as to the relationship between inner and outer. This relationship itself can also be expressed diagrammatically. It is clear that in Fig. 2.5 there is a relationship of inextricable mutuality between inner and outer: a change in one is part of a change in the other (for they are of 'one cloth'). Figure 2.4, in contrast, expresses a 'Newtonian' relationship of objects rebounding off one another at the behest of forces (and influenced by the differing constitution of the different objects).

In Fig. 2.5, the 'outside' is as always-already meaningful as we, the 'insiders' are. In Fig. 2.4, the inside gains 'knowledge' of the otherwise meaningless 'environment' (and changes accordingly) through its ongoing contacts with it (compare this, for example, with Piagetian constructs like assimilation and accommodation). As such, it is assumed that there are moments of distanced individual reflection that follow the experience of momentary engagement with real singular events (points of 'contact'). In Fig. 2.5, we are never 'outside' of our textuality – we *are* our textuality – and this textuality is immanent with power and the discursive.

Interrupter: That's all very interesting. But are you, in fact, saying anything terribly new? Haven't a few more eminent people than you been here before?

Beryl: I presume you don't mean my own *éminences grises*. Yes, in the sense I am giving to it, textuality can be viewed as fashioned out of the formulations of subjectivity provided by Vygotsky (1962), Shotter (1984) and Harré (1992), certainly in so far as they take the 'social' to be prior to, and constitutive of, the 'individual'. That having been said, I do think that adopting the term textuality is useful, and in that sense offers something new.

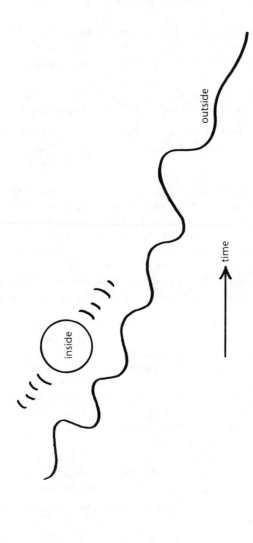

Figure 2.4 A representation of subjectivity predicated on the subject/object dualism – inside and outside are separate, as seen over time.

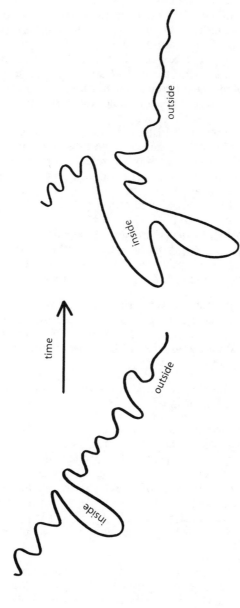

Figure 2.5 A representation of subjectivity where the inside is a fold of the outside, as seen over time.

To press home this point, we can briefly examine the earlier quotation from Foucault on sexuality. The beauty of this short and simple sentence is that it raises the possibility of the immanence of subjectivity, discourse and power. It suggests that the 'subjective' – in this case, the felt 'obligation to conceal' one's most intimate (subjective) thoughts and actions (whether these be shameful sexual fantasies, a lie one has told to a jealous lover, or whatever) is a folding or doubling ('another aspect of') of the discourses usually thought of as 'outside' (an 'externally' imposed 'duty to admit to it'). The implication being that, first, this particular 'subjectivity' (or inside) could not exist without this particular discourse (or outside) and, second (and more fundamentally), subjectivity in general could not exist without the principle of the fold.

Foucault combines these two insights in his concepts of 'subjectivation' and 'technologies of the self' where power and discourse are understood as being constitutive of subjectivity (and not merely regulative). The vocabulary of 'story' that we described earlier is one way of addressing the 'fold'. We can think of our-selves as 'storied' and 'storying' (cf. Sarbin 1986; Shotter and Gergen 1989) – what Christie and Orton (1988: 562) describe as *Homo narrans narratur*.

Such 'texts of identity', however, are never independent of their matrix of textuality (including power and discourse). A number of authors have addressed this by way of a concept of 'technologies of the self'. Foucault (1988: 18) for example, regards these as the discursive activities:

> ... which permit individuals to effect by their own means or with the help of others a number of operations on their own bodies and souls, thoughts, conduct and ways of being, so as to transform themselves in order to attain a certain state of happiness, purity, wisdom, perfection or immortality.

This reminds us of the politico-moral embeddedness of our self-narratives. Similar is Harré's (1983: 260) notion of an 'identity project':

> Self-knowledge requires the identification of agentive and knowing selves as acting within hierarchies of reasons. It follows that this kind of self-knowledge is, or at least makes available the possibility of autobiography. But as Hamlyn has convincingly argued, self-knowledge as history lacks the dimension of moral assessment that is at the heart of self-knowledge proper. I think it can be shown that self-knowledge as history cannot exist independently of self-knowledge as moral assessment ... Self-knowledge is coming to see oneself in relation to a moral order.

The point is not that a person may, say, go to the movies to see a John Wayne film, emerge from the cinema identifying with John Wayne, and begin to walk with a swagger, spit and speak in a slow drawl. This would simply be a matter of copying (or 'imitation' in the psycho-jargon of social learning theory). Rather, the point is more thoroughgoing. We are never outside of textuality. Of course, people do copy film actors sometimes. But this does not get close to the point that we can all be said to *live* stories.

> *Interrupter: Like, say, last night I had a 'show down' with my mother, and then she became all melodramatic – that sort of thing?*

Beryl: Well, we seldom actually narrate our lives in such an explicitly dramaturgical manner. But yes, our hopes, ambitions, fears, dreams, and so on are, in part, narrative in form. We cannot tell ourselves and other people who we are, who we have been, who we will be, and so on without narrative.

> *Interrupter: You seem to be saying people act out their lives as though they were actors in a play. Hasn't Goffman been there before you?*

Beryl: I think I am saying something more than that. Goffman's dramaturgical approach is mainly concerned with social interaction – that is, action. I'm talking about how people make sense of, and make, their life-worlds. Much more generally than how we act, I am suggesting that it is through the medium of narrative that we relate to others and construct ourselves as meaningful, knowable, accountable subjects. In a sense, we are made real by stories.

> *Interrupter: All right. Now I think I want to take stock a bit. Even if you don't care if we are going anywhere in particular, I would like to at least get some sense of where I'm going. Is that all right?*

Beryl: Fine, fire away.

> *Interrupter: Well I grant that you have done a reasonable job of indicating the importance of the so-called 'linguistic turn' under the climate of problematization, as you call it. The 'analytic' of textuality, as you narrate it, does seem to avoid the 'trappings' of dualistic thought, and I liked the way in which you didn't, as so often happens, avoid the issue of 'subjectivity' – although of course much more could be said on this matter.*
>
> *What troubles me, however, is the problem of relativism. Granted you manage to avoid the kind of naive subjectivist relativism which would claim either that 'if I don't know about it, then it doesn't exist', or that 'if I say it is true, then it is true', but do you not avoid this merely by replacing it with a kind of collectivist relativism whereby 'if everybody agrees on the story, then the story is true'? What worries me, then, is that you have produced an absurd doctrine of truth – a collective King-Canutism. If so, then surely you are in need of the parable of the 'Emperor's new clothes' – and I don't mean the Sinead O'Connor song!*

Beryl: In a sense, what you say is right: it makes sense, it's logical, and so on. But I want to insist that what we are saying only looks like a 'collective King-Canutism' if we are using the word 'true' in the same way that you do. When you say 'true' you appear to mean True, i.e. 'truth' as an accurate and 'observation-independent' description of the state of the world. When we say 'true', we mean rather that the story, observation or whatever is true-to-its-mark. From this perspective, the 'mark' – or what you are aiming at – is as important as the 'story'. In fact, like the dancer and the dance, it makes no sense to conceive of them in separation (hence we said, somewhat earlier, 'this interpenetration is textuality'). Each story comes 'pre-packed', so to speak, with concern (that is, the story is told always-already within a field of concerns which it addresses, and within which it may have 'grown'). If the story is good or true, then this is because it 'hits the spot': it works. This is not a matter of 'collective deception', but it does allow us to understand the fact that there are many different competing versions as to the 'truth' of any issue (why else would it be 'at issue'?)

Interrupter: But that's not the true meaning of true!!!

Beryl: Look – whose language is this? Anyway, I suggest you consult an etymological dictionary over that one.

Interrupter: All right. Leaving aside the meaning of 'truth' for now, doesn't your position still leave us prey to those ideologues who would thrive on such a 'flexible' conception of truth and turn it to their own dubious advantage? Doesn't this leave us floundering in postmodern apolitical and amoral hyper-reality?

Beryl: Well, one way of answering that old-chestnut is simply to point to the power that has been so obviously and so regularly wielded in the name of this 'absolute truth' that you seem so attached to and so jealous of losing (what are you getting out of your Truths?). Can you seriously maintain that Truth is innocent after reading, say, Foucault's *Discipline and Punish*? It seems clear that the 'fear of relativism' that springs up whenever 'postmodernism' or 'social constructionism' gets discussed is part and parcel of the discourse which would hold Truth up, not only as timeless and independent, but even as the saviour of humanity.

Interrupter: There's no need to get personal, I'm only playing Devil's Advocate.

Beryl: Well, don't take my word for it. Patti Lather (1990: 75) expresses the point very nicely when she says:

'If the focus is on the procedures which take us as objects and involve us in systems of categories and procedures of self-construction, relativism becomes a non-issue. If the focus is on how power relations shape knowledge production and legitimation, relativism is a concept from another discourse, a discourse of foundations that posits grounds for certainty outside of context, some neutral, disinterested, stable point of reference.'

Interrupter: Now hang on, it's all very well bringing in these grand quotations, but how does your work address these concerns? Surely the advantage of textuality is that it emphasizes flux and change and the interdependence of things – stuff that usually gets associated with people like Heraclitus who are more noted for stepping in rivers than engaging in 'political' or 'moral' matters. I've also read Patti Lather's paper, and now it's my turn to quote from it:

'All thought is not equally arbitrary, Bakhtin argued over fifty years ago; positionality weighs heavily in what knowledge comes to count as legitimate in historically specific times and places. The word is spoken from many sites which are differently positioned regarding access to power and resources. Relativism foregrounds the shifting sands of context, but occludes the play of power in the shaping of changing structures and circumstances. As such, it is what Haraway calls a 'God trick . . . a way of being nowhere while claiming to be everywhere equally'. In sum, fears of relativism and its seeming attendant, nihilism or Nietzschean anger, seem to me an implosion of Western, white male, class privileged arrogance – if we cannot know everything, then we can know nothing.' (Lather 1990: 75)

Beryl: Yes, well, I'm glad we've been able to reach some agreement. The point to make as I see it is that we need to go beyond a relativism which positions the human subject as the source of meaning, but not towards an objectivism which leads us to believe that the answer to our problems lies in an extra-discursive, non-human, independent realm of forces, structures and mechanisms. This is a 'false' choice. In fact, that last quote that you brought in provides a neat way of introducing the importance of our second analytic. Our current textuality is only possible against a backdrop of already historically sedimented human constructions, and it is this – the 'shaping and changing structures and circumstances' – and the interrelations between such formations, that we address as tectonics, which is where we move onto next.

Interrupter: Glad to be of assistance, Beryl dear!

Beryl: Happy to have you along, dear Interrupter.

3

Tectonics

The notion of tectonics has already been introduced in Chapter 1, and been mentioned several times in Chapter 2 in our coverage of textuality. In this chapter, it will become our primary focus. Initially, we adopted the term 'tectonics' because, beyond its desired denotation of construction/constructionism, it is (at least outside of the world of geophysics – and the concept of plate tectonics) a largely 'writerly' word, in the way Game (1991) uses the idea of 'writerly' – it is a word which requires the reader to expend effort in order to impute meaning and/or *make* a reading. Here we will explain more fully what we mean by it, and discuss why we think it is both a useful and, indeed a necessary, analytic within critical polytextualism.

What are tectonics? Constructing construction

As we will use the term, 'tectonics' refers to:

- the actions and inter-actions of textuality;
- the contours and topographies by which textuality may be read as constituted and bounded;
- the conditions of plausibility whereby specific textualities are narrated into possibility;

- the structures we read within those landscapes;
- the dynamics, including the change-through-time (temporality) we impute to the terrains of textuality.

Tectonics thus concerns the narration of how and why that which is presenced as textuality is produced, moulded and changed, and the notions of agency such accounts employ to account *for* the bringing about of such forms and changes. Whereas the analytic of textuality is primarily directed to the reading of knowledges as expressed – to the abduction of the apparent present – tectonics is concerned with the dynamic interplay of text upon text, and with how texts change over time and position.

We are not the first to use the metaphor of tectonics in this way. Indeed, it has a very respectable pedigree, having been used by Karl Marx himself:

> The so-called revolutions of 1848 were but poor incidents, small fractures and fissures in the dry crust of European society. But they denounced the abyss. Beneath the apparently solid surface, they betrayed oceans of liquid matter, only needing expansion to rend into fragments continents of hard rock. (Marx 1978: 577–8)

Deleuze (1990: 47), writing on Foucault's work, also made use of it:

> Strata are historical formations, positivities and empiricities. As 'sedimentary beds' they are made from things and words, from seeing and speaking, from the visible and the sayable, from bands of visibility and fields of readability, from contents and expressions.

And Foucault himself wrote (1970: xxiv):

> In attempting to uncover the deepest strata of Western culture, I am restoring to our silent and apparently immobile soil its rifts, its instability, its flaws; and it is that same ground that is once more stirring under our feet.

In order to apply this analytic, we have adopted the term 'tecton' to address the aggregates of textuality within and upon which tectonic processes operate. Although tecton clearly has resonances with notions like discourse, text and representation, we have introduced it in order to avoid the kinds of confusion which arise when terminology is used in widely different ways, to imply all manner of different things. All tecton denotes is that on which tectonic processes impinge. It is a technical device we use to 'freeze' textuality, in order to concentrate on tectonics.

> *Interrupter: Oh heck! Here we go again – another bit of ugly jargon. Is it strictly necessary?*

> Beryl: Well yes, I think it is actually – otherwise I wouldn't have introduced it, would I? It may seem as though I am creating words for word's sake, but I really am trying to avoid confusion.

> *Interrupter: Gotcha! You do realize you just said 'really'?*

Beryl: Come on, give us a break, it was just a turn of phrase. I was using it for emphasis, not playing a 'Truth Game'.

Interrupter: I suppose so. But no more jargon, OK?

Beryl: Look, I'm not making any promises. Just keep quiet for a bit, will you? Now, where were we?

Tectonic activity constitutes the processes by which different loci of textuality (i.e. tectons) are actively and ongoingly produced and re-produced in the course of human discursive, meaning-making activity. Put another way, wherever we find textuality, it is always engaged with the tectonic processes of establishing, maintaining or negotiating re-presentations of reality. We are thus all, as textual producers, located in an economy of knowledges, which (to a greater or lesser extent according to circumstances) positions us in the twin businesses of critically reading that ecosystem, and in re-writing it.

Change always requires the modelling of what is, even as one accepts that the very modelling is one of the conditions in flux. Of course, in practice both change and modelling are themselves multiple, critically polytextualized. It is this shifting dynamic of organization and re-organization that we seek to address through the concept of tectonics.

Encyclopaedia or workshop manual?

Over the first two chapters of this book we have given the term tectonics some located sense by treating it as if it were the post-structural moment of organization (under erasure) – as textuality (developed in the last chapter) can be helpfully entered as if it were the post-phenomenological moment of the life-world (also under erasure). The climate of problematization within which we see our work can be considered as a journey into the consequences of the mutual implosion of structuralism and phenomenology. In its guise as a treatment of the postmodern condition (e.g. Jameson 1984; Harvey 1989; Doherty, Graham and Malek 1992), the result is not a minimalistic venture but a densely painted, broad canvas.

The first texts of postmodern transdisciplinarity that such writers proffer have charted the new almost as did the classical encyclopaedists and invoke (if one still can use that mode of reading a text) the casting of their authors as new 'Renaissance Men'. Across the *nova panorama* they are rich in attributions of postmodern organization and lavish in imputations about the postmodern life-world. Our own ambitions are more pragmatic and less sited in ambitions of catholicity (let alone the search for a catholicon for the ills of modernism).

Interrupter: Hey, you saw what happened to Sinead O'Connor when she was rude about the Pope!

Beryl: Catholicon as explain-all, silly, nothing to do with the papacy.

Our ambitions are much more minimalistic – we want merely to develop the tools that can enable us, as craftspersons, to work on and work in the cultural ecosystem as the climate of problematization has delivered it.

The cultural ecosystem

The idea of an ecosystem is a useful allegory in relation to tectonics, for it is premised on the notions of interdependence and of competition.

Box 3.1   Allegory

We have introduced the term allegory here rather than, say, metaphor to highlight the implication that the symbolization should direct our gaze to the possibilities of moral–political readings of our allegoric. An ecosystem is rich in connotations. What was seen under high modernism as the cut-and-thrust of the marketplace of nature, is now being retold as an ideal of inter-dependence, which we upset to our peril. The reactionary possibilities of such politics, applied to culture, is just one vector of the allegory.

An ecosystem is inter-dependent in that it consists, at any moment of time, of a relatively stable arrangement of components, which, via certain forms of finely balanced exchange, maintain a dynamic equilibrium. At the same time, an ecosystem is always subject to change, both gradual and catastrophic. Remove any one component (e.g. take one organism out of a food-chain) and all the rest will be affected. The analogic transfers neatly to a cultural ecosystem – a change to one tecton does not only affect just that one alone, but, in its interaction with its neighbours, will alter them as well.

> *Interrupter: I can see how that works in terms of geophysics, but how would it operate in a cultural ecosystem?*

Beryl: An example might be the shift in political discourse from one where monetarism was so dominant an analytic it seemed to be stifling every other economic discourse, to one where the 'green shoots' of neo-Keynesian economics (rather than the growth it was supposed to engender) began to push through. This seems to be what is happening both in the UK and USA as we get into the 1990s. The point is that not only has the agenda and rhetoric of Conservative discourse changed, but, so too, in interplay, has the agenda and rhetoric of opposition.

> *Interrupter: Yet John Major won an election in 1992, George Bush lost one.*

Beryl: True, but then we should not think of cultural ecosystems as predict-able or lawful – and, for all the resonances between them, the local cultural-ecologies (and a lot more than the economies) of the USA and the UK are really quite different.

With our earlier caveat in mind, the interactive ecosystem-of-culture tectons and their associated knowledges, like species in a biological ecosystem, can be thought of as competing against each other for dominance within a kind of epistemological 'survival of the fittest'. Press (1980) has adopted from biological ecology the notion of 'sympatricity' for this kind of co-existence and competition:

> Sympatric species are those that compete, within any ecosystem, for resources and ultimately for survival, but at any point in time will be seen to be co-existing and more or less equally viable. The image is of sympatric theories that operate in parallel, at one and the same time competing and co-existing. (Stainton Rogers 1991: 7)

An example here would be the ways that, say, the discourses of conventional biomedicine and alternative medicine vie against each other for dominance. In recent historical times, in Britain certainly, biomedicine held an almost hegemonic epistemological position. As the anthropologist Young (1980) has argued, its proponents did not so much promote it as a 'better' way of making sense of health and illness, but as the only viable way to do so. All other explanations were treated as 'not really knowledge at all'.

But as Aakster (1986) has pointed out, as biomedicine lost its power as an explanatory discourse to offer solutions to the health problems of modern life, people (including medical professionals) have become more and more willing to countenance alternatives like homeopathy and Chinese traditional medicine. Today, while in orthodox practice biomedicine is still the dominant epistemology, its grip has lessened and discourses of alternative medicine have gained ground.

> *Interrupter: And, as you were saying before, biomedicine has itself undergone change as a discourse, as the challenge of alternative medicine has begun to become more acceptable.*

Beryl: Quite! It is, as far as I can see, becoming less dogmatic about its science, in some quarters at least, though there are still large pockets of resistance.

> *Interrupter: You seem to be saying, then, that even within a tecton there is a turbulent ecology of knowledges in play?*

Beryl: Of course, the geophysical analogy must not be taken too seriously, and this is why we need the notion of ecology as well. To shift the analogy again, I am reminded here of those glorious pictures of fractals – every time you shift the degree of magnification, new complexity, new activity becomes presenced. So too with tectons – at one level of analysis they may appear to act as singularities, but peep inside them, and a veritable maelstrom of activity will become apparent.

Working on the problematizing of the pre-eminence of expert knowledge

In so far as the climate of problematization needed to be established as a challenge to the existing intellectual order, it did so in part by developing critical analytics (like archaeology or deconstruction) of the orthodox groundings of knowledging. What can be applied to one's own foundations, it is argued, can also be applied to those of 'others. Hence the claim by some that the climate of problematization could foster resistance and offer a political agenda.

A common target (as we have seen above) is biomedicine and the paramedical practices (such as the therapeutic psychologies). When critical writers speak of the growing power of 'the psychobabble establishment' (cf. Rosen 1978), or of the powerlessness engendered by techno-medicine (cf. Ehrenreich 1978), there is often an implied simplification of the cultural ecosystem, a reduction to tectonic hegemony, knowledge of which is informed by friction and fraction against a critical discourse (e.g. feminism, Marxism). Whatever the virtues (in terms of political rhetoric) of claiming and slagging off such tyrannies, it can be as singularizing a piece of miscasting as dubbing lion 'kings of the savanna' and equally questionably predicated.

> *Interrupter: Did you mean to write lion there? Shouldn't it be lions?*
>
> *Beryl:* You are being pesky in this chapter! What's got into you? Yes, we *did* mean to write 'lion', which is the correct term in ecological discourse. It's a generic.
>
> *Interrupter: Oh.*

At least, that is what we are supposed to conclude from the reading of postmodern theorizing, which proposes that one of the main characteristics of contemporary life is the diversity of its cultural ecology. In consequence, the argument goes, whatever has been shaken and stirred up in culture over the past few decades, it no longer permits a distinction between the world of the ordinary and the world of the intellectual – the worlds of commonsense and expert knowledge. It denies as not only artificial but ideologically dodgy and practically untenable the division between 'lay' and expert knowledge (as posited, for example, by Moscovici and Hewstone 1983), arguing instead for viewing these as epistemologically equivalent (see, for example, Gleeson 1991; Stainton Rogers 1991).

> *Interrupter: Aren't you sliding into relativism here – arguing that every discourse is as good as every other? When I have a toothache, I don't go to my neighbour for treatment.*
>
> *Beryl:* Neither do I. By suggesting lay and expert knowledges are epistemologically equivalent, I'm not for a moment suggesting they are equally

practical in their application. Mulkay (1991) is good on this: 'Scientific knowledge can be seen as valid because it works . . . it seems to be objectively valid in the sense that it gives us efficient control over many aspects of the physical world' (p. 95). I go to my dentist because he (and mine is a he) has skills which appear to be effective, and, of course, he has the technology, my neighbour hasn't. But that does not mean that dentistry as a discourse cannot be subjected to deconstruction as Sarah Nettleton (1992) has so elegantly demonstrated.

If the gurus of postmodernism are correct, then no corner of our collective lives, no enclave of sociality is immune to its impact. We have, in this analysis, no 'cultura' carved up into sovereign states of plausibility and meaning, but a whole panoply of competing discourses which admit no single dogma as pre-eminent. What has changed, compared with previous times, is that the cultural landscape has become both more heterogeneous and more labile. A visual allusion might be to the opposite of the changes we can see in the English countryside, where a patchwork of small fields reflecting multiple ownership and use has, as ever larger conglomerates have built up their agribusinesses, been turned into a much plainer landscape of large-area fields. Hedges have been ripped up and from a 'plane one can see ever larger expanses sowed with single crops, producing as the seasons change, mile after mile of sulphureous yellow rape, followed by the golden yellow of barley.

Interrupter: Getting quite poetic, all of a sudden, aren't you?

Beryl: It was quite a sight the day one of me saw it.

In terms of cultural landscape, by contrast, the homogeneity of dominant discourses, in the past interrupted only seldom by small pockets of discord, has given way to an ever diversifying patchwork of competing, clamouring, alternative discourses wherein no single one holds sway.

However, as others tell this story, the production of the postmodern condition is often grounded upon a simplistic narrating of cultural history in which first pre-modern thought (based on theistic authority) and then modern thought (based on scientistic authority) have given way to post-modern thought which, as its central premise, denies any single epistemological authority. Postmodernity's consummate innovation, we are told, is the motley diversity of its canons. Graham (1992) terms this the 'periodicity' paradox of postmodernism, in that in presenting it as following modernism, it can also be read as part of modernism. And, in any case, the singular story of progress into which this so easily glissades is anathema to postmodern thinking.

If we view this genealogy, however, from an ecological perspective, the epistemic time-boundaries tend to dissolve. Instead of a linear progression, we see a more subtle shift. From a cultural ecological viewpoint there has always been (and doubtless will always be) a co-existing and competing multiplicity of sympatric ways of understanding and making sense of the world.

> *Interrupter: I see, so what you are saying is that we have been led astray by all this pre- and post- stuff, into thinking of modernism as an historical period, out of which we are emerging, whereas it is a condition, which does – and has, and will – co-exist with other . . . Hmm, other what?*

Beryl: Hard to find the words sometimes, isn't it? Yes, that is precisely what I am saying. It's not a question of one following the other, but them being different forms of epistemology, for want of a better word. It's to give this sense of sympatricity I am using the allegoric (I just slipped that one in) of a cultural ecosystem.

> *Interrupter: Slipped in or not, allegoric sounds like cough mixture to me.*

From this ecological perspective, we can now begin to ask why it is that extra diversification and, more arguably, de-hegemonization (or at least discourses about them) have arisen. What 'forces' have made the cultural economy of knowledges seemingly more open to diversity and discord?

We might look, for example, to the mass media as one catalyst via which the tectons of cultural life have become more labile. This has enabled issues and events to become not just local but global in their impact, but equally passing rather than ongoing in their issuance.

> *Interrupter: Watch it! Jargon-warning!*

Beryl: It's another word we argued over, I recall, but the jargonizers among me won. I agreed, in the end, that 'issuance' is sufficiently useful to be allowed. Look in the Glossary if you want a definition.

Whether we consider genocide in Bosnia, starvation in Somalia or the domino sequence of overthrow of old-style communism throughout the Eastern bloc, these events, constructed as 'news' by the ever more techno-logically sophisticated mass media, impinge on all of us with access to the means to receive their messages, and then dis-impinge as newer issues be-come 'news'. As the communications industries become de-regulated, their channels increased, their technologies up-dated and their productions farmed out, the rate and variety of information-flux expands not through a cultural imperative, but out of technological possibility (see Lowe 1991, for a more detailed exposition of this argument). Received notions such as the press as Fourth Estate can no longer be taken-for-granted. A postmodern economy brings with it a postmodern economy of knowledges in which it becomes increasingly hard to abduce stable, singularizing tectons.

> *Interrupter: Hang on, you seem to be going back on yourselves. First you are arguing against historicism, now you seem to be arguing for it. Which is it?*

Beryl: Both! The motley diversity of our contemporary cultural ecology can be discoursed as a product both of technological and political change – of what new technology enables us to do, and of what emergent neo-democratic ideology insists that we do, so I can argue for a postmodern condition in that resistance, once seen as a legitimate target for control (whether by the Inquisition or Macarthyism), which does at least appear to itself have become legitimated and institutionalized. But cynically I can say that rebels are now as likely to find a voice as pundits for orthodoxy, and that I take neither of them seriously.

Tectonic as metaphor

The notion of tectonics as we use it is clearly based upon the notion of plate tectonics as used by geophysicists. Its metaphorical resonances are deliberate, and to some extent helpful.

Box 3.2 Mapping *vs* geophysics

Potter and his colleagues (see Potter, Wetherell, Gill and Edwards 1990) observed the use of the metaphor of plate tectonics in the work of Parker (1989), and were critical of the call to 'invisible forces' they see in this form of modelling: 'great plates (discourses) on the earth's crust circulate and clash together; some plates grind violently together; others slip quietly over top of one another; volcanoes burst through while massive forces work unseen below. The limitation with this approach is that the discourses in this view become formed as coherent and carefully systematized (Parker 1989, p. 5) wholes which take on the status of causal agents for analytic purposes' (Potter, Wetherell, Gill and Edwards 1990: 209).

Elsewhere, however, Wetherell and Potter (1992: 1–2) make it clear that they *are* happy to use a cartographic metaphor themselves: 'In defining our task as mapping the language of racism in New Zealand we had in mind the notion of charting themes and ideologies, exploring the heterogeneous and layered textures of practices, arguments and representations . . . the metaphor forces us to see racist language in a new way. It emphasizes that discourse does have substance, it is a material which can be explored and charted . . . It is important to stress, however, that cultural maps and inventories keep changing. We do not want to suggest that the objects we discover will remain static or that the discovery is uncontested.'

In asking ourselves why a cartographer should reject the insights of a geophysicist, it is important to remember that these terms are being used as metaphors. What Potter, Wetherell, Gill and Edwards (1990) seem to be concerned about is that in posing issues of what it was that shaped the map, we may come to ignore how people negotiate their way around what the map is representing. We can see no reason why these two interests cannot be pursued in tandem, and indeed question the power of analyses that seek to assume they can be de-coupled. Hence, of course, the twin analytics we adopt of textuality and tectonics. The geophysical analogic draws resonances between efforts to reconstruct prior geo-continental conditions and the task of tracing archaeologies or genealogies of knowledge (i.e. attempts to reconstruct a text's prior epistemic conditions). In the former process the geophysicist offers us not just a re-presentation of the past, but names for past events and phenomena. For all that there was nobody around in prehistory to know about the continents of Gondwanaland or Laurasia, geophysicists, by giving those past land-masses those names allow us now to 'know' that they did exist.

Cultural analysis likewise gives us names for events and phenomena which are only 'knowable about' with hindsight, such as 'the Enlightenment project' or indeed 'Modernism' itself. Yet the analogy is limited, for it makes no sense for a cultural analyst to try to take culture back to origins. There is no cultural *Pangaea* lurking behind the historical 'land-masses' of knowledge s/he may excavate.

> *Interrupter: And where's that when it's at home?*

> Beryl: Okay, short geophysics lesson. It's the name given to the original proto-continent, before it split into two (Gondwanaland and Laurasia), which is storied to have formed the basis of the world's land-masses as we now know them.

It always needs to be remembered, then, that however useful metaphor and analogy may be in 'getting us thinking' in innovative and creative ways, we need to be continually wary of being too 'enchanted' by their superficial sense-making power.

> *Interrupter: I'm feeling distinctly disenchanted by now, I can tell you.*

> Beryl: Good, that means you are well on the way to becoming a convert. Dis-enchantment is *precisely* what we are seeking to bring about.

Indeed, one insight tectonic analysis provides is that what passes, on one reading, as received 'scientific wisdom' will, in another, seem little more than people being beguiled by the apparent commonsensicality of a discourse because of its allegorical and metaphoric resonances with deeply culturally sedimented stories.

A good example, which has been explored elsewhere (Stainton Rogers and Stainton Rogers 1992a: 39–42), is the 'alembic myth' of developmentalism in child psychology. There it was argued that the notion of development as an elixir, created out of the transformation of 'nature' mixed up with 'nurture', is a consequence both of allusions to chemical processes which create compounds from elements (e.g. salt from chlorine and sodium), and of resonances with historical myths ranging from fairy stories about changeling children to the modern story of 'Superman'. Aided by these allegorical foundations, developmentalists have singularized discourse over the young into formalized 'scientific theories' that purport to have the unique power to organize and explain 'fact'. By shifting our gaze from the child as subject, to developmentalism as subject, it becomes possible to recast its theories as narratives and to refer to them as 'Stories of Childhood'.

Interrupter: Nice opportunity to plug your amanuenses' book there, eh?

Beryl: Well, yes, but it was germane to what I was writing about. And with performance indicators to worry about these days, a little auto-citation never goes amiss, you know.

Interrupter: Do I detect a note of cynicism there?

Beryl: You bet! I'm pretty disenchanted, too, these days.

To return to milk our tectonic metaphor a little drier, when geophysicists consider Southern California, they see it in geological terms as the consequence of catastrophic clashes between tectonic plates. In this level of analysis, the workings of plate tectonics produce earthquakes – elsewhere, the same sorts of processes produce volcanoes or great mountain chains like the Himalayas.

The analogy as cultural tectonic works well in terms of California. More than geographical contingency allows us to see Southern California as also subject to cultural tectonics (a common postmodern theme, as portrayed for twenty-first century Los Angeles in the movie *Blade Runner*). The image generated is of culture clash not culture fusion, and this metaphor works far better than the dreary old socio-chemistry of the 'melting pot' or the liberal dream of a cultural mosaic or patchwork.

The analogy also works in the observation that mountain chains like the Himalayas were once barely detectable protuberances. Cultural landscapes, too, albeit rarely, may have their Krakatoas. Yet a critical difference also permeates all of these resonances. The geophysical plate tectonicist can claim a limited fixed point of knowledging to their work. They may experience an earthquake but it does not change their model (save by passing into that model in the form of data subject to the canons of natural science). Denzin (1988), in a postmodern treatment of *Blue Velvet*, suggests that this is precisely what the movie is narrating, on one reading at least. Its thematic is that the seething undercurrent of the archetypal battle between good and evil continues to simmer under the surface in comfortable, conservative 'small town America [*sic*]'. All that is required to release the pent-up miasma is some fault-line of vulnerability. Indeed, such a metaphoric was even more explicitly presenced in *Barbarella*, where the bubbling 'matmos' depicted ever-present, immanent evil, always ready to erupt.

For the cultural tectonicist, social 'earthquakes' present a change in the conditions of knowledging. Often referred to within the orthodox history of ideas as 'paradigm shifts' (cf. Kuhn 1970), where change is catastrophic, not only does the cultural landscape become rendered radically different (i.e. the relations between tectons undergo radical change), but the very tectonic fluxions themselves undergo radical change. To thoroughly mix metaphors, when the goalposts get shifted, so too does the nature of the game itself!

Cultural tectonics and subject tectonics

The analytic of tectonics thus both enables us to 'read' and to tell stories about the historical and cultural changes in conditions which render constructions-in-textuality live-able, plausible narratives. At the level of passing theory (i.e. subject to the always necessary acceptance of a rapid re-writing), we can initially address these conditions of plausibility separately for two rather different forms of hypothetical tectonic processes – cultural tectonics and subject tectonics.

The tectonics of virginity – or did the textuality move for you?

One route to testing the waters of textuality is the deliberate creation of sentences, which while well-formed, are perturbating of available knowledge systems. One such is 'Lost, one virginity: substantial reward for finder'. However we address this sentence, the missing virginity, *per se*, must elude us – as it would, of course, elude the reward seeker! It does so even if we enter the realms of the apocryphal 'problem page letter', where what is sought after is not the missing condition itself but the memory, the knowledge of that loss, dissolved, perhaps, in some alcoholic haze. Virginity has no strict antonym; in received Christian use, a woman has lost it when she has known (i.e. has sexual intercourse with) a man.

In terms of subject tectonics, this traditional Christian view posits two eigenstates in complementarity: virginity and non-virginity. There can be a personal transit in only one direction. Yet because the pool of virgins in the population at any given time is constantly being renewed through the fecundity of non-virgins (or indeed of the virginal in the case of the Madonna), while death takes its toll of the mainly non-virginal, the pool of virgins is relatively stable over time, thus allowing a meta-stable ritualization of virginity and its loss (or dedication).

Within such cultural tectonics, virginity and its loss have, of course, acquired massive concretions of added (and subtracted) moral, symbolic and economic value. Along with this has come considerable tectonic activity concerned with the establishment of virginity/non-virginity criteria. As we saw in Chapter 2, one result has been the search for bodily correlates of virginity and its loss, particularly in the form of the hymeneal substitution (i.e. the embodied notion of *Virgo intacta*).

Even if virginity had been consistently so embodied (and it is clear from pre-revolutionary French impotence trials that it was not; cf. Darmon 1985), this is not the place for a detailed genealogy of the semiotics of the hymen. What, however, is of interest, are certain continuities and discontinuities in subject and cultural tectonics of the discoursing of virginity (and its loss) and of the hymen (and its vicissitudes). While the medical (and indeed, lay) validation of virginity by hymenspicy [Editors' note: RSR insisted on this ugly term] is of considerable antiquity, and co-variant with concern for the phallocentric pursuit of the defloration of maidenheads, the semiotics of the hymen belongs to Modernism.

Under the gaze of human science, and specifically under the medical model, the hymen has been measured, classified, categorized in all its human variety (and indeed its variants of intactness). As concern for the preservation of virginity until marriage has declined under late Modernism, the technology of hymenspicy (and indeed that of the markers of other penetrable orifices such as reflex anal dilitation) has been increasingly focused upon children under the pursuit of 'detecting' child sexual abuse and upon the adult victims of sexual assault. (It is also favoured by immigration officers doubting the credentials of arriving 'brides' from traditional cultures, but that is another notorious story.)

For the mass of Modern persons, however, virginity and its loss are not gauged by hymenspicy (i.e. divination by hymen) but by the 'before' and 'after' of inception into sexual intercourse. It is that which allows young men (of whatever 'sexual orientation') also to experience themselves and to position others in terms of virginity and its loss.

However, we can also employ Modernism as the *deus ex machina* for the developmentalization of virginity loss. In the guise of sexology, accounts of sexual development (e.g. Schofield 1965) have enabled the laying of a Guttman scale upon inception into sexual activity. At the normative level for young lives passing through cumulative experience (and often within later sexual relationships also), there is a progression of growing 'intimacy' to be passed through in which coitus is the culmination (as in the bawdy song we sung on the school bus, 'Begin with number one, her bodice gets undone, roll me over, in the clover, do it again . . . Then there's number two . . . etc.').

The digitally 'deflowered' young woman (a technique once fostered by progressive sexological pundits to avoid 'wedding night traumas') who refers to herself as a 'technical virgin' is bringing to her subject tectonics a warrant drawn from the cultural tectonics of 'sex education'. What makes those tectonics different from the tectonics of, say, the *Kama Sutra*, are their different discursive warrants (i.e. Science rather than received wisdom).

This difference is crucial as a marker of the tectonics of sexuality under late Modernism, contrasted against traditional sex. In the former (but not in the latter) we can calculate the half-life of virginity (the age at which half of the studied population will have made the eigenstate jump into non-virginity). Not only is this held (and made) to 'matter' for us as a scientized culture, but it is held (and made) to 'matter' as we construct the vector of our subject lives.

Quite simply, that vast bulk of sexological work, in the Kinsey tradition, which has been based upon the accounts (the expressed texts) of its subjects has also come to shape its readers as subjects. Our concerns over virginity and its loss (and our whole credit–debit balance in the larger economy of sex) are grounded upon the magma of the human science project, even to where that percolates into the smallest capillaries of experience – the shared confessions between friends and lovers in the classroom, the bar or the bedroom.

Cultural tectonics

In accounting for the current physical geography of our planet, geophysicists do not, of course, just rely upon notions of plate tectonics. What the inter-action of plates may produce will, through processes like erosion or sedimen-tation, be moulded and modified. The term 'social sedimentation' is, by now, itself a well-sedimented term. At times it can be very helpful to think of tectons in that way, not so much as plates in action but as being laid down like strata (as is English case law); provided, of course, we also recog-nize that they are not thereby 'laid down in stone' – strata themselves are always subject to disruption.

There may also sometimes be the cultural equivalent of flies trapped in amber or living organisms (or at least their shadows) enduring through enfossilization – an historical fixing of a prior 'reality' in sufficient detail to be able to reconstruct it in the now in relatively unchanged form. Clearly, fossils and other cultural artifacts (such as cave paintings) allow us greater access to knowledge about some things than others – we can know more about, say, what kinds of prey pre-historic people hunted than the means by which they co-ordinated their hunting activities. At the same time, much of what is important about culture has left no such fossilized remains to be interpreted.

Furthermore, what has been retained has been subject to just as much distortion as the geophysical processes which have turned bogland plants into coal and proto-animals into oil. Attempts, for example, to reconstruct what were the salient discourses on intimate relationships in Shakespeare's time falter over what (to us) is the archaic language of his plays, which was idiomatic to his audience. Our understanding is also inevitably shifted by being perceived through a world-view steeped in knowledge about such ideas as psychodynamics and gender politics, and critically, by several hundred years in which his conceptions have been themselves woven into our cul-tural fabric of ideas. As the apocryphal innocent reader said, 'Shakespeare wasn't very creative, really, his plays are full of clichés!'

As we take the term 'cultural tectonics', it covers all the dynamics whereby the cultural lithosphere is (or more accurately is re-presented as) in restless movement of tectons, which are always subject to flux, while nonetheless (usually) seeming to its participant observers to be meta-stable. It is rather like sitting on a train assuming that it is you who is still, and it is the countryside which is flashing past.

At the same time, we need to pose two important caveats. The first is that cultural tectonics cannot be validated empirically because of the re-flexive narrative status of the concept itself. For example, we can make the argument that homophobic attitudes are sedimented in various ways – as religious 'natural law' discourses, as biomedical discourses and, critically, as biomedical discourses used to legitimate (i.e. laid one onto the other as part of a tectonic process) religious discourses. But this analysis, in itself, is a discursive production, and thus is itself subject to tectonics.

When somebody, for instance, argues that the emergence of the HIV has enabled a revival of religious bigotry about homosexuality within a modern, medicalized discourse, that claim itself is just as much a form in textuality, itself open to textual analysis, as the discourses upon which it offers commentary. Furthermore, the processes by which it imposes its gaze are just as tectonic as the tectonic processes about which they are narrating. Not only can we not avoid being located in discourse (it is part of our textuality), but we cannot place ourselves outside of tectonics. Some of the contrapuntal play of textuality and tectonics is covered in the next chapter (wilder flights of phantasy are reserved for the last chapter).

The second caveat effectively follows from the first – we are making no claim that in our analysis of cultural tectonics we are able to extrapolate or produce lawful descriptions of 'how tectonics work'. Any historicism we may argue as analytic is just that: our narrative device for 'telling a good story'. Only as narrative can it be written and read as if it were lawful. Thus cultural tectonics can only ever be the imputed organizational (and disorganizational) constructivities of cultural textuality. Looked at in this way, tectonics covers both those accounts of culture that draw upon notions of underlying structure, and those that reject such foundational maxims.

> *Interrupter: Let me see if I've got this right. What you are saying is that this stuff you are writing, like anything else, is a text. As such, its textuality is subject to tectonics, just like everything else. All right so far?*

Beryl: Yes, OK.

> *Interrupter: So in making an argument, you are not claiming to be telling how it 'really is', but just making an argument. Yes?*

Beryl: Yes.

> *Interrupter: So here you are, setting us out a grand meta-narrative all about how tectonics works, and then in the next breath (or, more accurately, the next keystroke) denying that there can be any meta-narratives! You are speculating over how tectonics might work even though, patter patter go the keys, you smile disarmingly (I can picture it well) and you then write that, of course, it isn't lawful or predictable; indeed, it's down right elusive. Is that right? Looks to me like you are really wanting your cake and to eat it.*

Beryl: Yes, absolutely. Don't think you are the first one to have spotted the paradox over postmodernism being a meta-narrative that denies meta-narrative. Graham (1992) has already raised it. But we think it's missing the point. Denying there can be meta-narratives is not to say they can't be told as language-games, but that they are not 'theories' in the accepted sense of the word. Really, all we are doing is being cautious and reminding you, dear interrupter (and you too dear reader), that just because we are beginning to read like scholars theorizing, in the time honoured way of academics, this is not what we are claiming to be doing.

If we are going to make the claim to transdisciplinarity stick, then the term culture, as we have attached it to tectonics, needs to cover all kinds of representational labour. In other words, we – just like art historians and students of film studies; journalists and professional moralists; psychoanalysts and Tent evangelists – are all of us engaged in a common trade of interpretation and telling clever stories. That business is the mongering of knowledges about organization and dis-organization to be found in the constructivities of their respective (and our) textualities.

The point we are making is that we – and you – need to be very wary indeed about the particular form of 'realist' knowledge-mongering we call theorization: i.e. the activity that involves the constitution of powers which may sound (or be told) as if they were natural dynamics where the narrative qualities of the story become rendered invisible.

What then tectonics adds to genealogy as an analysis, we assert, is a hyper-reflexivity, in which the metaphorical operation is made manifest and explicit. In other words, analysis is no longer a matter of just, say, abducing the sedimented political field against which the seemingly apolitical forms (such as its re-presentations of gender) of contemporary discourse acquire form and substance. What a tectonic genealogy attempts to do is to also bring to our attention the *reconstructional* labour necessary to such an abduction. It highlights the narrative effort whereby the purported conditions of plausibility of particular forms of knowledging (i.e. their niche in social ecology) are brought under a genealogical gaze.

What we are saying is that it is critical to acknowledge the implications of this argument for our own analysis. Clearly it enjoins us to accept that neither we, nor anybody else, has any exclusive executive lift to the penthouse of 'the truth': that much comes easily enough from our sedimented tecton of liberal pluralism, whereby we are positioned to find plausible a world in which there are no ultimate certainties, no ultimate expectation of consistency, no ultimate justification for assuming one has any unique handle on reality (whatever, if ever, that is!).

Of course, it is more or less inevitably a strangely 'schizoid' world, in which the transitive flux of realities will at any instant of engagement become intransitive, where conduct follows as though there are 'real things', as though people and events have at least some consistency – anything else would be to analyse into paralysis. But, as we have said, there is another, harder step that has to be taken. This is to acknowledge that critical poly-textualism offers a meta-tectonic analysis only in the sense that one can narrate it as such. When we take on that narration, we do so because it is useful, not because we regard it as 'true' other than through the affirmation of utilization. Its justification is, simply, its utility. It allows us to see, think and understand in ways that without it we could not. It is no more than that. In this we are doing no different than we have suggested for science – it (and our endeavour) is to be judged on the basis (and only on the basis) that it 'works'.

Subject tectonics

The domain of cultural tectonics (as we have just presented it) has some notable exclusions. What, it could be asked, is it saying about the artists, the directors, the politicians, the rogues, the patients or the persons whose progress through space and place generates those inscriptions that the cultural tectonicists (and cultural tectonicists *manqué*) read for us? What, to focus the issue, about the construction of the subject?

We propose that the subject is constituted both out of a narrative life and a life as narrator – in other words, the subject is *Homo narrans narratur* (cf. Christie and Orton 1988) – both a story-teller, and a-subject-storied-into-being. The distinction between 'subject' and 'cultural' tectonics is thus no more than heuristic.

The construction and the deconstruction of 'the subject' have been key concerns of the climate of problematization. It is useful here to quote from Henriques, Hollway, Urwin, Venn and Walkerdine's *Changing the Subject*: (1984: 3):

> Much of this work has been developed in France and the fact that it is written in French creates certain terminological problems – for example, the double meaning of 'asujettir', which at the same time means 'to produce subjectivity' and 'to make subject', is impossible to convey exactly in English in a single word. We have foregone the complexity of meaning in such cases and rather than load readers with an unwieldy term like 'subjectivity/subjectification' (asujetissement), we have plumped for 'subjectivity'... In brief we use 'subjectivity' to refer to individuality and self-awareness – the condition of being a subject – but understood in this usage that subjects are dynamic and multiple, always positioned in relation to particular discourses and practices and produced by these – the condition of being subject.

Thus, the experience of being a subject is itself 'subject' to a double tectonic – it is constructed within a construction (i.e. the discursive practices that Foucaultian tectonics ascribe to the social). It is probably fair to add that this statement can be reversed: the subject (at least, the subject in Foucaultian terms) is also constructive of that social. Thus what we have said of tectonic as metaphor or allegory fits the subject at least as easily as it fits culture.

This should not surprise us. For all the apparent novelty of dissolving person–society dualism, at the level of metaphor it has been done for some considerable time. Collectivities have long been 'personalized' (i.e. attributed personality, attitudes, even a collective cognitorium) in such forms as '... the British government takes a dim view of US policy in this instance...', 'the

Trade Unions have never been the brightest of institutions', and so on. Equally, at least since Freud, we have become familiar with the idea of the person as collectivity – the concept of the multiple self, the notion of being 'at war with oneself', and so on. In a parallel way, from sociological notions of a looking-glass self to those of 'role strain', have come the possibilities of seeing subjectivity as fracted, of being agonistically positioned between conflictual discourses. Hence it is as easy to accept the metaphorical resonances of subject tectonics as it is for cultural tectonics.

Once more, we find there is a contrast between the meta-stable state and the notion of violent disruption. Thus in developmental psychology we are told the story of how the present meta-stable landscape of the adult self has arisen through the process of development – we are invited to see ourselves as shaped and moulded, squeezed and stretched into adulthood. The process of development itself is often narrated in terms of brief but violent episodes of change, such as Piagetian or Freudian stages, or the 'storm and strife' of adolescence (see Stainton Rogers and Stainton Rogers 1992a: 52–3, for a more detailed analysis of this story-telling).

It is not difficult to see Freud's ideas in terms of boundary-plate eruptive conditions between *id* and *super-ego*. The emotions are often seen as acting in similar fashion to geological forces in these accounts of disruption (or perhaps we should say eruption). We can be, in popular language, 'like an earthquake waiting to happen' or, in James Taylor's volcanic phrase, 'a churning urn of burning funk'.

Most interestingly, we can also be in 'two minds', in other words, to have 'fragmented subjectivity'. For example we can be positioned simultaneously (or in very rapid time-sharing) within contradictory, agonistic narratives. This may be because we are simply 'making up our mind' or may be induced by hypnosis or, say, through a learned strategy of pain management (cf. Eccleston 1993). Faced with this purported geology of 'the subject', the human sciences have sought to foster the parallel of subjectification to scientific analysis. For all its complexity, the psychologist's and the sociologist's self is (like the Earth) held to be subject to study, revelational of lawfulness and – like recent efforts on Mount Etna – ultimately open to being shaped and controlled. (Sadly, as we write, one of our friends, Geoff Brown, was killed by an eruption he was seeking to predict, illustrating that tragically, working with geophysics as science practice is a lot more personally dangerous than working with metaphoric tectonics. It is a point worth noting.)

It is the claim to a scientific tectonics of the self that French theory challenges. It is not that subjects cannot be seen to be shaped and controlled; they do indeed have an embodied textuality that is the ultimate site of all discipline. Rather, French theory draws critical attention to the disguise of the discipline as science, and the productive role of the human disciplines in the generation of the managed subject. To parallel our assertions about cultural tectonics, subject tectonics are the imputed organizational (and disorganizational) constructivities of subject textuality.

Hence we are not giving to a Foucaultian reading any special status, save for what it makes possible, what it adds to the narrating of subject tectonics.

There are extant accounts of the subject that draw upon underlying structures (indeed, a Foucaultian archaeologist needs to employ them), just as there are those that reject such foundationals (as when a Foucaultian archaeologist speaks to us).

Once more, we will make the claim of transdisciplinarity, this time in relation to the notion of subject tectonics. One can pose, with Foucault, the question 'What is an author?', whether that author is the imputed agent of a book, a piece of visual art, a 'personality', a theoretical construct or a war. In a broader sense, we can now say of 'the artists, the directors, the politicians, the rogues, the patients or the persons whose progress through space and place generates those inscriptions that the cultural tectonicists and cultural tectonicists *manqué* read for us' that they too are in the business of 'the mongering of knowledges about organisation and disorganisation in the constructivities of their respective textualities'.

The tectonics of subject-in-culture and culture-in-subject

The drawing of parallels between cultural tectonics and subject tectonics is a sneaky, if not unpredictable, way of eliding over another boundary – that between culture and subject. To suggest that they may be mutually constituted and mutually constitutive has a neat ring to it. However, once we allow that neither subject nor culture can have a monopolar existence, that they are mutually implicative, then even such compounds as subject-in-culture and culture-in-subject also become illusionary demonstrations. Like a figure-ground visual illusion, they are products of the illusion, not the causes of it. (See Figure 3.1.)

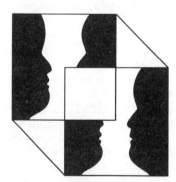

Figure 3.1 The ambiguous necker cube.

Hence we can expect (and certainly will find) that there is what we can call (again by re-cycling textual forms we have previously employed earlier in this chapter) a genre of treatments of cultural-subject tectonics whose agenda is the accounting of the imputed organizational (and dis-organizational) constructivities of cultural-subject textuality.

The various dialects of Marxism and feminism are obvious examples of such analytics in academic life; tectons in that manifold. They are prone to becoming, particularly in their respective moments of politicization (and hence intransitivity or substantivity), pandects – over-narratives that singularize their accounts into totalizing treatises. Arguably, this is exactly as they should be in order to function at specific points in space and place as ideology. In other words, to present a challenging account of cultural-subject textuality in terms of tectonics requires committed (singularized) engagement. But to be able to challenge the challenge, to move politically (and indeed intellectually), seems to require a different implement, one which enables us to address both moments of pandection and their challenge, one in which there is not certainty but multiple certainties – and, hence, uncertainty. As we see it, critical polytextualism is such a utility. It is not a thing in the sense of a meta-narrative acting as a pandect, but a fluxional device which is meta-tectonic only in the sense that a forum is meta-tectonic of its ongoing arguments or a novel is meta-tectonic of its thematic and characterological textuality.

Empirical and conceptual ramifications

What we are arguing for, of course, is a *critical* tectonics. If foundational notions of structure cannot be trusted, then either ideas of organization/ disorganization have to be abandoned as fatally compromised (leading to the 'horrors' of relativism or nihilism) or the texts of structure have to be read in order to be re-written. The language-game of tectonics is our best shot at such a re-writing.

> *Interrupter: It's your way round the meta-narrative that denies meta-narrative paradox, is that what you are saying?*

Beryl: Yes, that is pretty much it. The point is though, and it's an important one, as we use it (and indeed *why* we use it), critical tectonics does not warrant any particular political location, but it *is* open to – indeed, it demands – politicization. By this we mean explicitly that it specifically invites re-writing. In that sense it not only 'changes the subject' (the read or in-text-ualized) but also it 'changes the object' (the writer or the out-text-ualized). It also provides a passing theory or meta-stable basis for empirical operations. What we mean by empirical operations here can cover the kinds of research work we will introduce later in the book.

In that sense, we have adopted it because it makes possible investigation under the climate of problematization. However, we would argue that the expression 'empirical operations' can be applied with equal applicability to passing resolutions of the dilemma of the artist under problematization, or indeed of the subject, or even the culture in general under problematization.

Indeed, given that part of their problematics is that their position itself is problematized, their identity boundaries dissolved, they cannot but share in the same questioning we set at the beginning of this section – either they accept structure as fatally compromised or they read that diagnosis in order to re-write it.

Tectonics reflected and refracted

> No doubt the media's insidious chatter – that immanent white noise of postindustrial societies – has contributed much to the currency of postmodernism. But that currency also constitutes an act of self-apprehension by which a culture seeks to understand itself, presuming its uniqueness in history. Fashions often prove to be modes of obscure self-awareness as well as cultural desire. They beckon us to ourselves, somehow, under the twin aspects of our difference and solidarity with the past. Thus the fiction of the new becomes a tradition of novation – and the myth of a postmodern breakthrough yields to international conferences on the subject . . . Though postmodernism may persist, like modernism itself, a fiercely contested category, at once signifier and signified, altering itself in the very process of signification, the effort to speak it cannot be wholly vain. The effort a nissus[1] of unending discrimination, still merits our wakeful concern if only to adumbrate[2] our culture choices, our versions of historical reality, our images of ourselves – as we are, as we want to become. In our pluralist and dialogic universe, there may be no alternative to such transactions. (Hassan 1987: xi–xii; [1] impulse or striving towards a goal; [2] outline, overshadow, foreshadow)

Hassan, a long-time commentator on postmodern literature, captures much of what we wish to say of the analytic tectonics of subject and of culture, even if some of his terminology is even more obscure (or perhaps differently obscure) than that we allow ourselves!

Interrupter: Or I will allow you to get away with, you mean!

What is more, we find it heartening that he now casts his readings into a broader frame (owing much to William James) of 'critical pluralism' – a form of analysis which has much (but, as we shall see, not everything) in common with our own critical polytextualism. Hassan shares our affirmative doubt and doubtful affirmation, saying: '. . . I openly admit: I do not know how to prevent critical pluralism from slipping into monism or relativism except to call for pragmatic constituencies of knowledge' (p. 182). He reminds us also of the debt we owe to James for the narrative root metaphor, quoting from James' *Pragmatism* thus: '. . . the world is full of partial stories that run parallel to one another, beginning and ending at odd times' (James 1955).

The ironic dialectic of investment ('faith'), and hence concern, in these 'partial stories', in doubting that they can be foundationed, both problematizes and enables. On the one hand, both of our products (the tectonics of subject and of culture) and our own production by these tectonics, are open to multiple interpretation when considered in a transitive sense (another Jamesian term). On the other hand, only by knowledging them substantively, event by event, moment by moment, can we deal with them in any practical way. We are thus always in an endless dialogue between the specific and formed (substantive), and the global and fluid (transitive) or, in Hassan's terms, an 'unfinished pluralism' which:

> . . . is not mellow but exigent, harsh. Without dogmatism, it continu-
> ally demands moral, political, cognitive engagements on our part. If
> it 'rests' on anything at all, it surely rests on answerable belief, some
> ultimate trust in a universe gravid and stubborn with its differences.
> So long as two minds seek to apprehend that universe, no overwhelm-
> ing force or sweet seduction, no theory whatever, will reduce it to one.
> Pragmatic pluralism, then, is no philosophical system: it seems the
> very condition of our existence in the world. (Hassan 1987: 230)

Which is, of course, why it too must be worried; why it is worthwhile asking what does our engagement (our use of the analytic of tectonics of culture in this case) have to say about critical pluralism?

Whatever story we come up with does not bring a lot of comfort. Critical pluralism seems to have been originally adopted, around the turn of this century, to address a conflict between totalizing philosophies and nihilism. These are just the kinds of tension that we now seem to be facing in the recent disputes which have emerged between neo-Marxist and essentialist feminist dialects on the one hand and the postmodernists on the other.

The assumed 'relativism' of postmodern analyses (and it is here, for the passing moment, that we will position our critical polytextualism) has been vilified as 'dangerous', because it is seen to create a situation in which 'any-thing goes'. To allow that all texts have expressive equivalence is seen as, at best, voiding politics of meaning or individualizing politics as moral choice. At worst, it becomes an opening up of a Pandora's box, out of which will inevitably squirm, and then multiply, all manner of fascisms, bigotries and reactionarities that thrive on, only to seek to extinguish, relativistic toler-ance. Hence, of course, the continuing search for some way of anchoring analysis onto the real (e.g. the 'critical realism' of Bhaskar 1979).

It must be said that critical pluralism was, when it was first devised (and remains now), a particularly US story. As such, it does indeed carry the potential for relativism. So long as we partake only of its textuality, we can be located only as that positions us – as individualized, self-aware and self-determined actors, facing our own versions of 'High Noon', if only 'by the blue TV screen light' (to borrow Joni Mitchell's phrase); in other words, not answerable to any external reference as to the consequences of our actions.

The analytic of subject tectonics offers another (sympatric) story. The subject position of individualized actor is itself, of course, no more than a textual construction. It is not an inevitable component of critical pluralism, but rather it is a reading arising out of the modernism within which so much of superficially postmodern US culture remains steeped. If, as subjects, we can flicker in and out of polytextual positions (doing so, incidentally, fast enough to create the illusion of continuity, the 'secret' of both self and the movies) and, those polytextual positions include (as they could not for, say James, although we can now attribute them to him as he could not to himself) climate of problematization deconstitutions of the individualized actor, then we are as close as our resources in space and place allow us to be to realizing not a critical plural but a critical polytextual hyperspace of possibilities.

It is here, perhaps, that more than anywhere else we need to go beyond the geophysical and ecological metaphors which have, so far, been informative about cultural tectonics. There are two main limitations that we need to transcend. First, both root-disciplines operate within (in James' terms) a single substantive universe of reality – at any instant in time, what is there is *all* that there is. Any molecule of rock in any instant is either in the bowl of the volcano, or it is trapped in a stratum, or it is sitting on the seashore, or it is somewhere else. It cannot be in all places at once. It is either solid, or molten, or it has got so hot it has vaporized. It cannot be all three at the same time. To encompass such multiple possibilities requires a metaphoric shift into something more akin to the new physics of eigenstates, Schrodinger's live/dead cat and multiple universes. Tectons, in cultural terms, have transitive existence and influence all of the time; only when they are articulated (i.e. made substantive) are they fixed for a moment. But even in their expression, as they explicate they also implicate; and those not at that point explicated nonetheless are implicated within those that are. In other words, they are always immanent with other readings, other re-writings. Our tectonics, then, is a profoundly immanent tectonics, ephemeral rather than solid.

The second limitation is that within plate tectonics and ecosystems, nature allows for no moral analysis. Earthquakes and species extinction, no more than the evolution of the HIV or the development of holes in the ozone layer, have no *inherent* moral consequences. They acquire moral attribution only by their interpreted, attributed consequences, which are local and contingent to whomever is doing the interpreting. All may be seen as human catastrophes, but only by humans reading them as such.

There is a science fiction story (which exists for us as we write only as a fragmentary archive) which describes the panic and misery of a world as its sun went supernova, and all life on that planet was instantly destroyed. Many light years away and many eons later, three old men, riding across a desert, saw the explosion as a star appearing in the East, and interpreted it as a signal that the Messiah had been born. One world's cataclysm was, so the story went, another world's greatest moment (at least within a Christian discourse!).

Cultural tectonics, then, as we would want to use it, can be no mere 'detached' analysis of the shifting sands and species survival battles of text upon text. It is not just about 'what happens' or 'what happened' or 'what is happening' but, profoundly, it has to be concerned with consequences – both 'actual' and potential. Tectonics is not, say, just about observing that as one story gains ascendancy, it thereby mutes others. It is about the located consequences of such epistemological dominance – about who and what that empowers, who and what it disadvantages and oppresses.

It is precisely because, say, discourses over children's rights are both mutually conflictual and, at times conflictual with discourses of women's rights, that their manifold requires opening out. We may not like all that we thereby need to hear – for example, the paedophile dialect of children's sexual rights (cf. Chapter 8) or the dissolution of parental rights into parental responsibilities. But it needs to be heard in order for it to be re-said. To seek to censor out the expression of a tecton does not, *per se*, remove it from the cultural archive. Change requires work on that archive. Hence, we cannot align ourselves with those new ideologues who hold with control of the Pandorian boxes for fear of what may be let out if we dare to open them. But it does not mean we can open them and then dismiss all concern over what emerges.

4

Counterpoint

Interrupter: Otherwise 'Textuality and Tectonics get laid'.

Beryl: It would be the obvious next move in a story, wouldn't it, to see them conjoined into a relationship? But when did I do the obvious?

Romantic fiction, whether *Vanity Fair* or *Neighbours*, frequently gets woven around the theme of reconciliation, of star-crossed lovers, or erstwhile rivals or enemies. The same 'dream theme' of synthesis is to be found in stories as diverse as the combining of elements in alchemy to yield the Philosopher's Stone and the compounding of 'nature' and 'nurture' in socialization to make 'the person' (indeed their resonances, we have argued, have been used to construct an alembic myth of developmentalism; cf. Stainton Rogers and Stainton Rogers 1992a).

We do not see our analytics of textuality and tectonics, however, as operating in this conjugal fashion. Neither do we see them as in complimentarity (i.e. exclusively independent, immiscible universes of operation or meaning; see Box 4.2). We view them as more like political constructions such as 'freedom' and 'equality', where each informs our appreciation of the other in shifting textures over time, but where there can be no ultimate interpenetration of the two into a perfect politics.

Hence, we sought a more temporal, more fluxional metaphor for the interplay of textuality and tectonics. We found it in music – where textures do shift and transform over time – in counterpoint. Very much as in our own work, that counterpoint is built up as the product of two or more parts each with its own player(s), each open to its own consideration as they come together in performance.

Interrupter: We're not all musical you know!

Beryl: It's more or less a straight dictionary job. Counterpoint is built up by the simultaneous sounding (playing and or singing) of two or more parts or melodies. A simple example would be the adding of a descant to the main melody of a song. Didn't you do that at school?

Interrupter: Ah, how the melodies come flooding back! The on-going piece is a product of its tensions and resolutions – can only be heard because of its separate constituent parts, and yet is more than them, that sort of stuff?

Beryl: Exactly, and it also has a wonderfully eccentric adjective – contrapuntal.

Interrupter: Okay, okay. Stop showing off and let's get on, shall we?

This chapter is concerned with such a performance – dis-covering what emerges when the analytics of textuality and tectonics are placed in counterpoint, and with the overall appreciative position within which we employ them – not in a critical polyphonism, of course, but a critical polytextualism. By throwing into relief the contrapuntal interplay of our analytic devices in this way, we hope our audience will not only enjoy the performance, but also end up congratulating itself on its ability to appreciate how it was realized.

Interrupter: Bravo! Encore! Oops, sorry, got carried away a bit there. Do go on.

All that passes for knowledge, and all that knowledge passes for

Among other things, in this book we are interested in, to paraphrase and parallel Berger and Luckmann's (1967) ambition, 'everything that passes for knowledge'. We do not call it, as they do, 'a sociology of knowledge', because we see no reason to privilege one discipline, or indeed to identify with the notion of discipline at all. But the parallel remains valid, a concern not just with Knowledge (by whosoever capitalizes it) but with all that passes for knowledge. Berger and Luckmann were able to formulate their project, of course, because of, and in reaction to, another (larger) project – Modernism. Within Modernism, 'Knowledge' is often placed in opposition to opinion or belief (the doxa of pre-Modernism). It is Knowledge which enables the humanistic pursuit of the 'Truth that will set us free', the 'Nomos' which enables us to predict and control the vicissitudes of social being.

For critics of Modernism, there is 'something gained and something lost' in this epistemic leap: 'Where is the wisdom we have lost in knowledge? Where is the knowledge we have lost in information?' (T.S. Eliot, *The Rock*, Part 1, 1934). Part of the game T.S. Eliot may be playing with us is one of pointing out that within Modernism we are, always and ever, saturated in knowledge. Its operational canons (e.g. hypothetico-deductive method, falsifiability) demand the restless pursuit of ever more and more information. The Modernist cannot act from wisdom, but only on the basis of the current best condition of knowledge, the current best estimate of the information. In Modernism, all is conditional, all is tentative, however much it is wrapped in the rhetorical clothing of expertise.

Today, the other side of the Second World War and nearly half a century on from when T.S. Eliot was writing, nostalgia for a 'golden age' when the wise knew 'what to do' is once again to be found in much of popular culture. Yet now, it can become the subject of extensive cultural analysis through a hermeneutics of 'postmodern' cultural texts which 'take conservative political stances, while they valorise, and exploit the radical social margins of society' (Denzin 1988: 471). And by the same token, more general sediments of Modernism, and its parasitic critical forms, can be seen (particularly on the cusp of a millenium, particularly as forms of 'endism'), as still playing the false dialectics between uncertainty and order, the safe and the unsafe, chaos and anti-chaos. As Denzin also notes, there remains a viewer who 'still confronts the world through the lens of a nineteenth- and early twentieth-century political ideology' (p. 472).

If now we look back to Berger and Luckmann's project, it becomes possible to see how such viewing can be transcended: or at least, by-passed. The concerns spawned of Modernism, like the tension between knowledge and wisdom, can be bracketed into an ox-bow lake, a meander isolated from some other ongoing flow of ideas. They are still there, of course, but no longer in the mainstream as structures of debate. Rather, they are as formations upstream – the subject, if we choose to face the current, of tectonic scrutiny. By, as we have done, switching from noun (knowledge) to verb (as in knowledging), knowledge becomes not a thing-to-be-acquired but an endeavour in which to engage – a form of work and a condition of the worker.

Interrupter: This claim of yours to have made a verb out of knowledge has worried me for some time. I suppose it is some back-formation from acknowledge?

Beryl: Why do I acknow a trap?

Interrupter [Humming 'Air on the G string' and smoking a small cigar]: Very good. You know your Shakespearian English. But that was not my problem. I was more concerned that you were muddling participles with gerunds.

Beryl: I'm glad you brought that up because I'm not. If you look back over the book you'll find both because I want both. We can make use of both forms: 'a knowledging subject' and 'one cannot avoid knowledging reality'.

This shift changes the nature of the concern with knowing quite considerably. It, too, has flowed on from the primary problematizations of the 1960s, getting further downstream and, some would say, a lot muddier in the process (others might point to the greater fertility of its suspended silt!). Asking whether what we have now is an estuary or a delta, indeed where the river of discipline ends and the ocean of transdisciplinarity begins, may be pushing the metaphor too far, though it's an interesting question.

Thinking about knowledge not as a thing to be uncovered but as a production of human activity or a condition of the producer, troubles the boundaries between the making of things and making sense of things (cf. Christie and Orton 1988). What we make invites making sense before we make it. This is easiest to see in the domains of aestheticized productions (e.g. 'Pop Art') or moralized productions (e.g. an 'argument'), where there is an awaiting discourse of accountability – 'Who started it?' By bringing together in this way the aestheticized and the moralized, it becomes easier to recognize their commonality as knowledge productions. Just as 'Pop Art' had to result from a process of bringing into being, to become an 'it' of which the question 'Who started it?' could be asked, so too 'an argument' is not a given, 'natural' category but is also something brought into being, a created 'ithood'.

Box 4.1   Arty facts

Challenges to the 'ithood' of art have been common in the twentieth century. Dadaism (with its presencing of found objects like urinals as 'art'), the use of chance and hazard (as in the aleatory works of Jackson Pollock) and the most recent emergence of impermanent, 'conceptual' art (e.g. Koons' dog made of flowers), all seek to do that in their various ways. Magritte's painting of a pipe entitled 'this is not a pipe' makes claims to being art not because of its technical art-like qualities but because it problematizes visual re-presentation – a possible equivalent here might be 'this is not a text!'

We argue, of course, that a notion like 'causality', so central to Modernistic thinking, is also a created 'ithood', as is agency, as is – to close the circle – knowledge. This circle encompasses textuality (a created 'ithood' itself). But we need to make it clear that we do not wish textuality to be taken as a 'thing'. We see it, use it, intend it to be used as an analytic. It is also worth noting that whatever may be the universe of textuality for Beryl may not be identical to the universe for you (whatever is, is intertextual). This circle, of course, also encompasses tectonics (also with merely created, ascribed 'ithood', and also without thingness, but with intertectonicity). We have spoken for example of the accounting of the aetiology of 'Pop Art' or of 'an argument' – both accounts are tectonic.

More broadly, whenever and wherever accounts of the organization/disorganization of textuality are expressed, we are dealing with tectonics. Just as wherever and whenever accounts of the organization/disorganization of tectonics are expressed, that expression lies in textuality. Textuality and tectonics, in other words, enjoy, as we have tried to show, a contrapuntal relationship as analytics.

This is a theory – not!

It is important to stress what it is that we are *not* claiming. The counterpoint of textuality/tectonics is intended as anything but a form/content distinction. This is why we are not doing discourse analysis (cf. Potter and Wetherell 1987), nor discursive psychology (cf. Edwards and Potter 1992). We are not claiming to be able to 'uncover the structure of discourse' or to have more interest in 'interpretative repertoires' than befits any knowledge-mongerers who are also critics of knowledge-mongering. Of all the possibilities that the counterpoint between textuality and tectonics enables, it is the rejection of 'discourse', singularized as a performative arena, which is most salient here. Remembering how Roman coliseums could be flooded, we might say that we don't want to swim in a pool of 'all that is said and written' (Potter and Wetherell 1987), pulling out a magnifying glass for a closer look at the fauna, and hoping that by immersion we can somehow get a line on the common features of the discursive life around us. Neither do we claim any desire (or ability) to perch on the edge of the arena, and, without getting wet ourselves, trying to fish out a discourse, so that we can dissect it as if it were a living organism, to find out its natural capacities, its powers and its abilities (cf. Parker 1991).

The only 'life' we can detect within discourses is the life we bestow upon them when we bring the term into being to de-scribe the pattern which we create within the said and the written. Discourses are, to us, no more and no less than narrated textuality/narrative tectonics, a device whereby we can address 'discontinuous linguistic practices that variously intersect, juxtapose, and exclude one another' (Foucault 1970: 84).

In other words, quite explicitly, in suggesting that we may be able to learn something interesting by placing textuality and tectonics in a contrapuntal relationship with each other, we are not claiming, in any way or at any level, to be proposing a theory by which text, discourse or whatever can be better understood. Rather, we are suggesting that once you accept that all textuality is a matter of practice (e.g. language-practice), then all you can do is engage in practice (e.g. language-practice).

> *Interrupter: Let me see if I have got this right. What you are saying is that the stuff you are talking about, and the stuff you are going on to talk about,*

is not an exposition of a theory, but some suggestions about a set of devices that can be used to facilitate certain possibilities, is that it?

Beryl: Yes, that's right.

Interrupter: Well, pardon me for being a bit impatient, but aren't you making rather heavy weather of the distinction? Does it matter whether you call it a theory or a linguistic device?

Beryl: Yes it does matter. The notion of theory carries with it a lot of conceptual baggage, not to say more than a little arrogance. It is an idea and a practice intimately woven into and out of the Modernist endeavour, which we think can be shunted aside, ox-bowed. We don't like the word *qua* word much either.

Interrupter [snidely]: Theopathic are we?

Beryl: Actually, that's a religious emotion aroused by meditation about God (*Theos*). Theory has its roots in another Greek word *theorema*, a view. But to say something is a 'theory' is to assume you have a theomorphic (God-like) handle on what some-thing really means, how it really works – or at the very least a model worth testing. We are not making either such claim. Now we have got that clear, shall we continue?

The counterpoint of textuality and tectonics is not a theory to explain 'how discourse works'. In pluralizing and de-capitalizing 'discourse', we are giving a passing form to a working tectonic – the idea of discourses as semi-permeable social membranes which imperfectly contain the various ways of making sense and understanding knowledging. Constituted under this analytic, they acquire a level of trans-individuality, in the same sort of way, say, that accounts (by being authorially tied to individuals – some-body said or wrote them) do not do. In that sense, our work can be positioned as being closer to that of critical social psychology (cf. Parker 1991).

Abduction

The doubt about 'the real' inherent within the climate of problematization means we regard what we are doing as discursive abduction rather than, as we see critical social scientists doing, discursive induction and/or deduction. This in turn reflects the influence on us of the work of Will Stephenson (see Box 4.1). Abduction is an idea Stephenson took from the philosopher, Charles Peirce, who viewed it as covering 'all the operations by which theories and conceptions are engendered' (Peirce 1934: 414). In our words, that makes it a means to interrogate and explore (scrutinize) theories, not make them. Stephenson (1961: 11) himself said that abduction is 'inference, like induction, but concerned with explanation, whereas induction was descriptive – one proceeded from the sample to the whole in induction, but from the whole to an explanation or interpretation in abduction'.

What we like about the word abduction is that it is active and it is reflexive. It is active in that it does not, like the more traditional notions of deduction or induction, assume that knowledge can be derived canonically. Rather, it acknowledges that the process of knowledging is re-constructive (hermeneutic) because understandings, interpretations and explanations are 'read from' in a 'giving-to' as well as a 'taking-from'. Abduction is neither a scientific nor a philosophical technique. It is a practical craft, which can only be conducted by persons-in-culture (immanent with culture-in-persons). It is reflexive in that it acknowledges the part played by the person doing the abducing.

Interrupter: Why not use a simple word like abducer or abductor?

Beryl: Because that would mean somebody who abducts somebody or something, like a kidnapper. Language is sticky stuff.

Interrupter: I know – pass me a tissue.

Whatever is realized as text (broadly understood) can be abduced. This craft of abduction is often to be found as part of cultural analysis, but in a form in which the textuality of the text-analysed (author-ity) is less exposed than the textuality of the culture-analysed. Hence, the attraction to us of a further turn, that of a tectonics which proposes that a text-provider is not just enmeshed within the discourses of the culture which they express, but is also themselves active (i.e. abductive) upon those patterns. When we work upon (i.e. re-present) those expressed texts, we are sharing in a similar process of abduction, not claiming to be possessed of some unique extra-discursive craft skills.

Box 4.2 The work of William Stephenson

It was William Stephenson who invented the technique of Q-methodology, about which we will talk more in the next chapter. For now we are concerned with Stephenson's more theoretical work, which was not only sustained over many years, but also covered a very wide range. Stephenson applied his ideas to everything, from psychodynamics and theories of the self to how to buy a loaf of bread or make a cup of tea; from the notion of play to Newton's Fifth Rule.

In many ways, he was a man 'out of his time', in that for most of his academic career he was a lone voice in a positivistic wilderness which, at best, misunderstood him and, at worst, treated his ideas with derision. It was the former which made him most angry! He was extremely critical of virtually all orthodox psychology, and its locus in hypothetico-deductivism. He regarded psychologists as generally engaged in a 'vast fumbling about among the facts, with no rhyme and little reason' (Stephenson 1953: 1). Those of us who saw him in action were well aware he did not suffer those he regarded as fools gladly!

It is possible to identify in his prolific writing a great deal (but not everything he wrote and said) which resonates with our own approach, even though the terminology he used was generally very different. For example, he suggested that psychologists should be prepared to learn from the 'brilliant and penetrating analyses of famous novelists' (1953: 4) if they wanted to understand an issue, rather than trying to be purely scientific. He strenuously refuted attempts to measure psychological phenomena objectively. This, he said, was a meaningless task – 'blind empiricism' (1987b: 129). He could get very cross with it:

> [P]sychometry floods the US with pseudo testing of every conceivable kind – test intelligence, personality, skills, etc., and to assess one another at work and play, as teachers assess pupils and vice versa. Everyone in the US seems bent on measuring or assessing every manner of human foible and accountability, *ad libitum*. Every strike of a baseball player is counted, and every tackle of a football player. It implies objectivity, as if it matters . . . For myself, it is as unacceptable as the scholasticism of the early Christian philosophers: it is basically categorical only, and will one day disappear, one may hope, into a 'black hole' of grand illusions. (Stephenson 1987a: 134–5)

The only reality, in his terms, is subjective reality; the only thing we can explore is 'the world in [its] subjective respects' (ibid.: 123). This was radical stuff at the time – certainly in the 1950s when he first began really pushing these ideas.

He argued that the way any set of ideas is made sense of could be perfectly well investigated by exploring how a single person construed them (see, for example, Stephenson 1987a). It is pointless, he said, to go and ask a great crowd of people to express their opinions on a topic. Any single person-in-culture (to use our terminology) would have access to all of them, and could demonstrate them by Q-sorting. He was, however, explicitly not concerned with individual differences between people (Stephenson 1987a: 128) but with the ways individuals have access to ideas available to all.

Before his training in psychology he was a physicist, active in the period when Newtonian ideas were being challenged by the Theory of Relativity. He argued that there are a lot of parallels between physics and psychology, and adopted many of the concepts used in Quantum theory, such as that of complimentarity (see, for example, Stephenson 1979, 1982, 1983).

We have adopted a number of his terms, probably the most useful (for our purposes) being the notion of concourse. It is these ideas, as much as his technique of Q-method, which have been germinal in developing our own approach.

Concourse and discourse

Concourse is the term adopted by William Stephenson to describe the bounded universe of possible elements (propositions where we are dealing with text in the narrow sense) from which (and here we make use of time-bridges between his account and post-structural ones) discourses are configurated. We view concourse as a bounded universe (albeit a large one), because we take from Foucault the notion that discourses are themselves always inscribed within place and time. The discourses to which we have access are always limited by that which is locally and contingently at least think-able, if not say-able, present-able and do-able.

> *Interrupter: Isn't that something of a tautology – aren't you just saying that people can only think and talk about those things of which they can conceive – they can't think or talk about the, literally, inconceivable.*

Beryl: Sorry, it's going to be a 'yes and no' answer again. In strictly logical terms you are right. But that's not the point. It's a matter of practical observation.

Some inconceivables are a matter of linguistic convention. In Chapter 7, we will go on to argue that while one can be or feel jealous, it makes less sense to say 'I am jealousy'. Outside of poetry or other circumstances where we want to challenge doxa deliberately (as in this book), such a statement would simply not appear in the concourse on jealousy, because it is nonsensical. People simply do not bother with nonsense in their musings and their talk. Other inconceivables can only be identified *post hoc*. Lewis Carroll, for example, could not be said to have based his stories on Freudian notions, because he simply had no access to them (though, of course, we can make a Freudian reading of them today). This does not, of course, mean something is unthinkable merely if it has not happened or is, to present knowledges, impossible. Ardries wrote *The Doomsday Germ* (1975), a story about 'a super-resistant mutant virus, capable of exterminating 80 percent of humankind', well before the HIV entered the discursive arena. Trekkies 'boldly go' to all manner of fantastical worlds.

Nevertheless, stories cannot be told which are completely unconnected with what we can 'make sense of', even when that sense-making is derived from myth; indeed, as far as the past is concerned, there is nothing that we can think about other than that which is narrated as having happened (i.e. there are no 'real historical facts' but only 'historical facts as narrated'). Hence, for example, we can argue that the public hanging of a twelve-year-old is 'unthinkable' in British society as we currently know it, even though we know it did happen in 1814 and we may even have a good hunch as to why. What was 'thinkable' and therefore 'do-able' then is not 'thinkable' and therefore not 'do-able' today. If we were to do a study on 'delinquency' in contemporary Britain, we would not see as includable in the concourse of expressible propositions something like 'The child-thief should be publicly hanged'. Outside of phantasy or florid dementia such an idea is 'inconceivable'.

Needless to say, this exclusion is not an acknowledgement of some fundamental 'law of nature' about evolution in the nature of child discourse (e.g.
as deMause 1974, seems to be suggesting). It is an abducing of tectonic
change in the discourses available-for-use over time, and of the tectonic
ecology of the discourses available-for-use in terms of cultural location.

Nonetheless, not all 'conceivables' are equally think-able, say-able and do-
able. Within any concourse, some discourses will always be more pre-
eminent than others; more bolstered, legitimated, shored-up by the tectonics
in play (i.e. available-for-use) at a particular time and in a particular place.
These may be (as Berger and Luckmann suggest) a matter of institutionalized
hegemonic power (such as the dominance, in our time and culture, of biomedicine over other medical systems), or by other powerful interests, such
as in our time and culture the imposition of 'political correctness' on what
is say-able and (perhaps) do-able. In the professional world of those currently
engaged in child protection, for example, it has become virtually impossible
to raise the proposition that children may be capable of consenting to sex
with adults, without being accused of being an apologist for the paedophile
lobby.

But the observation that some discourses have expressive dominance does
not preclude the abductive potential of members of a collectivity to express
and draw upon the muted discourses available in sympatricity with those
given prominence. Sharing in a concourse as a system of signs and symbols,
people are always capable of expressing variedly from its range of discursive
possibilities (i.e. of giving different accounts).

> *Interrupter: So there can be different accounts of textuality and tectonics
> and their counterpoint?*

Beryl: Of course. Over these pages I have expressive dominance but you can
still butt in and as for the readers, well . . .

> *Interrupter: Don't bother, I can guess. A reader can resist, set up a critical
> re-writing, impose a dialogue, or simply stop reading.*

Beryl: Yes. Though of course the last, the 'put down', is undoable in *this*
discourse! The work we are doing in variously offering-for-use the
analytics we have ourselves crafted (like tectonics) or more openly
appropriated (like Stephenson's notion of 'concourse' and Peirce's
of 'abduction') is not intended as either primarily didactic or polemic
(although we admit this may be how we come across), but as an
invitation to make use of ideas we ourselves have found useful. How
they get used, of course, is up to the user.

Indeed, we are critical of others when we see them as denying such 'openness'. When we read the work of our contemporaries in discursive studies,
we often are struck by the way even the neo-structuralists among them (e.g.
Kristeva), while very prepared to focus down upon the minutia of 'discourse',
nevertheless seem to approach 'it' as a broad, amorphous and unspecialized
unity. Such a panchrestonic (why not explore the Glossary?) approach can

result in an impression that there is but one kind of material to focus upon, but one kind of research question to ask, but one kind of knowledge to be addressed.

To take a specific example, questions of re-presentation seem to present particular problems. For postmodernists, of course, representation is a term under erasure (hence, cf. p. 140, rXe-presentation). Within social psychology, it is the troubled treatment of representation by Moscovici – his concept of 'social representations' (cf. Parker 1991; Ibañez 1993) – that feeds the disease. Moscovici has indeed presented social representations unreflexively as to his own representational labour, and employed them in the same explain-all way.

However, in that critical gloss, there is a danger of adopting a destructive rather than a deconstructive stance and, in so doing, rejecting the possibility of any analytic focus upon the more imaginal facets of knowledging. In other words, it runs the risk of being iconoclastic rather than iconologic. In the next section, we will explain how we have sought to open up the possibilities of addressing what abduction, as a distinctive facet of knowledging, can achieve.

Texts representational and rhetorical

The labour of knowledging can be expressed in a variety of media, in diverse codes (e.g. iconographic and linguistic). We will follow current convention and call all such expressions texts (see, for example, Christie and Orton 1988). This is not a reifying move, but a good-enough-for-now analytic strategy to enable attention to be paid to the kinds of knowledges abducible from text. To draw you, the reader, into our argument, we will suggest that your knowledging of 'Textuality and Tectonics' has led you to abduce both:

- representations (i.e. descriptions, properties, characteristics, qualities) *of* Beryl, her alter-egos like the Interrupter, 'the book', textuality, tectonics, and so on; and
- discursions (i.e. arguments, debates, understandings, action agendas) *about* Beryl, her alter-egos, 'the book', textuality, tectonics, and so on.

Obviously, we have an agenda for this call to personal affirmation. It is that differentiating representations from discursions increases the analytic power of the counterpoint of textuality and tectonics. By suggesting, in other words, that representations are, at one and the same time, abductible from discursions and yet dialogically (in some sense dialectically) related to discursions, allows us to gain certain kinds of insights and understanding (i.e. it is a functional 'language game' to play).

This latter assumption allows that the objects of discursion, and discursion itself, are intimately related in that they emerge in the same process (Foucault 1972). According to this argument, representations of 'the mad' can, say, inform discourses about madness; and, in turn, theories and beliefs about madness can feed into popular images of 'the mad' (we will demonstrate this more fully in Chapter 6). However, there is no inevitable contingency between the two – a culture's ways of portraying 'the mad' will, at times, be ontologically quite independent from that culture's explanations of what madness is, what causes it, and so on.

Consider, for example, the Jekyll and Hyde mad character (Stevenson 1886). While it can, in one reading, be seen as anchored within the discursive tension between the rational and the irrational which dominated discourses about madness in Stevenson's time, in another reading, it can be seen as a contemporary re-casting of an older representation – the lycanthropic archetype.

Interrupter: You mean an image of a wolf in creep's clothing?

Beryl: Something like that.

In other words, there will seldom, if ever, be only a singular one-to-one mapping between an understanding of madness (i.e. a discursion on it) and a particular set of representations of 'the mad'. The point can, of course, be generalized. If we employ tectonics as a metaphoric here, although discursions and representations may be seen to abrade, polish (even infiltrate) one another, we can argue that they also usually remain, for all that, stratificationally separate formations (i.e. tectons).

A second reason for distinguishing between the 'of' mode (construing, representing) and the 'about' mode (making sense of, discursion) is that we observe that representations and discursions frequently differ in their modes of mutability. Representations, once constituted, tend to acquire a considerable degree of functional autonomy and continuity – they seem to be more resistant to change. Of course, over time and space they can come to be addressed by new and emergent discourses, or by differently located ones. As new stories are told around old representations, new flesh may be formed on the bones of the old, but the bones themselves go marching on, and remain archivally accessible (see Chapter 6). The innocent child, for example, may be fashioned and re-fashioned, as Kate Greenaway gives way to Mabel Lucy Attwell gives way to Disney as successive genres of representation, but the iconography of 'childhood innocence' itself persists so long as it has representational utility.

By contrast, discursions are more open to being re-written and re-read, and are hence more subject to the potentially catastrophically tectonic dynamics impinging upon all synchronic social products. An example here is the shift from a discourse on 'self-abuse' to one on 'child sexual abuse', as the moral climate over childhood sexuality has been brought to mutation in resonance with discursive change over sexuality in general (see Stainton Rogers and Stainton Rogers 1992a and Chapter 8). Which is not to say, of course, that discursions may not sometimes be abduced as meta-stable, showing a relative fixedness which provides the critical cultural analyst with the grounds for imputing the workings of power–knowledge synarchy. Discourse on sexuality more generally is a good example, seen as changing and variable in its specifics but always acting as an enduring locus of 'concern' across time and space.

Interrupter: Hang on, are you saying that there is some kind of 'essential' difference between representation and discursion? Surely not?

Beryl: Not 'essentially', no, but pragmatically, in the sense that when we examine them (either in empirical studies or by cultural analysis) they do appear to work in somewhat different ways. We are not, as I went to some pains to explain (were you listening?), putting this forward as 'a theory' of knowledging to be evidenced or disproved. Rather, we are suggesting something like: 'look, isn't it fascinating, it does seem to us that representations and discursions are different. We wonder why that is? Perhaps scrutinizing this will throw up something interesting.'

Discursions, explanatory and conative

Discursions, it appears to us, come in a variety of forms. Some seem to be mainly about understanding. The sort of thing we have in mind are propositions like: '*Textuality and Tectonics* does for the disciplines of the social what Attila the Hun did for the Roman Empire.' Others seem to be more about conduct – what ought to or could or should be done. An example here would be: 'Teachers who are concerned about having too many students to teach need only make *Textuality and Tectonics* a set book for the course, and their classes will empty at a stroke.' There are undoubtedly other ways of classifying discursion, but it is these two we have found the most generally germane to the work we have done.

Presentations, understandings and conations

We would like to argue, therefore, that for any topic, discursions concerned with explanation, understanding and so on will have a somewhat separate propositional concourse from those discursions concerned with conduct. If we add this distinction (about which more will be said later) to the previously argued differentiation of representations from discursions, we end up with an analytic template like that in Fig. 4.1.

Basically, we are seeking to divide up the domain of knowledging, for purposes and reasons we will explain in more detail later. In our 'topology of knowledging' (our abduction of the contours of the textual territory map, if you like), the counterpoint between textuality and tectonics has its points of expression in text. Text, in this sense, is that which is constituted as 'at issue' through the local and contingent operation of that counterpoint. Thus, for a student of English, the manuscript of 'Waiting for Godot' may be the text, while for a researcher working on the topic of AIDS, it might be 'HIV' which is the text.

Triadic tablature

Across a wide range of texts, we want to suggest, knowledging (as we in our cultural location know it) can be applied within these three moments:

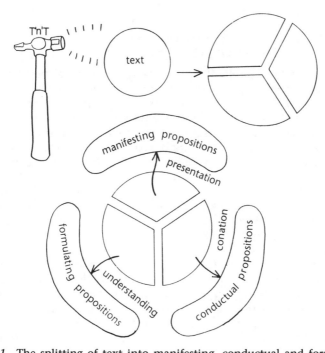

Figure 4.1 The splitting of text into manifesting, conductual and formulating propositions.

presentation, understanding and conation (see Fig. 4.1). In received science, these correspond to, respectively: variables and parameters; hypotheses and theories; and technologies and applications. In most other locations in culture, these take the form of, respectively: representations, explanations and policies. We see that isomorphism between science and non-science as important, and as laying the ground for the incorporation of scientistic knowledging under a critical polytextualist approach. But we also see it as meriting more detailed treatment than is possible here. Hence, having noted the possibility of a parallel we will move on.

Taking up the example of 'Waiting for Godot', we can illustrate how our working tectonic classification of manifesting, formulating and conductual propositions relate to text. Consider the following propositions:

- Has a clear sense of purpose
- Is boring
- Seems to exist outside the real world

- Operates as a metaphor for the human condition
- Uses humour to make its point
- Is seeking to tell a moral tale

- Should be read by every psychology student
- Is something children are better kept away from
- Needs very careful staging to be effective.

The first set of three propositions are rXe-presentational possibilities that could be 'tried for fit' upon textual entities, whether those be Beckett himself, one or more of the five characters in the book (Estragon, Vladimir, Lucky, Pozzo and the Boy) or the only-alluded-to Godot or, indeed, the play itself as object. The second set of formulational propositions offer understandings (readings or meanings) that, once more, can be tried for fit on the play as a story (others could address the characters as entities-to-be-understood – propositions *about* the characters). Finally, the last three propositions imply actions that could be proffered about what should be done about/with/to a text, here the play (again, others could be applied to the characters, as in what should Vladimir do, or how should Godot's non-appearance be handled?).

> *Interrupter: Stop right there! It's all very well telling this – I will admit alluringly convincing – story of how to classify the three moments of presentation, understanding and conation. And it is a pretty diagram. And I accept you have some support from classifications elsewhere which carve up epistemology in similar ways. But you have to admit it does look awfully like 'Boom, boom. Have we got a nice new theory for you?' I thought you had turned your back on that kind of razzmatazz?*

Beryl: I have. Look, I'll let you into a secret. Our classification did not (even though we may be making it look as if it did here) arise out of painstaking scholarly labour. It came about as a consequence of the search my bits were doing. The division into (re)-presentations, understandings and things like social policy or action-prescription was, at first, purely pragmatic. It's what seemed to work. Will that do, as an explanation for now?

> *Interrupter: I think I understand. There is much rationale you have to elide over to make the narrative here work. And we are not to read too much into what you are saying (particularly not a theory) and just be patient.*

Beryl: Precisely.

It is, we trust, clear that there can be no finality to these moments, no way that we can find 'the truth' about the characters or about their story. What we will find, if we ask people to respond to the propositions, is dispute. 'Waiting for Godot' no less than 'social class' or 'child sexual abuse' throws up issues in contention. As within politics itself, there are positions to take up, parties to align with (or against) – whole sets of ways to knowledge, in which a range of propositions can be configurated in distinct and distinctive ways.

Indeed, in so far as we think that there are, say, liberal-intellectual, feminist, or 'middle majority' views on 'Waiting for Godot', social class or child sexual abuse, then scrutinizing these issues may well inform us more about the textuality and tectonics of knowledging *per se*, than about the issue in question itself (more about this will follow later). In fact, although we have usually done the studies we did because we have a particular interest in the way certain issues are knowledged, our main interest has been in the textuality and tectonics of knowledging itself.

For example, we have used our work to enable us to abduce about what regimes of knowledging produce what issues in the first place. This is, of course, the domain of archaeotectonics (as in Foucaultian archaeology). But it is precisely the indeterminacy of the flux between the dispute of issues and the constitution of regimes of disputation that demands a counterpoint of analytics – textuality and tectonics.

From this it is clear that within a 'climate of problematization', critical polytextualism regards issues of cultural agency and subject agency as unpickable apart. It can, of course, recognize attempts so to do (and to valorize one or the other modality). But its analytics cannot offer any route to resolution because they locate all such claims within the manifold of knowledging, and in a doubting that there is anything outside that manifold. However, this is not to confer any 'ithood' on the manifold. The textuality of the manifold is subject to tectonics of space and place. The manifold in, say, the space and place of the philosopher Kant is not the manifold of today. Like the universe of the cosmologists, the manifold of knowledging changes (or we knowledge it to be changing, which is the same thing).

Political counterpoint

However tempting it may be to story them that way, the purported political hazards of the 'climate of problematization' (cf. Box 1.1) are not new issues arising *de novo* in the current 'crisis' in the human disciplines. They have a considerable history in the field of social theory. The work of Weber provides one obvious anchor into an analysis of the consequences of 'relativizing' knowledging. It has given to social constructionism (through Berger, in particular) a doubt and dissolution of faith which it is possible (although politically misleading) to label conservative (Berger's own politics are not the issue here).

What it is – and it is more than enough to worry the radicals – is agnostic over Utopia, and in particular agnostic over notions that the application of disciplined, directed knowledging shall bring about the Good. What we see as distinguishing our approach of critical polytextualism from, say, radical social psychology, is not so much understanding as implication. It is the failure to engage the analytic with a singularizing utopian implication which feeds accusations of political impotence or conservatism. We would argue that the very contrapuntal quality of the analytic provides the basis to resist any such appropriation. It puts one, borrowing Berger's terms, in:

... the predicament of one who tries to see the world as lucidly as possible, who suffers from the radical 'disenchantment' such lucidity almost invariably brings ... who nevertheless is committed to humanizing interventions, political or otherwise, in the course of collective events. (Berger 1982: 14)

Clearly, those who doubt singularizing utopian implication are aware of the risks in doubting it. There have been several attempts within the 'climate of problematization' to resolve this dilemmatic. Perhaps the most effective so far is Rorty's (1989) constitution of the 'liberal ironist'. Our own resolution begins by adding a further moment to Berger's analysis – almost the opposite of dialecticizing it away by the Stalinist injunction 'the personal is the political', as some radicals might prescribe. Rather, we would argue, a further level of complication is required. This 'one' of whom Berger speaks he has already divided (cf. Berger 1966: 16) into a professional (the sociologist) and all else that makes up 'the totality of [his/her] existence as a human being' (i.e. who is in the 'nevertheless' in the earlier quotation).

Rather than fragmenting the subject in this way (and in doing so, asserting an underlying whole), we would prefer to talk in terms of local operating rules. Such rules of engagement cannot be clearly located as of the subject rather than of the culture; they are features of subjects-in-culture (and thereby of culture-in-subjects). Within the language game of critical polytextualism, we use the analytics of textuality and tectonics to explore the diversity of knowledging. To those who might wish to mute certain forms of knowledging or valorize one form over others, critical polytextualism is subversive, but it is a procedural rather than political subversion. That it can be said to be conservative against the standards of radically utopianized practice is evidence enough of that. Within other language games (such as those which can be read as active within our 'ordinary lives'), we can engage in re-writing texts rather than concerning ourselves with the manifold of knowledges currently brought to them. Some of those re-writings could be called radical, but they are neither uniquely derived from nor uniquely warranted by critical polytextualism.

But there is more, for we cannot go along with Berger's division between a 'professional' and 'personal' plausibility system. An illustration may help here. In the studies of 'jealousy' described in Chapter 7, a number of alternative understandings are outlined. These include accounts of jealousy as 'natural', as 'psychological immaturity', as 'a sign of love', and so on. When occupying ourselves with scrutinizing understanding, to unpack and reveal them is neither to endorse or refute one or other of them, but merely to engage in re-scription. Equally, we cannot lay upon ourselves as participants nor upon others as participants any greater implication of endorsement or rejection. Like a carpet-salesperson laying out their wares, we are saying 'here are some of the ones that are on offer'.

As no more than an abduction of understandings, with no implicated warrant at any remove, these different accounts for jealousy have, we would argue, no intrinsic moral value (positive or negative). One is no better or worse than another, they are simply different. The case can be made even more strongly for rXe-presentations. (Each 'peculiar' just *is* in the cast of the mad.) Where issues of ideology and morality arise is once we get beyond even the abduction of conation-as-textualized and into conduct-as-inscribed, and here getting off the fence becomes an issue. To observe, for instance, that an understanding of jealousy as 'natural' can be used to justify 'a crime of passion' (as in 'he could not help it, he did it in a blind rage') introduces a moral dimension. Where it results in institutionalized inequitable treatment (e.g. men being more likely to avoid being charged with murder, because of assumptions about lack of premeditation) it becomes a matter not just of personal morality but ideology.

In Chapter 8, we will look specifically at the ways understanding and conduct may be discursively linked – the way a particular understanding may warrant or imply certain forms of conduct; how a certain action or a policy may be predicated upon or justified by recourse to a particular understanding. Such contingencies are the very weft and warp of the fabric of our social lives – start teasing out the strands, and the whole cloth seems to fall apart. But tease it we must, for the simple reason that there is no 'glue' of causality holding it together, and within a 'climate of problematization' that needs to be exposed.

The notion of 'voice'

Put another way, we are suggesting that 'believing that' and 'believing ought' are linked only in so far as they are subject to an additional politicizing tectonic. Indeed, one could argue that the tectonics of politicking, as we understand it, largely concerns the construction of such links. We have adopted the term 'voice' to express how such tectonics may operate. Let us try an illustration again to make the point. In Chapter 8, we will be looking at conduct-prescriptive and policy-prescriptive discourses on 'child abuse' and how these may be linked to different understandings of 'the problem'. There we will see that certain ideological discourses provide the links – it is these which weave the two together. For example, we will see that liberal-humanism and feminism are voiced as different understandings of 'child abuse', respectively attributing it to 'family dysfunction' or to 'patriarchal power'. Voiced as conduct-prescriptions, these become apparent as different warrants for policy. Policies of 'working with the family' and 'treating the abuser' are warranted by the liberal-humanistic 'family dysfunction' understanding. By contrast, the feminist 'patriarchal power' understanding warrants policies of 'removing the child' and 'punishing the abuser'.

From this analytic, it is the voicing of ideology and not causality or the operation of 'natural laws' which provides the cohesion holding the whole fabric together. Hence we argue that far from being an apolitical, ideology-insensitive (and therefore 'dangerous') endeavour, critical polytextualism places ideology as central to its analytics. It is here, perhaps, that the counterpoint of textuality and tectonics is most evident, for ideology (in this sense) has to be able to be seen as operating in both of these ways – in textuality (in the sense of the discourses within which ideologies are knowledged) and as tectonics (in the sense of the voicings by which ideologies weave one kind of discursion onto another). It is worth noting that we are using the term 'ideology' here in its broadest sense, to cover any system-of-knowledging, including not just the overtly political (such as feminism and liberal-humanism) but also other formal systems like science and more informal ones such as traditional wisdom. All of these, within our analytic, must be read both as forms of textuality, and as tectonics.

Subject/culture counterpoint

Part of our motive for adopting the idea of 'voicing' as the conceptual glue that binds different discursions together is that although it implies a person able to 'give voice' to an ideology at particular times in particular places, it equally conveys the context which 'gives voice' to those discursions. The emphasis is on the expression, not upon hidden-hands in the person-expresser or the context-expresser. This at least gets us around the regression problem, wherein, beyond the realm of textuality, there has to be a *deus ex machina* doing the ideological action, by drawing on some extra-textuality universe of moral truths to make the necessary evaluations.

This still leaves us with the problematics of subject and agency, which cannot so easily be dispatched. Our own position is very vulnerable here. In expressing our discomfort with much received knowledging, it should be clear that we are, thereby, concerned with re-writing. Our suggestion that the subject/culture counterpoint is indeterminate is deliberately designed to trouble an area subject to much theoretical (and other) politicking. Whereby may seem to lie a neat paradox. In generating that re-writing, are 'we' not falling into the trap of valorizing the subject, the author of that re-writing (i.e. us)?

Beryl is a help here, but only as an *aide-mémoire* to the problematic. More to the point is our own position 'in' textuality. Any attempt to position us as the authors of this re-writing is itself a tectonic – part, if you like, of the story of authorship. It could just as plausibly be asked, what texts are being re-worked by these writers? What are the archaeotectonics of 'their' ideas? In other words, all efforts to apply any kind of causal attribution are themselves texts, no different in kind from the text they are trying to attribute. This may seem para-doxical, but is, of course, exactly the position we are seeking to foster.

Now it is perfectly true that no such analysis is possible until there is a text 'at issue'. It is also true that many texts are the result of authorial labour.

Interrupter: What's all this appeal to truth all of a sudden?

Beryl: It's a narrative device, a manner of speaking.

Interrupter: But the first 'true' is a necessary or logical 'truth', the second an appeal to a particular kind of reading as you would call it.

Beryl: In a manner of speaking, yes.

However, that certain texts can only 'be' through the agency of an author is saying little more than certain texts can only 'be' through a television set. Those are statements of necessary contingency not of agency. Nor does the need for a text to be 'at issue' demand any universal recourse to an agentic analysis of the tectonics of issuance.

Of course, there are local and contingent narratives in which agency does matter. An example is the drawing up of a legal contract, like the one we signed to produce this book. Beryl is written into it as its author, and then 'explained' by a list of our names. One pragmatic reason for this is we have no wish for the advance and royalties (however minuscule these turn out to be) to disappear into the æther, and sadly, thus far, Beryl has no bank account. We are prepared to go that far in deconstructing authorship, but not so far as to forgo its rewards!

Interrupter: On the other hand, 'no taxation without representation'?

Beryl: Alas the Inland Revenue is critically polytextualized that way. Just as they can legally 'live on immoral earnings'.

Subject agency (and at times cultural agency) are constructions whose attribution clearly do matter to the working of our collectivity. Thus we are not denying them, but rather, like everything else, stressing their narrative rather than their absolute truth – their textuality and tectonics. Not only is this a matter of keeping faith with our analytics, it is significant because it allows us to turn the spotlight onto the ideological 'work' that agency performs within tectonics, by way of its textuality.

Moving on

To summarize, then, and to re-state once more (hopefully not to the point of boredom), textuality and tectonics have been presented here as narrative devices which, in counterpoint, provide a means to scrutinize narration – the telling, re-telling, reading and re-writing of the stories (see Chapter 2) by which we knowledge the world. Further, dividing narration up into three moments – presentation, understanding and conation – has been suggested as a means by which to enable empirical scrutiny of each in isolation from the others in the chapters which follow. The notion of 'voice' has been offered as an analytic for exploring how, by recourse to ideology, they are made contingent. This does not constitute a theory but a 'tool box' of analytics that we can now take up and use. Before we can do that, however, we need to consider the methods of scrutiny – the crafty dodges – available to us for using these tools. This we will do in the next chapter.

Interrupter: Is that the end of the performance! Is this where we clap?

Beryl: Well, it's the end of the chapter, certainly. Whether you applaud or boo is up to you.

Interrupter: Actually, I'm more interested in a swift drink. Shall we slip out before the crowd?

Beryl: Good idea. What's yours?

Interrupter: A T 'n' T of course, tequila and tonic. Make it a double.

5

Crafty dodges: the question and questioning of methods

Prolegomenon

Interrupter: What? Even the late Frankie Howerd settled for a prologue.

Beryl: I couldn't say prologue could I? That means 'before the discourse' – a very dodgy ontology. Prolegomenon is the *mot juste*: a critical intro- duction to a lengthy text.

Interrupter [adjusting toga]: Poor dear, her prolepses are playing up again. No, don't laugh; don't mock the afflicted. She's been a bit over-rupted recently. Show a little pity, humour her. Let her think she's resolving objec- tions before they arise.

Over the previous chapters we have presented textuality and tectonics as simultaneously that which we are studying and the means by which we study; in other words, as analytics. Thereby we claim to both scrutinize textuality and tectonics, and reflexively to recognize that our scrutiny is itself textual and afforded by tectonics. In some people's minds, this is bound to raise the spectre of a vicious circularity. Certainly, our enquiry is circular (self-consciously so). Whether this implies a 'sub-text', a viciousness, a dirty tricks campaign upon sense and understanding is a different matter. Doubtless it will prove frustrating for those who want to know 'the answer' to any given question. There are two, related aspects to the climate of problematization which may particularly be drawn upon in defending such a circularity:

1. The interminability – under Modernism – of debate on any given question. This will be explored later in this chapter as the *interrogation interminable*.
2. A suspicion of attempts to close debate by recourse to the singularization of truth.

Truths, in other words, are service stations on the road to nowhere.

In such a critical polytextual position, it is possible for us to recognize that 'human life' is neither clear *nor* singular; debates are not 'won', 'culture free' at critical junctures by the success of enlightened thought, but are forgotten – subducted under other debates (cf. Kuhn 1970). Likewise, an effect is always multiply attributable; effects (issues, concerns) precipitate accounts of their causation – effect thereby precedes cause.

Thus positioned, it comes to be surprising that anyone could think that there was a single answer to questions of 'human life' (as if human life were a question) in the first place. Hence, the circle does not appear to us to be a *problem* but as a *necessity* for any who wish to avoid singularization: 'What is decisive is not to get out of the circle but to come into it in the right way' (Heidegger 1962: 195). (See Figure 5.1.)

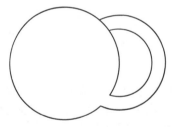

Figure 5.1   Coming into the circle.

Interrupter: 'To everything there is a season . . .'

Beryl: That's for the Byrds. But are the Talking Heads most postmodern?

This co-incidence (textuality and tectonics being both what and how we study) has been hinted at previously in our distinction between 'theory' and analytic. Here, theory – in order to be gauged against its subject – must necessarily be separated from, and then linked to, this subject by methods *which are designed to permit a clear view* (methods which render invisible their textuality and tectonic provisioning: their positionality). An analytic, in comparison, depends upon no such contrast and hence no such bridge and no such requirement for transparency. This is why, for us, 'methods' cannot stand as means for the generation of validation or falsification: method, when paired with analytic as opposed to theory, is not forced to bear any burden of *proof.*

The credentials we require of method can be stated as follows: a method must permit an effortful engagement which recognizes and embraces the forehaving and foreconception (the taken-for-granted) involved in any knowing.

Agenda

In this chapter, then, we explore some of the methods of empirical investigation – and other, non-empirical ways of addressing texts – which have been developed within the climate of problematization. We will . . .

> *Interrupter: Hmm. Isn't the empirical/non-empirical distinction just the sort of thing your 'climate' sets out to 'problematize'?*

Beryl: In my most pedantic incarnation, I'd have to agree with you. We're in trouble with words – as usual. 'Empirical' is a very slippery term, it can mean anything from experimental to quack. I guess you want me to 'define my terms'.

> *Interrupter [ironically]: I don't want to cause you unnecessary distress.*

Beryl: What is an author but a site of sensation? Okay, investigation is, literally, to be 'on the track'. What empirical adds to that is a sense of being *methodical* about it, of adopting an ordered approach, one capable of yielding similarly *organized* (not necessarily the same, of course) output from one instance of use to another. This stands in contrast to being *a-methodical* in approach – taking a *laisser aller* line and accepting markedly varied *kinds* of output from one instance to another.

So, for example, you dear Interrupter (or you dear Reader) could investigate this book 'creatively' – as variously a fly swat, a fire-lighter or a cure for insomnia. That might be great fun but it would not qualify as 'empirical investigation', as I have just glossed it. But if you were to approach the book in a systematic way (even better in several systematic ways), asking by procedures like discourse analysis ('how can it be read?') that would be an 'empirical investigation' by my definition. Have I kept 'on track' over your question?

> *Interrupter: Methodically!*

Once again, we are using the notion of a climate of problematization as a device to imply tectonic change – here to highlight a shift in the landscape of method (and the landscape thereby methodologized). To put the point directly, the craft skills of the climate of problematization are, inevitably, going to be in tension with those that went before them. Thereby, they are not proposed as 'new, improved' replacements for received methods but as both challenges to the kinds of questions and answers those methods enabled and as means to doing something other than that which received human science does. In one sense, they are not methods at all as conventionally understood in much social science (i.e. technologies of research that can be taught), but explicitly acknowledged crafts or skills acquired in the doing. As Parker (1992a: 5) notes of Potter and Wetherell (1987): 'the reader is told, quite rightly, that discourse analysis is like riding a bike'. Hence, it is helpful to constitute research, or as we prefer to call it scrutiny, under a climate of problematization, not so much in the language of paradigm shift (see the Glossary) which implies translation of position in some implied fixed geometry of enquiry, but as a paradigmatic warp. Following a shift to a climate of problematization, everything changes – the warp is climatic!

Before those tectonic events, and with the benefit of the 'hindsight' those events engendered, methods served the various discipline-bound projects of enquiry into the social and the human. They were, in other words, implicated in governmentality (see Glossary), offering a means towards, and a unique warrant for, positioning investigators and practitioners as policepersons of the soul and mentors of the great and the good (cf. Rose 1990).

Methodolatry

Under Modernism, 'methods' held a very special status, not just for full initiates into the mystery religion of human science, but also for those serving their apprenticeship. In particular, in the socialization of putative social scientists, there was (indeed, still is) often a *methodolatry* in which method was accorded a kind of meta-stability, treated as a tecton in its own right – to a considerable extent separate and separated in syllabus from the more shifting sands of topic-ality.

In other words, irrespective of where one is located in terms of specialization within a discipline (one's intra-discipline speciality), methods have often been treated as generic to the discipline and accorded special syllabus status. Further, while theory is often presented as a disputed plurality of alternatives – one in which a major focus of teaching is to help students acquire the skills to argue this theory against that – method is presented as a minefield of error. The task is to learn how to follow the map, keep on the 'right' track and avoid getting 'blown up' when matching method to research question. Variety in methods (e.g. qualitative/quantitative) is put across not so much as a matter of disputed alternatives but as a test of choice-competency, making an appropriate decision in terms of the kind of topic being pursued, and the level of analysis required.

The special place of method is, thereby, re-emphasized by its style of teaching which tends to the canonical rather than the disputational. The clear prescription is fostered (and enforced in training by such things as marking criteria) that there are 'right and wrongs ways' of doing method, stronger and weaker procedures to address whatever specific 'research questions' arise.

These institutional circumstances, then, afford a special position for the category 'method'. In the ideal-typical case, 'Method' for a human science under Modernism stands outside of specialism and regulates the investigations that go on within specialisms. The overall impression is of 'method' as a value-neutral and ever-improving set of procedures which can be brought to bear upon any specific issue. The ultimate warrant for this special status lies in that project of methodolatry, which is itself grounded upon the combined status of method and methodologist in the 'Truth Game'.

> *Interrupter: This is drifting into 'the Pot calling . . .' if you ask me. Your account of these 'curriculum tectonics' and their bearing of the stigmata of modernity, strikes me as caught up in the very logic you question.*

Beryl: You may find this hard to believe but I rather agree. As it says in Ecclesiasticus: 'He [sic] that touchest pitch shall be defiled therewith.' I do rather have a sense of 'beach tar on my feet'. That is one of the problems of the 'questioning' mode. But it got us to the 'questions' didn't it?

> *Interrupter: You're a lovely textual mover! But in this book you have also teased apart your analytics and methods using the device of separate chapters. Aren't you simply going along with the convention of first deciding on an area of study and then choosing the most appropriate method to study it empirically?*

Beryl: Yes and no.

Certainty and surprise

At its worst, research can become yet another taken-for-granted presencing practice, in which the link between aims and the means of solution are almost as automatic as reaching for a hammer to drive home a nail. We're thinking of the 'got an issue, do a public opinion survey' kind of knee-jerk research. However, even if we think about that empirical investigation, which is a thoughtful linking of aims and objectives to ways and means of realizing those aims and objectives, then research boils down to a skilled craft of matching up tasks to tools.

> *Interrupter: So we are going to get Beryl's Big Book of Q-It-Yourself?*

Beryl: No. That is a book that wasn't. It never got further than an outline proposal because it seemed to us un-writable – it could only have been cast in the same, old, established mould.

Our concern with scrutiny departs quite radically from the modernist research endeavour of 'finding the right tool for the job' and its methodolatrous inversion – frantically trying to 'find the right job for the tool'. [*The person with a hammer in their hand sees the whole world as a nail.* Apocryphal Sayings of Beryl.] We can be critical of that endeavour in a way that those still immersed in Modernism cannot – by troubling its project not just by laying judgements on specific instances of its realization. This is because we can make use of a shifted viewpoint – a re-vista – from which we can look out on the modernist landscape. This narratal postmodern panorama point (and we have no illusions it is anything else) provided by the climate of problematization renders what it presences as a tectonized terrain; moreover, one for which the major tectonic events which produced it occurred sufficiently long ago for the dust to settle, for a strata of unsurprise to become sedimented, for a lack of criticality to become established. What now appears there has become familiar territory. From our privileged (and we use the term under erasure) vantage point we can see its landmarks more clearly. We can see how institutional power, sustained by the sedimentation of its vulgarized knowledges as commonsensical, became the informed approach to human questions.

By contrast, the tectonic events that allow us to discourse as we do (e.g. as critical polytextualists) have occurred far more recently. The climate of problematization is still intensely active, and therefore all we can see within it is a still rough and discomforting topography. Moreover, we are here, as it were, making the terrain – not 'out there' looking out over it. These involvements both make it difficult to observe the contours of our transit and to claim any prescience about where (indeed if) things are going to end up.

What we can feel is the disturbing pleasure of taking methods and analytics as connate. This means that the simple task of finding 'the right tool for the job' no longer makes any singular sense. As an analytic, textuality is not only permeable to and permeated by anti-philosophy (e.g. Heidegger 1971; Derrida 1982) and post-structuralist interventions in the humanities (Rorty 1989) and human sciences (Foucault 1972), but is also sensible to the practice of the problematizing mode of reading texts around which these interventions were written. The idea of tectonics is similarly perforate to and impregnated by critical concerns (Parker 1989, 1990; Burman 1990) over the politico-moral relativity (or even power, place and space opacity) that can attach to the modes of practical involvement which our engagement with post-phenomenology/post-structuralism occasioned. These matters are discussed further in the last chapter.

> *Interrupter: Let me guess the next step in the argument. You are about to release one of Woolgar's (1988a) 'horrors'. Namely, that investigation is impossible without prior representation. Hence, every observation is enmeshed with the methods used to achieve it. Hence, each and every method and derivative observation is, **a priori**, theoretic, that is, constructed.*

Beryl: Couldn't have put it better myself. Have I got a convert?

> *Interrupter: Hardly. I think you have just caught yourself in your own trap.*

Beryl: Exactly. It is just such a critical reflexivity I was after. Remember what I said in my prolegomenon? Circles and all that?

The point we are making is that the separation of analysis and method is both devisive and divisive. However, these are not intrinsically troublesome (we would argue nothing can be foundationally perturbating). Indeed, it gives us no grief at all since we are engaged in a scheme of ecologically interdependent analytics and methods. What is worried, though, is the modernist notion that it is possible to separate theory and method – that theory is subject to formal judgment via an independent tribunate or juristic programme of method (i.e. study, outcome and evaluation). Like the workings of more literal 'supreme courts', the notion of a completely neutral, objective judiciary of method simply will not wash and cannot, in fact, accomplish the tasks given to it. Like our law courts, its pronouncements are always local, contingent and subject to challenge.

This is not to say that in more mundane terms such research does not 'work'. It is certainly not a call to reject any and all received 'data' in some orgy of empiricist nihilism.

> *Interrupter: No? That's what a lot of your colleagues say. Only the other night in the 'Three Tuns' . . .*

Beryl: I really think that sampling of discourse is a little local for most of our readers!

Rather, it is to argue that such research is representationally ortho-doxical. Even down to the verdicts it can yield, it can challenge a conclusion but it can never challenge the institutionalization of knowledging.

Given that as researchers we wish for information that may surprise us, that can disturb any tendency to set up new incipient ortho-doxies, the climate of problematization offers an attractively para-doxical ambience. It implies, in Michael Taussig's (1986) glorious phrase, a 'nervous system' of methods, where in our pursuit of the empirical we are always 'troubled' as well as 'troubling' . . .

Beryl: Some would say 'troublesome', just to get that in before anybody else does!

> *Interrupter [Still in tritunic mode]: Hmph!*

In other words, the first thing we ask of methods is that they must be open to reflexive self-criticality. They must be sufficiently 'open' to alternative readings that we cannot be accused of dogmatism; yet sufficiently methodical to avoid being accused of being ineffective, or no more than relativistic.

Interrupter: In other words, you want to avoid being seen as 'soft'?

Beryl: It's a bit more complicated than that, but the notion of 'hard' versus 'soft', if you can avoid smirking, is not a bad place to move onto next.

The implications of understanding

Although it provides far from an absolute distinction, the traditional divide between 'the arts' and 'the sciences' has often been expressed in terms of their different methods of enquiry. We have drawn upon that commonplace wisdom (and also signalled our doubts as to its ultimate substance) in the last chapter when suggesting some translation rules between the scientist's knowledging of a scientific issue and more mundane knowledging of day-to-day issues.

Nevertheless, we would be the first to recognize that in the construction of scientized knowledging, the highest emphasis has usually been placed on competence in appropriate methodology. Indeed, one still hears it suggested (particularly by experimentalists!) that there is a scale of value running from 'experimentation' (the highest, best and most desirable form of controlled enquiry) to 'unstructured examination' (the lowest, messiest and dodgiest form of enquiry). Underpinning that notion are ideas of the place of theory. The 'best' theory is that which allows the quantitative expression of an hypothesis, through whose falsifiability via experimentation comes the only true march of knowledge. (Note that we have already raised questions about the place of theory in the last chapter.)

On such scales of values, not only is the knowledging of the arts and ordinary life found wanting methodologically, it is also found wanting in conceptual (theoretical) rigour. It stands condemned as mere opinion or belief without empirical validation (armchair knowledge, lay beliefs, metaphysics or 'old wives' tales'). Tales of the growth of scientific knowledge frequently stress the power of empirical methodology, whether in the collation of 'true' knowledge (e.g. Durkheim's study of suicide) or the debunking of 'false' knowledge (e.g. Phungst's demolition of 'Clever Hans' the horse that could, purportedly, count).

So-called 'soft methods' in the human sciences (e.g. interpretational, participant observational, case study, *verstehen*) have often been presented as 'soft options', at best tolerated (until more rigorous, 'harder' procedures and statistics overtake them), at worst condemned as worthless. This story of scientistic knowledging, and challenges to it, are oft-spun in the critical literature. We are not reiterating it here as though it were some new insight. Rather, our purpose is to suggest how it enables a particular tectonic in critical reaction. Where scientizing has become the 'enemy' (e.g. in some dialects of feminist research, because it is identified as 'masculine') attempts are often made to reclaim its counterpole. A case in point is the 'agentic'/ 'communal' distinction:

> 'Agentic' research, which involves 'separating, ordering and quantifying, manipulating, controlling' is contrasted with 'communal' kinds of

scientific enquiry, involving 'naturalistic observation, sensitivity to intrinsic structure and qualitative patterning of phenomena, and greater personal participation of the investigator' (Carlson 1972: 20). Traditional modes of enquiry, it is argued are 'based primarily upon agentic features'. (Wilkinson 1986: 10)

Box 5.1 The qualitative/quantitative tension

The agentic/communal divide is a re-formation of the quantitative/ qualitative distinction which has long been used as a regulative, reality-maintenance device in methodological debates in the social sciences. An easy way of reading the moral valuation involved is to note that qualitative (i.e. non-numerical) data are frequently transformed (e.g. by content or structural analysis) into quantitative data. Then, of course, they can be subjected to the mystery craft of statistics – a crucial element in the tribunate judgement of the 'Truth Games'. However, such 'transformed' data are taken as 'less' than data gained by theoretical translation into mathematical operationalization. It is these latter 'truly quantitative' data that are seen as maximizing the objectivity of the operation at both the researcher and researched-upon ends of the investigation.

Outside of this agenda, it may seem strange that quantity and quality have been so often treated as tensional opposites, each pitted against the other (cf. Silverman, 1985, for a fuller treatment of this oppositionality). Within it the investment in this oppositionality reflects the tectonic formations that constitute the human disciplines – specifically, how they sunder the 'subjective' from the 'objective'. For Foucault (*The Order of Things*, 1970), this distinction constructs us dualistically as knowing subjects who can then examine themselves as objects of inquiry. The autonomy and self-sufficiency of the categories 'subject' and 'object' have been, respectively, problematized by Henriques, Hollway, Urwin, Venn and Walkerdine (1984) and Woolgar (1988b). Both these troublings, of course, reflect upon the other through their mutual predication. Together they allow a warp away from the constitution of subjecting–objecting as fundaments of the human disciplines.

Instead, it now becomes possible to narrate them as melo-drama; a dialogue between meaning and accuracy (as we will illustrate in Box 5.2 by the badinage between Spock and McCoy in the soap 'Star Trek'). If accuracy dominates the work-world of Science, meaning dominates the play-world of Life. Recall, for example, the opening sequence of *The Prisoner*:

'Who are you?'
'I am number two.'
'Who is number one?'
'You are number six.'
'I AM NOT A NUMBER!'

Some such move towards 'communal' methods has also been the hall-mark of other challenges to the orthodoxy. As the magma capillaries of the climate of problematization began to seep into the bed-rock of social science, Harré and Secord (1972), for example, called for a new ethogenic method-ology for social psychology, one which focused upon the accounts people (as rule-following agents) give of their behaviour. The ethnomethodological school in sociology (cf. Garfinkel 1967) also turned to the study of accounts in everyday life in their focus upon the negotiation of rational accountability.

Some sense of the heterogeneity (or inconsistency, if you prefer) of the notion of 'communal' methods can best be conveyed by noting that it variously implied both late structural (as above) and late phenomenological commitments. Thus in parallel to the above developments, existential soci-ologists were happily employing similar 'soft' methods to uncover the cen-trality of feelings to experience (cf. Douglas and Johnson 1977).

More recently, 'communal' methods have drawn together in a variety of ways. One major recent statement is Denzin's (1989) 'Interpretative Inter-actionism'. Of it, he says:

> The approach advocated in this book should only be used when the researcher wants to examine the relationship between personal trou-bles, for example wife-battering, or alcoholism, and the public policies and public institutions that have been created to address those personal problems. (Denzin 1989: 10)

However, the book extends considerably beyond this agenda because, in so doing, 'Interpretative Interactionism seeks to bring lived experience before the reader' (Denzin 1989: 83). In thereby adopting an *auteur* function, Denzin also turns to *auteur* craft. This is quite self-conscious, for he notes that, 'All interpretation is fictional in the sense that it involves either the observer's or the subject's accounting of what has occurred or what something means' (p. 137). Hence, 'thick description' ('deep, dense, detailed accounts', p. 83) is pursued not just as method but as device. It enables not just interpretation but 'thick interpretation' (that which 'elaborates and builds upon thick de-scription', p. 112). It is no accident that Denzin can equally well turn his hand to the movies, for they too 'speak to the problem of presenting and doing interpretation' (p. 138).

The idea that methods should reflect theoretical commitment and faith harkens us back to the argument in the previous chapter about the press for a link between understanding and implication. We have suggested that this is a key element in the tectonics of politicization. Hence, for example, 'hu-manistic' theories, such as Harré and Secord's (1972), often make a specific plea for 'human methods', just as, more recently, feminist theorization has been linked to calls for feminist methods.

From the critical polytextualist perspective, of course, the idea of operating within a politically consistent textuality is not an axiom-to-be-followed but a possibility-that-can-be-explored (one of many potential tectonics). In that regard, it does rather seem as though the looser or more open the political agenda of an approach, the less it tends to go in for doctrinal methodolatry. A case in point is social constructionism, whose roots in such eclectic traditions as those of Berger (e.g. Berger and Luckmann 1967) is paralleled by an equally eclectic stand on methods (e.g. Antaki 1981; Shotter 1993).

Interrogation interminable

As critical polytextualists, we do not enter this particular methodological debate by taking one side or the other. To do this would be to claim a privileged access to some social/psychological reality, be it with regard to the passing laws of the quantitative researcher or the authentic experience of the qualitative researcher. Instead, we treat both modes as emblematic of research practices which, like any other text (cf. Chapter 2), conceal or 'repress' certain readings in order to produce meaning. Both modes ('hard' and 'soft') claim to reveal some 'truth' about the social or the personal, and it is this search for truth which necessitates the concealment of the opposed attitude. This is also the case for the 'triangulation' (cf. Cosminski 1977) of such methods, which is also performed for truth functions (such as validity).

Looking to the tectonics that call for and enable these textual negotiations, the hard/soft, qualitative/quantitative distinction begins to resemble another melodrama of interrogation – the 'nice guy/nasty guy' interview routine beloved of police and intelligence work (and their re-production as entertainment). The 'nasty guy' backs the target into a corner of the interview-room and demands 'just the facts ma'am' and simple ('thin') yes or no (quantifiable) answers. The 'nice guy' operator offers a cup of tea and a cigarette, and empathizes with the participant, even to the extent of appearing to defend her from the 'blow cold' operator – and draws out 'thick' (qualitative) information. Whichever approach to interrogation is taken, the purpose is still to break down the resistance of the subject, to get them to yield a testimony to the truth.

> *Interrupter: And, of course, you don't do that?*

Beryl: Like any other researchers, we take up people's time and use our skills of persuasion or cash from research budgets to get them to participate. But we are not into a 'Truth Game', we do not demand 'honesty' or 'openness'. We treat all our participants as textual transducers, not as 'souls' (open or closed) to be scanned and judged. Usually, we also participate in our own studies, and show our data alongside those we have gained from others.

> *Interrupter: Well, I've done a few Q-sorts in my time, and I can tell you I felt 'put on the line' sometimes.*

Beryl: In the quasi-normal distribution, you mean! And I thought you enjoyed strict discipline?

The craft of textual curiosity

At the risk of provoking the Interrupter again, a contrast is needed to develop our tale. If the Modernist style of research can be compared to interrogation, what is it that the interrogators are after? What result could bring the interrogation to an end? The answer many well help to clarify why the interrogation interminable (for *The Prisoner* from the last Box, or that earlier germinal figure in the worrying of modernity, Kafka's 'Joseph K') has become such a dystopian semiotic in present-day culture.

Modernist research is interminable because it aims at uncovering 'the truth', whether that comes in the form of general laws (and modifying corollaries) of human conduct, or in the form of the experiential truth of a group or an individual. Once discovered, each fragment of 'the truth' (which is an in-finite resource not unlike the pickled parts of saints distributed around Christendom) is given the role of the start of an explanation of the matter at issue. This is built up into a knowledge [which might be Levi-Strauss's structural universals of anthropology (1966) or Becker's *verstehen* fix on the mind of the 'dope-head' (1963)], which is itself foundationed upon axioms of the lawfulness of the generation of objective social behaviour or the openness of souls in accounts of experience generated by knowing subjects.

We argue that this focusing in of investigation, this assumption from the start of a singularity underlying the issue at hand, works (i.e. makes the 'invisible' more 'visible') not just through the highlighting of instantiations of that singularity (i.e. where it is detected as represented) but also through suppression of all else (i.e. readings that emphasize the variation, contradic-tion and intertextualities of the texts to hand).

> *Interrupter: Hang on! If I had just been bitten by a rabid dog, it is precisely that 'singularization' and 'suppression of alternatives' that I would be des-perate to get.*

Beryl: So would I! But that doesn't mean I want a singularized account of Louis Pasteur (be it psychoanalytic 'the great man story of medicine' or 'data faker'). Applied science and technology can mandate singularization where it deals pragmatically and effectively with a local singularity (be it treating rabies or mending a puncture on my tricycle). But scientific discourse *as discourse* falls clearly within the remit of textuality and tectonics.

This form of argument is quite common in climate of problematization work. It is argued generally for the discourse on science by Knorr-Cetina (1991) and Mulkay (1991). More specifical it is applied, for example, of the production of the concept of attitude in experimental social psychology by the discourse analysts Potter and Wetherell (1987). One of me (Stenner 1992) has made the same case over emotion (cf. Chapter 7).

Box 5.2 Science (fiction) and emotionality

The original television series *Star Trek* and its spin-off movies are ideal texts to illustrate the textuality and tectonics of emotionality and to explore many other themes in this chapter. In this allegory, the 'mission' narrates the ongoing drama between three central characters, Spock, McCoy and Kirk. To explore their 'new worlds', 'to boldly go' depends upon the provision of solutions not primarily to singularities (such as diseases of dilithium crystals) but to problematics that draw upon tectons of 'ration and passion'. Spock, the technocrat, is a creature of almost total rationality who continually quizzes McCoy (the doctor-healer) about his 'human emotions'. McCoy typically responds with accusations of heartlessness. At times of crisis, Kirk, being the Captain of the ship, seeks advice from both of them and then conciliates their divergent *modus operandi*, producing solutions which are a carefully managed integration of clear thinking and compassion.

By observing that characters who are only narratively embodied can be storied as having plausible emotions and faculties of thought makes visible the textuality of our own emotions and rationality as opposed to truly 'embodied' characters. So viewed we can appreciate that emotionality is not contained by the reading of our or of others' bodies as affectized texts, but extends into a situation, covers a field of morality in which emotionality or calculating 'cool' can be evaluated. Our engagement (scopophilic and identificatory) with this melodrama is not a spontaneous value- and ideology-free textuality, but follows the tectonic topographies of discursive productions such as Romanticism and Classicism; Patriarchy and Imperialism.

Boxus Interruptii: But what has *Star Trek* got to do with real emotions? With natural selection and the biological bases of emotion? Alternatively, with the subjectively real experiences people have of emotion?

Boxus Berylii: Shame on you knave! That is the modernist question. We know perfectly well that modernist methods (quantitative and qualitative) that are brought to bear upon it. As I am agnostic over singularizing essential truths, I don't pose that question and, hence, don't set about trying to answer it. My trajectories do not project back onto a thing 'emotion' but warp off, boldly go onto the textuality and tectonics of emotion. 'Beam me up, Scottie, to Chapter 7.'

Indeed, there is a marked degree to which no matter what the texts addressed within the climate of problematization (including the constitution of scientific knowledge), the dominant analytics have all been textual (i.e. primarily operating in language). This has tended to be true whatever the texts under analysis (e.g. filmic, visual artistic, architectural or discursive). This is what makes for transdisciplinarity, for the move is to address all fields of textuality in a way that modernistic methods could not. For French theory, with its roots in philosophy, this is hardly surprising. But it is equally true of feminism or neo-Marxist critical methods. To an extent, this is reflective of the politicization operant in much of that work – texts, once viewed *as* texts are available and amenable to having their ideologies unpicked, to being debated, to being rewritten. But it would be unfair and misleading to suggest that thereby lies *the* explanation. At least as salient (as we noted in Chapter 1) is the common concern with the problematic of language itself.

Discoursing discourse

When working around the problematic of language, several difficulties arise. It is perfectly clear, for example, that what might be called a purely formal linguistic approach is not what is required. What may trouble a 'postmodernist' about the writings of a 'modernist' is not the use made, *per se*, of grammar. The same holds true for analysis of accounts in ethogeny or ethnomethodology. The grammatical well-formedness or otherwise of the participant's sentences is not what is at issue. Even where, as in the case of, say, Derrida (cf. Chapter 1), the language seems chosen to disturb; any breaches of received use are there for a purpose that goes well beyond teasing grammarians. It is relevant in this regard that linguistics itself now increasingly recognizes a level of analysis beyond that of words and sentences, i.e. that of discourse (cf. Coulthard 1977). What discourse analysis brought to linguistics was a new emphasis on function (cf. Labov 1972). Of course, the term discourse (as is typical of a new 'buzz-word') has been widely taken up and acquired a variety of meanings (cf. also Parker 1992b). The specialized use which Foucault makes of the term is discussed in Chapter 1.

Nevertheless, it is often used in a very general sense (e.g. by Gilbert and Mulkay 1982; and later by Potter and Wetherell 1987): 'to cover all forms of spoken interaction, formal and informal, and written texts of all kinds' (Potter and Wetherell 1987: 7). The idea that discourse could be analysed, of course, existed long before the emergence of 'discourse analysis' as a name for the activity. Freud, for example, was offering an analysis of text and 'speech acts' ninety years ago. The content (i.e. objective) and structural (i.e. subjective) analysis of oral and textual language has been a common feature of 'soft' methodology since at least the 1930s, when it was employed in the interpretation of 'projective' tests (often derived from Freudian notions). It is an almost taken-for-granted skill in social research, finding its way down to secondary school project work. Hence, we need to ask what is 'new' about the structural analysis that now gets called discourse analysis?

> *Interrupter: Right on! I thought DA meant a funny hairdo until I discovered Potter and Wetherell.*

> Beryl: That dates you!

One answer would appear to be that contemporary discourse analysis is informed by much that relates to the climate of problematization. Work in neo-linguistics, in ethnomethodology and ethogenics, as well as concepts from semiology and social constructionism, has given discourse analysis a new sensitivity to the user-features of language as well as to the problems of its study.

Nevertheless, it often seems to retain a functionalist, pragmatic and agentic (used here in the sense of implying agency) approach. 'People', Potter and Wetherell (1987: 32) inform us, 'use their language to do things'. Hence, one major task of the discourse analyst is '"reading" the context' (p. 33) in order to unpack the function of language in a text. This does, of course, raise an old problem. On what basis, one might ask, should one accept, say, Potter and Wetherell's readings as any more plausible than, say, Freud's? Or, to broaden the net, just what is the status of any claim (from literary theorist to discourse analyst) that we are being told, say, what Hamlet (or indeed Shakespeare) is doing with language?

To a critical polytextualist, of course, that is exactly the point and indeed is acknowledged by Potter and Wetherell. Such readings as we make can constitute a concourse of possible knowledgings, each such knowledging having its own tectonics of interpretation. Applying one such tectonic, we can recognize the possibility that discourse analysts (just like anybody else, and like all those who offer readings of texts) 'use their language to do things'!

Hence, when we offer readings of texts (as will be seen in the latter half of the book), we try to make explicit just how minimal are the claims we make. A 'thematic decomposition' (cf. Stenner 1993), for example, as we call our 'discourse analytic' work, is just that – a story of function or a tale of meaning.

We are not suggesting, by the way, in asserting our own critical reflexivity, that discourse analysts are unaware of their own language functions. Rather, we are suggesting that the genre of textual analysis *per se* still has a tendency to warrants of certitude – there is little place for the psychoanalyst or the critic who confesses: 'Could mean this, could mean that? Who can say?' The punters like a good story too! Which is not to suggest that story-tellers are only concerned with entertaining their audience. They may also want to change them and indeed the world. Stories can also be parables and the (post?) modern teller of parables may have other warrants – a 'politics of discourse analysis' (Parker 1992a: 22). But even in that, those politics can only be structurations to be found in the current concourse of possible political knowledgings. And the identity-presentations of their raconteurs can only re-produce the desired *personae* of story-tellers.

> *Interrupter: We have to 'accept' the author as a story-telling 'personality' as we 'accept' their text as parable?*

Beryl: Jesus! He's got it.

> *Interrupter: Blaspheme not phantasm! While I've got your attention, aren't your 'thematic decompositions' **auterial**?*

Beryl: Yes, which is why we also try to worry the author function.

Senior Editor: Please note the deliberately polysemic quality of this badinage (cf. Derrida's 1991 discussion on Joyce, *Ulysses Gramophone*).

Displacing the analyst?

That we can so easily come to consider the *auteur* in so much climate of problematization work – that their unique hand and performance (textual identity) is so much part of every *œuvre* – may be picking up upon no more than a hangover from Romanticism. We have come to expect our commentators to be 'personalities' and, reflexively, putative commentators have certainly made 'personalities' of themselves.

> *Interrupter: Are you deriding bouffant hair-do's?*
>
> Beryl: Did I say that?
>
> *Interrupter: You didn't need to, your look said it all.*

It is a genre in which the stamp of the raconteur can lead to a situation where the reading becomes personified – hence we can have Baudrillard's 'America', or Wim Wenders's 'America' or Alistair Cooke's 'America'. Which is one good reason to question whether this personification is justified. Are we being given the 'unique', the 'creative leap' or are we all just hooked on 'going to the analyst'? If readings can only reflect the current concourse of possible knowledgings, then it at least seems worth exploring whether the analyst might be redundant. Why not, it could be asked, just collect readings as lepidopterists once did butterflies or nosologists once did with diseases, and allow the taxonomy to emerge by way of a formal calculus of comparisons and contrasts? As to whether this is a viable endeavour (and what needs to be added to make it viable) occupies the next section.

Pattern analytics

Wherever data are dirty, you will find a statistician. Wherever data are really dirty, you will find a meta-analyst. Twentieth-century statistics of pattern analysis owe much to two dirty disciplines: agriculture and psychology. The problem of unpicking association among variation has considerably occupied both. Environments, whether fields used for seed trials or schools used for testing some new educational innovation (cf. Danzinger 1990), vary in complex ways, and those variabilities have a nasty habit of interacting with the very thing you are trying to test. The solution was the development of modern statistics of association amidst variation. As commonly used, these statistics reveal associations (e.g. correlations) between variables.

> *Interrupter: Aren't the associations within texts (i.e. between words used) employed to explore the authorship of that text?*
>
> Beryl: Yes, it is one product of being able to correlate variables. It is even employed as an 'objective' form of discourse analysis. Another utilization is in computer packages that will test the density and grammatical complexity of one's language.
>
> *Interrupter: I don't suppose you've used one?*
>
> Beryl: I would not gainsay your assumption of a negational respondence on my part!

If one adds more and more variables, then more complex statistical techniques (such as factor analysis) can be employed to reduce the complexity to more simple patterns of association. How this works is easiest to see in terms of so-called 'mental testing'. The questions we can ask that supposedly tap, say, personality or intellectual ability can be reduced, using the psychometrician's statistical procedures, to a limited number of basic traits (e.g. numerical and verbal ability; extroversion/introversion). This might seem to, but does not, meet the need we expressed earlier for a calculus of similarities and differences. It does not because it produces taxonomies of measures, not taxonomies of knowledging (cf. Brown 1980).

We can illustrate the difference quite clearly by considering how we might knowledge Prince Hamlet. Traditional statistics of association and variation are designed to tell us whether measures (for example, of quality of parental relationships, sexual orientation, unconventionality, proneness to fantasy, self-destructiveness) vary together (are intercorrelated) across various cases that we measure (e.g. people).

> *Interrupter: Let's see if I've got this. They are useful for telling us whether, in a group of people we study, a measure of 'poor parental relationships' goes with a measure of 'self-destructive tendencies'.*

Beryl: Spot on – they intercorrelate so-called traits.

> *Interrupter: But not whether the quality of an individual's (say, Hamlet's) parental relationships more characterizes him than, say, how prone to fantasy he is.*

Beryl: You're good at this logical stuff.

> *Interrupter: According to the psychometricians, we men are logical you know. Talking of logic, Prince Hamlet can't be tested at all. He doesn't really exist.*

Beryl: Yes he does, in textuality – and in that many times over. That's the point. We don't need a 'real' Hamlet to be able to get measures like this, only access to Hamlet as storied. It's a neat demonstration several of me have used to occupy undergraduates in practical classes for years (cf. Semin and Rogers 1973). What we hope it shows them is that if you only need a storied Hamlet, then how is that different from them storying themselves? Try it sometime.

> *Interrupter: I imagine you set Gergen and Shotter's **Texts of Identity** as homework?*

Beryl: You bet!

Q-methodology

What we were looking for as a method was the 'opposite' of correlating 'traits', something which correlated whole structures of readings (e.g. about people) in order to disclose how they 'shake out' into sets of very similar accounts, i.e. shared stories. Following the work of Stephenson (see Box 4.2) and Steve Brown (e.g. 1980), we will call the first (the unwanted approach) R-methodology and the second (the wanted approach) Q-methodology. In the next section, we will set out how Q-methodological work is done.

Sampling a concourse

Q-method begins with the task of establishing a concourse in respect to the topic in question. In our example, this would be the concourse of descriptions (i.e. re-presentations) of the character of Hamlet. It is here that our division between presentation, understanding and conation is salient. In our studies, we have found that they work best if, in respect to any topic, we seek to treat these three as separate concourses. In simple, practical terms, people find it easier and more meaningful to consider propositions in relation to one another if they are all either to do with re-presentation or understanding or conduct/policy.

The way we gain a handle on a concourse is by exploring as wide a gamut of the available texts as we can discover. This itself is a pretty daunting and demanding task. For example, we would seek out statements about Hamlet's character from scholarly works, both written and oral (e.g. from conferences as well as academic journals and books). We would look for different ways he has been portrayed in film and television, both by watching the productions ourselves and reading press reviews and commentaries. With a subject like this we would also look at educational materials used, for example, at 'crib' texts for teaching at different levels. We would engage in conversations in formal interview settings (e.g. with a range of 'experts' working from different perspectives) and in informal settings like dinner party talk or in the pub or at the hairdressers.

In this way we could arrive at a large number of propositions describing the character of Hamlet (the man, not the play). Typically, we would expect to generate several hundred such statements. These we would see as constituting, as best we are able to discover, an estimate of the concourse on Hamlet as re-produced. Of course, we could not hope to cover everything that is or has been said on the matter, and this is one place where Q-method is noticeably a craft. Ultimately, our ability to generate worthwhile, useful data from our Q-studies is heavily reliant on our ability to arrive at a reasonably comprehensive explication of a concourse. This depends on our craft skills, as persons-in-culture, to gain access to the discourses by which any topic is knowledged. This we do in part by sampling as widely as possible. In part, it is also a matter of speculating about the ones we might find expressed to make sure that the means of their expression are covered, such as, in the case of Hamlet, Freudian readings, Marxist readings, feminist readings, and so on.

Interrupter: But that makes it circular.

Beryl: No it doesn't and that is the beauty of it. First, you cannot force a reading because the participants have the power – they structure the items. Second, any proposition gets its salience (or irrelevance) in use. For example, the statement 'loves his mother' will be understood quite differently from a Freudian reading compared with a feminist one.

Devising a Q-set

Our next task would be to sample the concourse to generate a Q-set of items. We do this by grouping statements which appear to carry similar meanings and selecting one to represent them, and by eliminating direct opposites. We also usually simplify statements and recast some in order to make them comprehensible to as wide a range of people as possible. This is usually achieved by a mixture of pilot testing and using our own judgement. In this way, we could arrive at a sample of perhaps 80–90 propositions capable of expressing a reasonably representative range of statements about Hamlet as a character. This is about the upper limit of what people appear to be able to manage. At least 30 or 40 are needed, in most cases, to offer a reasonable coverage of the alternatives.

The next stage is merely technical. The statements are printed out on small cards or on sheets of paper that can be cut up, so that each statement is separate, the 80 or so of them forming a Q-pack that can be sorted. Usually, we accompany this by a list of the statements, set out on sheets of paper so people can add open-ended comments. These are not necessary to the statistical analysis we shall do, but we find them a crucial part of the craft of giving sense to the data which come out of the computer.

Selecting participants

Finally, we would ask some people to sort the statements. In most studies, we would include a proportion of 'ordinary folks' and some people selected in the hope of gaining expressions of particular 'viewpoints'.

> *Interrupter: In other words, you hypothesize alternative results; just like an experimentalist.*

Beryl: No. We may have certain culturally derived expectations but these are 'up for grabs'. We are as happy to be surprised, as not. Beryl herself has come up in some strange company at times!

> *Interrupter: You are a subject in your own experiments?*

Beryl: You tease, of course. I am a participant (usually) in my own scrutinies. In any case, all research is participant observational whether people recognize it or not.

In the case of a study of representations of Hamlet, these would include people like critics working from a range of perspectives (e.g. feminism, psychodynamic theory) and 'experts' like English teachers, playgoers and actors. As we have noted, we also usually participate in our own studies. The main reason for this is that when we report our data we can indicate the viewpoint we ourselves have expressed. This means that the reader can draw conclusions about the ways this may have influenced the readings we lay upon the data.

An important point to note is that unlike in R-methodological studies (e.g. orthodox studies of attitudes), we are not at all interested in finding out what particular individuals or groups 'believe', or gaining access to a 'representative viewpoint'. Thus we make no attempt to select participants in our studies as a representative sample of a population. Representativeness, in Q, is a matter of the concourse (and hence Q-sets of items are often called, confusingly, Q-samples). Rather, our aim is more taxonomic – we want to identify and describe the range of alternatives (here representations). Hence selecting participants is more a matter of seeking to ensure diversity and comprehensiveness – we want to make sure we include a medley of people who, between them, are likely to express lots of different viewpoints.

Often information about who a person is or 'where they are coming from' can also be useful for interpreting the data, and so we usually ask participants in studies to tell us something about themselves. For example, if they state that they are 'Christian Spiritualists' or 'social workers' or that they have had particular life-experiences (e.g. of severe illness or having grown up in care), these may be salient in terms of the topic in question.

Q-sorting

We ask our participants to sort the statements along a dimension we provide for them. This, in the case of representations of Hamlet, would be something like from 'most descriptive' to 'most undescriptive'. Usually, we ask people to begin by sorting first into three piles: positives (descriptive); negatives (undescriptive); and a middle pile of statements about which they are uncertain, see as non-salient, or have ambiguity towards. Having done that, we ask them to sort all of the statements into a pattern which is then entered into a grid like that in Fig. 5.2. Thus into this grid they would select the four statements they felt were 'most descriptive' of Prince Hamlet and place these into the +5 spaces. The four chosen as 'most undescriptive' go into the –5 spaces, and so on.

Interrupter: Not much room is there?

Beryl: Each proposition is given a number, here from 1 to 80. It is the number that gets written in and moved on to the next stage.

Q-analysis

We would then enter these data into a factor analysis program, adapted so that it correlated whole Q-sets between people's sorting patterns, rather than

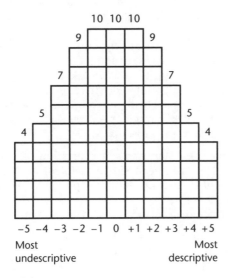

Figure 5.2 Q-sort grid.

the conventional manner of correlating across people and between responses. The reported sortings from each grid will then be correlated with those from each other grid and, just like data from mental measurement, reduced by factor analysis into a limited set of bunched-together similarities (factors rotated to 'simple structure'). But unlike with R-methodology, in Q the factors (at least when we have re-expressed them in grid form) correspond to different construals, which was just what we wanted.

The analysis typically yields somewhere between three and ten factors. There has been considerable debate between those of us who use Q-method in the UK and those using it in the USA (indeed, with Will Stephenson himself, when he was still alive) about how factors should be selected for interpretation and how many we should attempt to interpret. We do not intend to get bogged down in these debates here (the really keen could follow them up by referring to Stainton Rogers and Stainton Rogers 1990a).

Factors may be exemplified by the sorting of a number of people or, in some cases, by the sort of just one person. What this means is that each factor can be re-cast as a pattern of sorting. For each factor, the analysis gives a loading measure (a correlation with the factor) for each sorting pattern of each participant in the study. Exemplificatory sorts are those which have a high loading (usually somewhere between +0.7 and +0.9) on that factor and only very low loadings (usually we set this point at >0.3 or thereabouts) elsewise. Where several people's sorts are exemplificatory, a weighting and averaging procedure is used (see Brown 1980: 238–43) to derive an 'ideal' pattern, which expresses the factor best.

Factor exegesis: Exploring textuality

Interpretation, at one level, is relatively simple. We reconstitute the sorting pattern by, say, laying out the statements on a table (some computer programs do this for us as a print-out). We then interrogate the pattern, by looking at what statements are placed where. It is usually fairly straightforward to gain a sense of what is being expressed by looking at the statements placed at the extremes. For example, take the case of a factor which placed the following in the four +5 positions:

- Item 10: As a character, Hamlet is an expression of masculine power.
- Item 53: Hamlet is best understood as a violent criminal.
- Item 57: The role of Hamlet displays how patriarchy allows brutality to be expressed as romanticism.
- Item 59: Hamlet could never be re-cast as a woman.

It does not take too much 'insight' to dub this a feminist reading of the character. Other patterns would indicate other readings. In each study we would use these kinds of observations to generate a description of the reading being expressed. This is where the additional data form a crucial part of the whole exegesis. To discover, for example, that this factor was expressed by the sorting patterns of three people, all of whom adopted the self-description 'feminist', would be further indicative that it is a feminist reading being expressed. If, say, we also found open-ended comments from these participants written in terms of 'ruling men', 'patriarchal power' and 'man-made world', then these too would help us to flesh out our interpretation and locate it within some dialect of feminist discourse.

Here we are using a very transparent example to illustrate how exegesis works. In most studies we find that some factors are like this – everything 'hangs together' and the story told is easy to recognize and therefore easy to recount. But also in most studies we find factors where it is much more difficult, at least initially, for us to make sense of them. It can take many hours of puzzling and speculating before we can make a reading. Often, in cases like this, we go back to the participant(s) whose sorting pattern exemplified the factor, and ask them to help us. We also go and look for texts from the cultural archive (sometimes suggested by participants) to assist us.

Interrupter: Isn't that very frustrating?

Beryl: No, quite the opposite, it's one of the most exciting aspects of the work. It's like being set a puzzle or conundrum you have to solve, it's like a riddle. And like with a riddle, it feels great when, at last, you do get the sense you've 'cracked it'. One of the things we most enjoy about the work we do is that we always learn something new from it. Steve Brown (1980: 39) expressed this nicely when he wrote:

'Q samples provide a launch pad for an investigation, an entrée into a phenomenon, the scientist's [*sic*] best initial guess as to how a particular administrative situation, social consciousness, or whatever operates. The data gathered with the Q sample may lead in quite different directions . . . There is never any guarantee, in other words, that splash-down will occur in the same area as the point of departure.'

In other words, one of the benefits of Q methodology compared with, say, discourse analysis, is that it can force us, as researchers, to strive to express accounts or readings of a topic which would not otherwise have occurred to us. Participants in our studies can and do set us puzzles by the factors they bring into being, which we would otherwise have missed.

At this stage, having identified and described each of the factors, we usually expand the task into a more thorough cultural analysis. For example, where we can identify certain themes being expressed, we might look for other places where they have been made manifest. For example, in a study on understandings of health and illness (Stainton Rogers 1991), a theme of 'will-power' was identified as highly salient to a factor emergent from the sorting patterns of a group of people which included both entrepreneurs and alternative healers. It was then possible to link its expression into recent theorization on the role of the notion of self-control in the US capitalist system (e.g. by reference to the work of Crawford 1984) and back historically into the writings of influential Victorian thinkers about the importance of 'the will' with respect to health and illness (e.g. Hack Tuke 1872).

In this way, a Q-study generates a number of alternative (statistically they are orthogonal) 'accounts' or 'descriptions' of the way the topic or issue in question has been knowledged. In simple studies, we use only one Q-sort and focus in on just one of our three moments. For example, the study on re-presentations of 'madness' described in Chapter 6 looked only at representations. Sometimes we conflate moments in a single Q-set, usually for pragmatic reasons. One of the studies described in Chapter 8 examined in a single Q-sort alternative understandings of childhood together with views on child-rearing and social policy towards children. Other studies use just one Q-sort, but participants are asked to do it twice (e.g. Owens's (1993) study of the 'self' in coupled and uncoupled settings).

Exploring textuality and tectonics

In other studies, we have sought to look at more than one of the moments by asking people to complete two or, in a few studies, three different Q-sorts. This not only allows us to examine the textuality of topics and issues in greater breadth (since it allows us to explore two or three concourses at the same time), but it also enables us to scrutinize their tectonics; in this case, some of the ways in which 'voice' may operate between one moment of textuality and another.

Three of the studies we will describe in the chapters that follow were ones in which we explored more than one moment. The study on understandings of jealousy to be described in Chapter 7 includes a second Q-sort on the different kinds of advice to be given to people experiencing jealousy. One of the studies on social policies/conduct towards 'child abuse' to be described in Chapter 8 also looks at understandings as well as social policy/conduct. In other words, participants were asked to complete two Q-sorts: one on understandings of 'child abuse' and the other on their views about what social policy we should adopt towards it.

The other study to be described in Chapter 8 looks at three aspects of child sexual abuse: understanding, social policy, plus a third seeking to address 'voice' more directly, by exploring the rhetorical/ideological discourses within which 'the problem' can be constituted. Hence participants were each asked to sort three different Q-sets: one on explanations of why sexual abuse happens; one on definitions on what it is, its location within an ideological framework and views about its moral connotations; and a third on 'what we should do about the problem'.

In these linked Q-sort studies, we sought to gain some indication of the tectonics of knowledging by looking for patterns of response across Q-sets. For example, where people with certain backgrounds (e.g. men convicted and serving prison sentences for sexual assaults on children) all articulated, via their Q-sorting, a particular explanation for child sexual abuse, and these same people's Q-sorts expressed a particular view on policy, this gave strong clues that something common was being voiced. Where another group (e.g. men describing themselves as proponents of 'boy love') voiced a different explanation, and a correspondingly different view on social policy, we could begin to build up, from this empirical data, a reading of the kinds of tectonics which might be in play. For instance, we could begin to speculate about how some discourses may act to warrant or enable certain forms of conduct. In the former case, we could speculate, for example, that prisoners are only too well aware of what 'story' needs to be voiced in order to evidence the contrition and 'self-awareness' required to aid their chances of parole.

> *Interrupter: Notice I have been very quiet for a while now. It's all been fascinating. Indeed, I'm getting keen to hear about these studies right away. Can we move straight into them?*

Beryl: Sorry, you are going to have to be patient for a while longer, though I'm delighted to have whetted your appetite. We will go on to discuss and pursue these possibilities in more detail pretty soon now. But I'm afraid there's a bit more on method we need to tackle first.

Other pattern analytic methods

These, then, are the bare bones of Q-methodology and it is the most frequent method that we use. There is much we have simplified in this description, and if you want to know more about how we use Q-method, we suggest you look at two books which have devoted more space to describing constructionist uses of Q-methodological research in more detail, Kitzinger (1987) and Stainton Rogers (1991).

There are other procedures that can be analysed in this way, e.g. fixed construct Kelly Grids (cf. Bannister and Fransella 1971), even conventional variables (cf. Stainton Rogers 1991). For those who like playing statistical 'Happy Families' there is, in fact, a whole clan of pattern analytics (cluster analysis, smallest space analysis, facet analysis, multidimensional scaling, correspondence analysis) to collect!

Proponents of each will argue their corner vehemently, illustrating their case with the power of their findings. Obviously, we find Q-methodology works for us and we think our data are impressive. Rather than become bogged down in internecine strife about its drawbacks and its merits, it is probably more informative to consider what these pattern analytics (mostly) have in common.

We would stress two features. First, they all involve direction. There is a universe of solutions to any complex intercorrelation matrix. Researchers go for those that 'work', those that yield data that 'make sense'. For example, if we find that a solution gives factors that can be interpreted to generate accounts that sound like stories we know or at least ones for which, with effort, can be given a reading, and draw the stories from common sources together (e.g. this one from four psychoanalysts, that one from three self-styled 'Hell's Angels'), we are likely to find that solution more viable than one of which we can make less sense however much effort put into trying. In practice, Q-method does this for us, so we stick with it. Whether you think that makes the procedure circular or whether you think it is a strength depends on your story.

> *Interrupter: I thought it might. I suspect Q-methodology is your extra-discursive fixed-point.*

Beryl: Think about it pragmatically. If an issue is in dispute, we have found Q-method always comes up with the goods – so far, over what amounts to more than a hundred studies, we have always got factors we can make sense of, and they are always interesting. If it works, as they say, don't mend it.

> *Interrupter: Not very critical polytextual that argument is it?*

Beryl: It is if you focus on what work it is doing. Namely, presencing the manifold of available textuality, which has been tectonized into a concourse. If its transformation you are after see pages . . .

> *Interrupter [wincing]: Forget it.*

At an anecdotal level, we find that criticism of Q-method tends to fall into four main camps. Some statisticians hate it because its use of factor analysis smacks of 'inversion' (but then people used to say that about gays). 'Agentic' researchers reject it because they find it too subjective and indeterminate. They worry about its replicability and argue that, lacking any external reference, it cannot be validated in the conventional manner. 'Communal' researchers distrust the use of statistics in any shape or form. They argue that in selecting the statements for the Q-set and constraining the pattern of sorting, Q-method, like any other psychometric approach, merely sets out to reinforce the researchers' preconceptions. Finally, realists see it as dangerous, because they regard it as according epistemological equivalence to all viewpoints, thus risking the consequences of endorsing (or at the least failing to deny voice to) ideologically unacceptable views (e.g. the 'boy love' argument for decriminalizing adult–child sex).

Paradoxically, we find this disputation most encouraging! (see Stenner and Eccleston, in press). First, we do not give one whit about violating statistical preconceptions, so long as our method works – which, in our terms, it does. Second, we are perfectly happy to be seen as failing to have any external reference by which to validate the accounts we uncover, since we deny any such 'truth' is available. This we have argued throughout the book.

Third, we refute the claim we are imposing our own preconceptions. The data produced from a Q-study are generated by its participants, not by the researcher(s). Even though what can be expressed is, admittedly, limited by our craft-skills in designing the Q-set, the potential number of alternative patterns which could be expressed is enormous. In practical terms, from the many millions of possible patterns that could be expressed, we find only a handful actually emerging. And wherever two or more participants express a similar patterning of propositions, then their Q-sorts will, of course, be strongly intercorrelated. Where two or more sets of participants express two or more alternative patternings of propositions, these will emerge as distinct 'factors' almost whatever the statistical analytic adopted.

The issue of relativism we have also dealt with extensively in the book already. The point is simple. Were we only to elucidate factors, then we might stand accused of the dangers of relativism. We do not. The factors and their exposition are always only the starting-point of interpretation. Once explicated, our data analysis consists of a careful, 'open' and power-sensitive interpretation and discussion of their contextual consequences. Indeed, as we have indicated, we specifically used Q-sorts in conjunction with each other to explore the tectonics of 'voice' by which knowledge is ideologized and/or mongered. In this we are no more relativistic than the most politically informed of discourse analysts, of whatever hue.

Discourse analysis by any other name . . .

We have devoted effort and space to explaining Q-method because, on the one hand, it is a technique we have found extremely useful and, on the other, it is not well known and frequently misunderstood (indeed, ill-used; see Stainton Rogers 1987, for a full treatment of its appropriation for 'agentic' research). We would like to stress once again, so that there can be no misunderstanding, that the actual Q-sorting is just a small part of the process.

The work done in devising the Q-set beforehand and in interpreting the factors afterwards both take up the bulk of the time and effort involved (often several months of work in contrast to the few hours or at most weeks involved in administering the Q-sort), and are by far the more important. Frequently, the preparatory work of exploring and seeking to elucidate a concourse involves a range of other, more conventional 'communal' methods. For example, Worrell and Stainton-Rogers (1992; see also Chapter 8) conducted more than forty individual and eight group interviews, in order to devise her three Q-sets. Similarly, our approaches to interpretation have much in common with some forms of discourse analysis, in that we look for common themes between our factor interpretations and other texts (e.g. theorization in the field, cultural metaphors). In other words, we make readings of our factors, informed from within the 'climate of problematization' about issues of power, agency, purpose, salience and ideology, in ways very like those used by cultural analysts. We would argue that the crucial difference is that the participants in our studies have – by their Q-sorting – controlled the number of stories expressed and the structure of these stories throughout the exegetical process – in a way that, say, the originators of the texts studied by more conventional discourse analysts have not.

> *Interrupter: But if you are also conducting interviews and subjecting them to analysis, aren't you just doing 'discourse analysis' by another name?*

Beryl: Well . . . we're certainly bringing analytics to texts. In the case of the preparatory work to a Q-study, the Q-study itself acts as a check on the thoroughness of our cultural analysis.

> *Interrupter: Junk in, junk out.*

Beryl: Yes, another aphorism I find it hard to shake off. But there's another reason for looking at texts as expressed. Stories usually flow through time (even just the textual time to tell them), while a Q-study standing alone is a snap-shot.

Thematic de-composition

Q-method can be used to follow a story through time (for example, where participants are asked to describe themselves through a bereavement: Hale 1993). But it is demanding and doesn't effectively address the shifts that can occur in ordinary narrative (e.g. as when people are moving ground as they talk). This is typical of both story-making (see below) and story-telling. Hence, where we want to explore the manifold within a text, we will employ something that looks rather like discourse analysis or the kind of critical reading that can be brought to a book or a movie. To stress, to ourselves as much to an outside audience, that it is, strictly, a reading, we call such work thematic de-composition. Thematic de-composition played an important role in Stenner's work on jealousy (see Stenner 1992; see also Chapter 7). Where something is conventionally narrative – and there's no doubt that jealousy can seem to ebb and flow, move in and out of lives and loves, take on shifting forms of accountability – then to respect our concern, we need to scrutinize that concern narratively.

Interrupter: What about the 'green-eyed monster'?

Beryl: I'm not saying that jealousy is only narrative. Which is why you will also find in Chapter 7, Q-method brought to it.

Interrupter: Which also gets you off the hook you were earlier trying to impale discourse analysts upon?

Beryl [reeling in]: It was only a sprat to catch a mackerel.

Interrupter: I thought some of Beryl was vegetarian?

Beryl: And for my flora generation . . .

Seeded thematics

Furthermore, as will become clear in the chapters which follow, we usually augment Q-studies by using other methods to 'get a handle on' an issue, topic or whatever. Overall, we call these 'seeded thematics', and we are currently developing a range of approaches in this mould. They are generally used with small groups of people, in order to gain access to the more rhetorical aspects of talk, although they also have potential for use with individuals. They are similar in approach to some of the methods suggested in Antaki's (1981) book on methods suitable for exploring 'ordinary explanations'. All rely on providing the group with a small amount of 'seeded' information, and asking the group, as persons-in-culture, to develop stories, arguments and speculations about consequences.

Analysis of the expressed material from these techniques is also scrutinized by 'thematic de-composition', by which the conversations between group members are scrutinized, in order to make readings of the themes, arguments and ideas expressed.

Seeded stories

This approach was developed by Stenner to address understandings of jealousy (see Stenner 1992; see also Chapter 7). The approach here is to ask a small group of people to imagine they are in a setting in which they might realistically be expected to engage in collective story-telling. For example, they are passengers on a bus which has broken down, spending several hours together waiting for a spare part to be delivered.

They are 'seeded' with the beginning of the story – any incident in which jealousy is expressed or implied. Their task is to devise, together, a credible continuation of the story to reach a believable ending. The aim is to observe both the outcome (i.e. the story produced) and the discussion by which it is generated.

Seeded judgements

This began out of times when we explored what happened when Q-sorts were completed by pairs or small groups of people rather than by individuals.

We observed the discussions which went on, and found these illuminating, yielding large numbers of statements which we found useful in interpreting the factors which were subsequently generated. However, with 80+ sets of items, the procedure was time-consuming and unwieldy. We thus designed a sorting task which was less time-consuming and more manageable.

It consists of devising about ten short vignettes around the topic in question. For example, Worrell (see Worrell and Stainton-Rogers 1992) devised ten vignettes describing different incidents or forms of sexual abuse, varying such features as the age, ethnicity and gender of the child concerned, the number of children/abusers involved, kind of sexual assault, the relationship between the child and the abuser (e.g. stranger, family, person in position of authority) and the consequences (e.g. injury). She then asked small groups (10–12 people) to sort these from 'most abusive' to 'least abusive' by way of group discussion.

The data from this kind of approach are not the rank order eventually agreed between the group so much as what was said in discussion. In making judgements about relative 'abusiveness', participants articulated some of the reasons for their decisions (e.g. they made statements like 'It's far more damaging if the abuser is somebody in a position of trust'; 'Intention matters less than the actual harm done'; 'It's less abusive if the child sees it as normal, even if it's not').

Worrell used this approach as a means to get groups talking, as the basis for her group interviews. The data she collected were both analysed in their own right, and as the basis for devising her Q-sets. O'Dell (1993) has used the same technique in individual interviews, as a means to get people talking about the 'harmfulness' of sexual abuse, as an alternative to more direct structured interviewing techniques.

Dreams and nightmares

This approach was originally devised as an exercise in training. Here the task consists of describing to a group a set of circumstances, for example a young child giving evidence in court. The group splits into pairs to explore different aspects of the situation – the building and furniture of the court, the people involved, the rules governing what can and cannot be done, the timing of events, and so on. They begin by describing the 'nightmare' worst-case scenario – everything that could go wrong. In training they then go on to discuss to what extent these conditions apply to the court in which they work, and what can be done to improve the situation.

As a research method, it has been used by O'Dell (1993) to explore understandings of harmfulness with respect to sexual abuse. A case illustration is provided to the group, and they discuss the various worst-case outcomes in terms of harm done to the child, and what can be done to avoid or ameliorate the harm. Again the main purpose of the approach is to 'seed' an agenda for discussion, and create conditions in which people are more comfortable and willing to express opinions than if they are simply asked direct questions.

Subject and culture, textuality and tectonic

In keeping with our own worries about subject/culture dichotomization, our procedures, whether Q-methodology or seeded thematics, float ungrounded between subject and culture. We will read a text under thematic decomposition without concern as to whether it purports to have unique authorship or whether it seems to be a collective product. The stories we collect from Q-methodological studies are expressed through individual 'subjects', yet they normally end up in communal factors. This seems to us one of the great powers of the technique. Either is, taking the word loosely, a 'social representation' (though note we are not using that term in the formal sense given to it in recent European social psychology; for climate of problematization critiques of that work, see Potter and Litton 1985; Parker 1989; Ibañez 1993).

This does not mean that we will not allow people to 'own' their discourse. Sometimes this is achieved via the highly 'personalized' open-ended glosses or by negotiating our reading of a factor with those whose sorting patterns served to exemplify it. Sometimes it is in the nature of the study that is the 'autobiographical' aspect which dominates, in which case we will pseudonymously identify participants. However, where this happens we do not impute from text to essence – we consistently recognize that a person's story only becomes evidence of an 'inner essence' by narrative fiat (of course, much autobiography asserts that *droit de raconteur*).

There is an unexpected pay-off to our subject/culture dissolution. By not claiming to probe the self, to intrude on the 'personal', we are operating outside of the domain of most ethical anxieties about research (Hicks 1993). (We hope we are collecting and diffusing stories ethically, of course.)

This can be most clearly seen in the last technique we have developed – that of seeded thematics. The key to seeded thematics is collective generation and refinement. By, for example, asking groups to create stories or plays around a matter at issue and to subject them to group criticism and refinement until they feel 'right', we can enable the expression of collective knowledging. The story 'settles' into a tectonic 'good form' or gestalt.

Individuals in the group, thereby, are not being asked to express their 'own' feelings, to recount their 'own' experience or whatever (a crucial recasting where that experience is illegal, immoral or fattening). Critically, they are involved in a collective endeavour – to create a narrative in which feelings and experiences known to them (of their textuality) are fairly reported. The resultant story then itself becomes a text open to forms of thematic de-composition (no more or no less than would say the text of a passion play).

Interrupter [sulking]: Is that the methods over? Can we get onto the studies now?

Beryl: Yes, nearly there.

Interrupter: Good. I was beginning to feel very neglected. I thought you'd forgotten all about me.

Beryl: Do I detect a hint of jealousy?

Interrupter: What me? Jealous? Of a figment of the collective imagination of a gabble of authors? You'll be accusing me of hearing voices next!

Beryl: Cooee! It's epilegomenon time.

Interrupter [omnes]: Oh no it isn't.

6

Topologies of representation

Interrupter: Uh hum!

Beryl: Now, just hang on a minute. I haven't even begun to tell my tale. How dare you interrupt me before I have even spoken!

Interrupter: Well I feel I have a perfect right to do just that. I want to challenge the inclusion of this chapter in the book.

Beryl: You don't even know what this chapter is about yet.

Interrupter: You have a title, and a space for a chapter that seems to be exclusively focused on representation. What I want to know is, why? Why look at representations at all? I thought they had conveniently gone out of fashion as objects of scrutiny with social psychologists after McKinlay and Potter (1987) and Litton and Potter (1985) effectively demolished what they called Moscovici's Social Representations Theory!

Beryl: Just hold your horses. If you had better manners you would have given me the chance to address those very questions. And a lot more interesting ones as well. So curb your tongue, knave.

Representation, according to Foucault (1970: 17) once occupied a key position in European thought:

> In the sixteenth century resemblance played a constructive role in the knowledge of Western culture. It was resemblance that guided ex-egesis and the interpretation of texts; it was resemblance that organized the play of symbols, made possible knowledge of things visible and invisible, and controlled the art of representing them. The universe was folded in upon itself: the earth echoing the sky, faces seeming themselves reflected in the stars, and plants holding within their stems the secrets which were of use to man. Painting imitated space. And representation – whether in the service of pleasure or of knowledge – was posited as a form of repetition; the theatre of life or the mirror of nature . . .

But applied to present-day epistemology the term representation is among the most popular targets for the heavy artillery of the climate of prob-lematization. Across the spectrum from critical art history to the sociology of scientific knowledge it has become *de rigueur* to doubt claims that any craft can actually represent (i.e. re-present) some naturally (observer-free) presentative reality; can capture, in Foucault's phrase, 'The pure gold of things themselves'. Rather, it is argued that representation (i.e. knowledging prac-tices) precede and enable our sense of the real (the represented or signified). However, there is an interesting conflation in popular usage between repre-sentation and presentation which can be exploited to develop the scrutiny of re-presentation. For example, one's representations (such as the verbal and iconic text of a talk) are spoken of as one's 'presentation'; we say we are 'making' a presentation. Explored more closely, this sense of presentation is replete with connotations of power. The presenter opens up themself or their product (not necessarily willingly or even knowingly) to critical scrutiny. This is most obvious in that sense of 'to present' (e.g. one's buttocks to a superior conspecific simian or one's symptoms to the medical gaze) which is then taken as a laying before, exhibiting or offering for consideration. The presencing practice that is then laid upon the presented then re-presents it (gives it manifest properties which then allows it discursive location) as a sexual submission to the attributing ethologist or as a condition (i.e. a set of diagnostic signs rather than a person) to the physician.

Human beings, human products and the humanized natural world are always ever immanent with presentation and have an openness to critical scrutiny. Presentation is always thick with representation (i.e. prior represen-tational labour). In that ordinary language sense, we can take the term re-presentation to mean those structurations of attributes-in-presentation which can invite presencing practices but which do not uniquely 'contain' any specific discursive location. Representations are, in other words, verbal or iconic texts 'cut from' or 'pasted into' textuality. A neglected family photo-graph album lost at the back of a drawer is an archive replete with such immanent representations 'snapped out of' the textuality (and tectonics) of a family saga located in past time and space. Once they are rediscovered the photographs can be 'read'; represented as propertied social objects (e.g. a 'bonny baby'). Presented to a social historian (or the family in question), they will also be re-told – re-presenced into a given, specific, discursive, narrative practice different in the 'now' from what it was in the 'then'. In this chapter it will be on the a-discursive moment of 'reading' and the taxonomies of typifications which it reveals that our interest (and meaning of) representation will focus.

Pomo-reductionism

When we read the work of many of our contemporaries in 'discursive psychology' we find that, in addressing social knowledge, they do tend to privilege spoken and written language as thick and flowing, and usually only mention representations while they are taking a sideways swipe at Moscovici's work on Social Representations Theory. These days it seems that few apart from Moscovici's faithful followers (and even this is contestable) appear to be interested in representations *qua* representations. Writers and researchers such as Fairclough, Parker, Potter and Wetherell, who explore discourse in its minutiae, seem thereby to approach textual knowledge at the level of expression as a broad amorphous and unspecialized unity. However much they may differ in their treatments of texts, they seem to concur that their concern must be upon Text in the generic.

> *Interrupter: Now just hang on a minute. You claim to be talking about your contemporaries here, but basically you are just talking about a bunch of social psychologists. They, and perhaps other social scientists, use representations in a very particular way; and not in the same way that say an art historian or a linguist would.*

Beryl: All right, you have a point. I can see I am going to be forced into asking my friend the Box to help out here. If I can show that I am sensitive to the more general debates around representation, perhaps then you will allow me to get on with my argument about specifics without too many interruptions.

Box 6.1   Representing representation

Representation of the world, like the world itself, is the work of men; they describe it from their own point of view, which they confuse with the absolute truth. (Simone de Beauvoir 1970, quoted in Keller 1985: 3)

The argument is that the reality represented does not determine the *representation* or the means of *representation*. Instead, the process of signification itself gives shape to the reality it implicates. (Henriques, Hollway, Urwin, Venn and Walkerdine 1984: 99)

Our ability to speak as if realities exist independent of our knowing them is a key function of language and *representation*. But can an object exist independent of our practices of *representation*? ... In a classroom situation, the challenge to students (those with realist proclivities) is to demonstrate the existence of any object (fact, event, thing) without recourse to a form of *representation* ... Students quickly see the difficulty of the task. Indeed, no one has thus far succeeded in demonstrating the antecedent existence of a fact or a thing independent of some representative practice ... in [a] spirit of exasperation ... students suggest that a punch in the face might finally convince sceptics of the reality of the physical world. In this un-happy event, the bruised relativist would again have to remind his [Woolgar's] audience that physical assaults also constitute a form of *representation*/communication. (Woolgar 1988b: 56–7)

For those writing about medical imagery in particular 'realism' implies a progressive move towards accuracy, which takes as a paradigm the sup-posedly unmediated eye of the camera. This is built on the assumption that the camera, like the eye, sees what is really there and that the goal of *representation* is the recreation of the original perceptual act. *Representation* accordingly consists of recording or transcribing an objective, natural world. This approach is as seductive as it is fallacious ... those who offer *repre-sentations* are always selecting and choosing, both consciously and uncon-sciously, rather than merely reflecting a pre-given world. (Jordanova 1989: 46)

Over the last twenty years or so there has been a crisis in authorisation: Who can speak for the other? From what position and on what basis? What has been called into question is the justification of *representation* with reference to a logic of society, or from a position of a political doctrine or movement. (Game 1991: 86)

Accounts of a 'real' world do not, then, depend on a logic of 'discovery', but on a power-charged social relation of 'conversation'. The world neither speaks itself nor disappears in favour of a master decoder. The codes of the world are not still, waiting only to be read ... no particular doctrine of *representation* or decoding or discovery guarantees anything. (Haraway 1991: 98–9)

[Our emphases throughout]

What Box 6.1 shows quite clearly, and what we have earlier also tried to outline, is that representation is a polysemic term. Not only does its meaning shift between different discursive arenas, it also takes on different meanings within the same one. Why then to make the point before getting interrupted again, are we making trouble for ourselves by trying to re-use the word?

As we outlined in Chapter 4, we have found the term useful when talking about relatively concretized or imaged descriptions which crop up in our research endeavours and are detected by our participants as distinctive forms of knowledge. We (and they) recognize that these are somewhat different in kind from the accounts of arguments, debates, and point positions which people and other kinds of texts offer to us. We (and they) are basically talking about the difference between describing what something (e.g. a table) is like (its height, material, number of legs and all the other things which make up its tableness), and discoursing on what tables are for, how we might use them, whether they are good or bad, where they originate, and so on.

As a rough approximation, then, representations in texts are 'pasted in' verbal images that stand out, indeed can be 'cut out' by human pattern analysers as distinctive forms of story-telling. They can 'stand in for' visual images, by received translation conventions, but they are also textual devices in their own right – descriptions (to use another troublesome word) rather than agendas for action, narratives, arguments or rhetoric. To mute attention towards the conscribed (representations), while valorizing the discursive, seems to us a rather odd thing to do. Why, then, do contemporary psychologists working with discourse seem to have this fascination with 'thick' texts, with language at its most 'linguistic'? Why, for example, do Potter and Wetherell (1987) assert that 'This book is about language and its importance for social psychology' (Potter and Wetherell 1987: 1)?

> *Interrupter: Well, why not? Why shouldn't they decide to focus on language if that is what they find interesting?*

Beryl: Why not indeed. We are simply suggesting that it might be of interest to explore what is being covered up in this uncovering.

Parker, for example, argues that to focus on language serves a very particular purpose. It diverts us away from a path well-trodden by social researchers, which leads them directly into the laboratory:

> ... we have to be aware of the way language, as the cartilage of culture, produces through its own distinct metaphors of social mechanisms, ways not only of understanding the world, but also ways of 'understanding' other ways of understanding the world. This work of language in accounting for action, and becoming part of the action itself, brings us to the alternatives to laboratory experimentation. (Parker 1989: 17)

Indeed, not only are we told to pull away from old-style deductive research, we are directed to approach language itself as the means by which we can come to understand the role that language plays in constructing social reality and our understandings of it:

> We are concerned with the nature of knowledge, cognition and reality: with how events are described and explained, how factual reports are constructed, how cognitive states attributed. These are defined as discursive topics, things people topicalize or orientate themselves to, or imply, in their discourse. (Edwards and Potter 1992: 2)

> *Interrupter: So where is the harm in that?*

Beryl: Because of what may be getting obscured. In focusing their concern this way, they imply that it is only *expressed language* that matters (gainsaying Parker's point that it is only 'part of the action').

More generally, the stress on the discursive appears to singularize the thickly texted as the *only* home of social knowledge. In taking this line, Potter and Wetherell have placed themselves in a rather tricky position. In their critique of traditional conceptualizations of 'attitude' they argue: 'It is clear that the attitudinal object can be constituted in alternative ways, and the person's evaluation is directed at these specific formulations rather than some abstract and idealized object' (Potter and Wetherell 1987: 54).

When Potter and Wetherell refer to specific formulations of the attitude object, one could reasonably ask: 'Are they not referring to its various re-presentations?' Indeed, in order to raise the problem of the singularized attitude object as an argument against traditional attitude theories, one needs to address the range of different representations of a social object which are available in culture, and which are discursively related to the 'attitudes' (i.e. opinionations) which are expressed. Given that Potter and Wetherell seem to be arguing that people can 'have in mind' (or perhaps 'in discourse') varied conceptualizations of the social object opinionated about, why do they eschew the term and/or the notion of representation? It does, even in quasi-*realist* theory-language (cf. Semin and Rogers 1973), do dreadful damage to the received concept of attitude. Yet they seem patently to avoid addressing the even more punishing argument that notions of culturally relayed and related *imaged* understandings bring to traditional psychological attitude theory. However, eliding over the issue of representations is part and parcel of the consistent emphasis in their work as a whole and its focus on texts as a generic.

> *Interrupter: Well I can see their point. As you yourself admit, the term representation is highly problematic. So many of its synonyms (depiction, illustration, resemblance, for example) could be referring to representations as things which stand for something else – or stand in for something. Surely it invites being drawn into the very realist frame that you say you are trying to avoid. If something is standing in for something else, what is it standing in for if not something real?*

Beryl: But why assume that that which is represented is 'real'. Look in any comic book or fairytale and you will find representations of extra-terrestrials, ghosts and frog-princes. You're not saying those are real, are you? The task is to find effective ways of talking about images and descriptions as social knowledge. Maybe we just need a term that's less dodgy and confusing.

> *Interrupter: I don't see why I should do your work for you, but why not use one of your devices to warn the reader that 'the representations word' is both necessary and is a problem?*

Beryl: At times, I'm so glad I represented you. What a jolly good idea. I'll put the 're' under erasure – rXe-presentation – this pushes the focus onto presentation, i.e. showings and manifestations. It will also help to disrupt its continuity with previous ways in which it has been used, and yet show that I am basically interested in the same territory. And I'll still have the 're' there somehow, to remind people that representations do have an iterative quality. Yes, that will do it nicely.

Interrupter: OK, explain to me what the difference is between a representation and a rXe-presentation.

Beryl: A rXe-presentation is a 'showing' – a description or portrayal or imaging *per se*. There is a subtle change in implication – a representation might stand for something, while a rXe-presentation allows a sense that 'it' simply is.

Interrupter: Now all you have to do is to say why you are so keen to study rXe-presentations in the first place. And I warn you, after all that struggle, it had better be worth it!

Why look at rXe-presentations?

Social knowledge about any topic or issue can always be expressed as, and gained from, a diversity of cultural modes of expression – at least as much, say, through acoustic, iconic or haptic texts as through verbal texts. Within that polytextuality, indeed, within the different modes themselves, there are local conventions of expression and impression that (in their breaking of as much as in their adherence to this nomic order) bring into play a variety of kinds and forms of social knowledge. Thus, for example, a description of the appearance, qualities and properties of the computer used to record this text as it is keyed in can be appreciated as a different order of knowledge-in-use from that which is involved were we to enter into a debate about computers, civil liberties and data protection. Others have also found it useful (indeed necessary, to meet the life-worlds of their respondents) to make this distinction in their research. Thomas (1987), for example, felt it important that she should be able to make a distinction between images (and stereotypes) of masculinity/femininity *per se*, and the discursions which constitute accounts and debates which focus on them, and discursively locate them as Gleeson (1991) did for 'the mad' and explanations of madness.

It seems, then, that the activity of knowledging as practised in ways that are ordinarily understood by and seem to make sense to people involves the negotiation of both rXe-presentations and discourses as different aspects of textuality. Consequently, we as researchers and commentators need to be able to address both the debates/arguments/understandings about objects, events and issues, and the descriptions/properties/qualities/characteristics of objectivities, events and issues. We are, in other words, reflecting back the distinction made to us between the knowledging activities of 'conscribing' (noting the attributes of) and 'cognizing' (discoursing upon) first developed in Chapter 4.

What are rXe-presentations?

We use the term rXe-presentations to refer to the expression or showing of 'imaged' understandings which are shared, and drawn upon, as a common stock of knowledge, in a culture (cf. Gleeson 1991).

> *Interrupter: Such as?*

Beryl   [staring wildly]: Well, how about a rXe-presentation of a crazy woman? A psychiatrist (or a psychiatrized culture) might well be ready to ask how does this madness present itself? And the answer might be a woman who is passionate, out-of-control and destructive.

> *Interrupter: Are you talking about someone like the character played by Glenn Close in **Fatal Attraction**?*

Beryl: Yes, or by Sharon Stone in *Basic Instinct*, or Eve Black [*sic*] in *The Three Faces of Eve*, or Lucia de Lamamoor in Scott's poem, or Crazy Kate . . . do you get the picture, so to speak?

> *Interrupter: You mean the same basic sort of image of a mad woman is being used over and over in a variety of different stories. But aren't you just talking about stereotypes available for women, or roles available to women?*

Beryl: Now, it's interesting that you should ask that. RXe-presentations do have some of the qualities generally attributed to stereotypes and socially circumscribed roles; they have the same kind of intransigence. They are repeatedly relayed and replayed in culture to such an extent that many members of a collectivity will be able to both recognize and describe them. However, a rXe-presentation doesn't just refer to a character in the way that terms like role or stereotype might. It can be used to refer to a wide range of social objectivities both tangible and conceptual.

> *Interrupter: I already feel a regret coming on, but, such as?*

Beryl: Well, why not a rXe-presentation of the psychiatry that might be expected to dispose of the mad woman I have just mentioned? You don't have to search very far in either the professional literatures of psychiatry, or in the popular media of our culture, to find a range of different rXe-presentations of psychiatry. For example, we might have a rXe-presentation which focuses on the positive nature of psychiatry which intervenes and controls the lives of mad people in a benign way 'for their own good and that of society in general'. Alternatively, there is the cold and uncaring face of institutional psychiatry, managing and manipulating our minds, denying our civil liberties, and so on.

> *Interrupter [putting down* **The Sun**]: *GOTCHA! Here you have to admit that you* **are** *basically saying that rXe-presentations stand for something else, they are replicas or models of things that exist in the real world like, psychiatry and mad women.*

Beryl: Not at all. Listen . . .

Any idea that we model some substantial reality would pull us into a particular kind of relationship with Truth, of the kind put forward by the Representationalist school of Frege (1960), etc., in which we have to address representations again, for example, in terms of whether or not they are accurate reflections, and where questions of correspondence and misrepresentation come up. We are not interested here in the question of the distortion of reality or adequacy of representation to 'Truth'. Those kinds of arguments we can explore when we look to alternative understandings (cf. Chapter 7). Presently, we are interested in rXe-presentation as a part of textuality.

The concept of rXe-presentation may depend on the notion of a locally agreed realm of objectivities which are represented. But this does not mean that we depend on the notion of the existence of an independent pre-represented reality to which the rXe-presentation refers. If this were the case, how could we have rXe-presentations of Father Christmas, and other overtly fictive constructions? To talk about rXe-presentation does not mean that we need be constrained by a materialist perspective. We do not perceive rXe-presentations by looking in a mirror which we hold up to the real, for that which we call reality in our everyday lives is comprised of rXe-presentations, discourses and all other elements of textuality. Just as the sense of words is in their use, so too is the sense/meaning of a rXe-presentation in the discursive location in which we find it.

> *Interrupter: But if rXe-presentations are so enmeshed in discourse, is it any wonder that some theorists want to collapse rXe-presentation into language, and reduce everything down into discourse (or social representations for that matter)?*

Beryl: It may explain, but does it justify? It only makes sense to ignore distinctions between different kinds of social knowledge if by doing so we add something to our discussion of it. I can see no evidence of this. Yes it is interesting to consider a rXe-presentation embedded within a particular discourse. But that isn't the only thing we can do with a rXe-presentation. If it is possible to access, explore and discuss rXe-presentations in their own right, so to speak, then why not consider them as removable pieces of the jigsaw puzzle of social knowledge rather than considering all forms of social knowledge as simply more of the same, i.e. discourse? Now where was I, oh yes, a presentation gains its meaning from its discursive location.

When someone evokes or de-scribes a rXe-presentation, they are usually in the mode of trying to tell us something. People draw upon rXe-presentations in the course of communication, but that communication depends on the extent to which the simulacrum is accessible to, i.e. shared in by, others.

> Someone paints a picture in order to show how he [*sic*] imagines a theatre scene. And now I say: 'This picture has a double function: it informs others, as pictures or words inform – but for the one who gives the information it is a representation (or piece of information?) of another kind: for him it is the picture of his image, as it can't be for anyone else. To him his private impression of the picture means what he has imagined, in a sense in which the picture cannot mean this to others.' – And what right have I to speak in this second case of a representation or piece of information – if these words were rightly used in the first case? (Wittgenstein 1953: 96–7)

Thus the product of *representational* effort can only be regarded as a rXe-presentation when it is embedded within a context which imbues it with meaning, and allows for its recognition as a rXe-presentation, that is, when it becomes 'public' property.

> *Interrupter: Hang on a minute. You've slipped something in there. Are you saying that rXe-presentations have no meaning in their own right?*

> Beryl: Well that depends on how you are using the term of course. If you mean the product of representational labour (i.e. the presentation) has no auto-genic meaning, then I would agree with you.

Regardless of what the originator of a text/picture intended (as if we could know that) the meaning is not built into the object constructed. The meaning remains located by and in the agora of social negotiation. If, however, you are talking about rXe-presentation as we are using the term (i.e. to refer to relatively concretized or imaged understandings and descriptions which are available in the collectivity), then of course it 'has' meaning. If it had no meaning, it would not achieve the status of a rXe-presentation. Presentations created by artists and authors have to be read to be constituted as rXe-presentations.

> *The Virgin Mary* [easily recognizable amid the rocks]: Excuse me. Speaking as one who has been represented rather more than most, I feel I must point out that there are those who disagree with you here. When an artist paints my image they are trying to convey a clear and very particular meaning.

Certainly, the once dominant hermeneutic/iconological approach within art theory (and indeed within media studies and cultural studies), has resulted in a search for culture-specific lexii, in order that signs and symbols in visual displays might be deciphered. Indeed, the notion that, within specific discursive agora, certain visual forms have particular meanings is not exclusive to disciplines which draw upon art theory. Within the psychodynamic tradition, for example, visual symbols to be found in dreams quite directly implicate particular meanings. The manifested umbrella or the woman with rounded contours are read as presencing the latent (inherent) meanings of phallus and fecundity. Indeed some psychoanalysts take this even further and use these shared interpretations to deny culture-specific and located relationships between signifier and signified (cf. Jung's 'universal' archetypes).

However, the practice of deciphering signs and reading the components and forms within such pictures permits the obscuration of the difference between a picture or visual and a rXe-presentation, as evidenced by the Wittgenstein quote above. We have made this point already in our discussion of hymenspicy (cf. pp. 39 and 70). Barthes (1972: 110) has argued that '. . . pictures . . . impose meaning at one stroke, without analysing or diluting it . . .', but not because they fuse a concept with an image. Rather, 'Pictures become a kind of writing as soon as they are meaningful: like writing, they call for a lexis' (ibid.). We are no more interested in the picture as 'object' than we are interested in written words as 'object'. Once visuals become meaningful (i.e. are invested with meaning by their discursive location they are no longer pictures but rXe-presentations which happen to be provided in visual form rather than as language texts. The study of the symbolism within a painting is much like the study of the symbolism within a poem. Over both, the reading of rXe-presentation requires that we study the discourse within which it is embedded, and that we regard the rXe-presentation as comprising a set of interconnected and mutually dependent immanent meanings.

> *Virgin Mary:* So basically, you are saying that certain art theorists have been over-focused, centrated in their attempts to get at the meaning of a particular work?

> *Beryl* [less than reverentially]: Not exactly. Like the same kinds of theorists of literature, at their best they have tried to make an anthropological leap into an alien culture (like the Renaissance) to read a product from that world-view. But they have not been able to resist the authorial trap of giving an 'authorized reading' of individual pictures, plays or whatever.

> *Virgin Mary* [gnomically]: Funny that. Just what He says about theologians.

Here the deconstructive move is straightforward:

> Once the Author is removed, the claim to decipher a text becomes quite futile . . . refusing to assign a 'secret', an ultimate meaning to the text (and to the world as text), liberates what may be called an antitheological activity, an activity that is truly revolutionary since to refuse to fix meaning is, in the end, to refuse God and his hypostases – reason, science, law. (Barthes 1968: 437)

That said, we can now move on to our own rather different agenda. While we can enjoy disturbing pleasure in the troubled territory of representational effort or the act of representing, and author-izing effort or the act of authoring, we have also come to be interested in rXe-presentation for what it can tell us about the way products become re-socialized as they are 'cut out' from somewhere else and 'pasted back' into contemporary discursivity. Our special guest in this chapter, the Virgin, is a case in point. Bartlett (1932) was one of a very few psychologists who took rXe-presentation seriously. Facing subjects with the task of reproducing ambiguous figures, he found that:

> ... the presented visual pattern seem at once to 'fit into' or to 'match' some preformed scheme or setting. The connecting of the given pattern with a special setting is obviously an active process, for, speaking in an abstract sense, the setting used is only one of a large number, any of which might be brought into play ... I shall call this fundamental process of connecting a given pattern with some setting or scheme: *effort after meaning*. (Bartlett 1932: 20)

Put into more contemporary language, when they are cut from context the traces (fossils) left behind in pictures and textual descriptions can potentially evoke images of objects/ideas, such as when they are told within contemporary discursive contexts, for example. These products have no meaning in their own right, but they are scopogenic for us – they invite a reading they exhibit, they present, and thus they have meaningfulness. Each has the potential to be worked over discursively, to be 'meaninged'. And of course they will be 'meaninged' differently in different discursive contexts. Thus images, whether fashioned in language or paint, come to be available in the culture and provide us with ways of representing objects and ideas in the same way that discourses provide us with culturally accepted ways of discussing, debating and taking positions on ideas and objects.

Interrupter: You mean its like that song 'If a picture tells a thousand words . . .'?

Beryl: Not at all! Far from it. We need a thousand words to re-tell an image. Presentations do not provide world-views, they do not provide prescriptions or instructions, or even portray a particular understanding of how the world is. Presentations are merely expressed objectivities. An image only becomes a rXe-presentation when we make use of it in discursive praxes, when it is embedded in a context. There is no meaning in the presentation of the stars in the sky until someone draws notional lines between them and calls the groupings constellations.

*Interrupter: But surely some rXe-presentations work because the presentation has an in-built meaning. What about the rXe-presentations of women in pornography. These serve to oppress women. You can't be saying that the picture of a woman with naked breasts on page three of **The Sun** doesn't carry an in-built meaning! We all know what that kind of picture is saying about women!*

Beryl: Do we? Such a picture only has meaning when it is discursively located. There is nothing inherently oppressive about any image. Remember the Virgin has her breasts exposed in several images of the
'Madonna Lactans'. Imagine the shock that would be caused if she
were shown like *that* on page three of *The Sun*.

Now, it may well be that some rXe-presentations are for a time, in a
specific localized place, allegorical of ideology: one can think of images like
John Bull or Uncle Sam. Equally, a 'page 3' picture is 'pasted into' a ready-
made location and hence it, too, is given an iconic quality by the reader.
However, just like a National Emblem, it can be re-written – for example, as
a token of the rXe-presentation of a particular kind of objectification and
fetishization of women, an 'effort after meaning' involving the setting of
(say) a feminist discourse as in the work of Jo Spence and Barbara Kruger.
But the presentation *per se* doesn't carry with it instructions as to its reading
(only contextualizing it as 'page 3' or 'pornography' or a 'feminist critique'
does that). Indeed, it is precisely because the image does not import a specific
reading that it can be appropriated, and can become a matter of contention.
One can think of many cultural contexts where nudity is not of significance
or certainly not something to be remarked upon.

> *Beryl and the Interrupter [as one voice]: Ah Club Mediterrané, that's my
> idea of a token economy!*

There, uncovered breasts need evoke no special reading, for they are the
only presentation around in the visual marketplace. However, once naked
breasts are painted or photographed or textualized for consumption (e.g. in
the stylized fashion typically used on page 3 or in the Sistine Chapel), then
the image may come to be marked off as a rXe-presentation. Much the same
happens when objectivities such as a lavatory or a vacuum cleaner are marked
off as 'Art' (e.g. by being shown in an 'Art Gallery'). They are, thereby,
transformed by this discursive location into rXe-presentations.

Presentations as objectivities have become particularly interesting to us
precisely because they are in-and-of-themselves devoid of ideology. Hence,
in their rXe-presentations, we can gain a handle upon the tectonics of social
knowledge by exploring the ways in which they are worked over and ideologized within particular discourses. This is not to say that presentations are
ever 'empty'. To present at all they have an immanence of meaning, they
have an openness to discursive appropriation. Foucault, in his chapter on
'Representation' (1970: 59), makes this point explicitly:

> the whole domain of the sign is divided between the certain and the
> probable: that is to say, there can no longer be an unknown sign, a
> mute mark. This is not because men [*sic*] are in possession of all the
> possible signs, but because there can be no sign until there exists a
> *known* possibility of substitution between two *known* elements. The sign
> does not wait in silence for the coming of a man capable of recognizing

it: it can be constituted only by an act of knowing it. (original emphases)

But there need be nothing within an image as such which tells us in what direction the rXe-presentation should be aligned, what meaning it should take, until the moment when it is appropriated discursively. If we think back to the crazy woman we introduced earlier in the chapter, we can see the same character entering the stage at particular historical moments – doing more or less the same things but being understood very differently. The sthenic mistress in *Fatal Attraction*, driven by libidinal pressure to hound her erstwhile lover, can be played against Crazy Kate driven to excess when her innocence is betrayed – and in that counterpoint we can almost hear their respective tectons of knowledge grating against each other.

> *Interrupter: The sound in your metaphor there rather serves to highlight, by contrast, how far even rXe-presentations take you into the visual mode. I still suspect you may be more caught up in iconic talk than you realize.*

Beryl: I take your feeling. However, within my research I am far more likely to approach the study of rXe-presentations through written descriptions. Indeed, it is hard to imagine how some of the rXe-presentations I study, of such things as jealousy or psychiatry, could be approached otherwise.

> *Interrupter: Now you are losing me again. I could deal with the notion that Bartlett offered, there are some pictures – like the illustration in Fig. 6.1 that one could variously contextualize and therefore interpret differently. It could be a fish tank, a shoe-box, an ice cube, for example. But how can you put pre-discursive presentations in front of people in verbal form?*

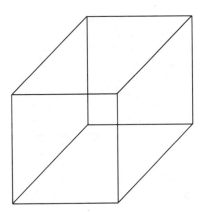

Figure 6.1 Ambiguous picture, which could be a fish tank, a shoe-box or an ice cube.

Beryl: I think it is now you who is having troubles because of iconic talk. Let me explain. Bartlett had his own realist 'safety rail'. He thought he could index changes between that which he presented and that which his subjects represented (drew) as what they saw. How the *same* line drawing (i.e. containing the same conscribing of lines and angles) can become different things shifts the concern completely. This is what a rXe-presentational Q-sort does, but now 'before our very eyes' (sorry to be iconic).

We provide, from cultural sources, the conscribing of propositions, and the participant makes a rXe-presentation. It is those structurations which we are interested in, textual gestalts rather than picture-objects. However, verbal imaging has not before been made within such delineated conventions: we cannot 'paste in' great Q-sorts from the past! By contrast, because some rXe-presentations have been laid-down in a stable a-verbal form (as pictures), visual imaging does have a kind of intransigence. This means that a rXe-presentation in the form of a picture may endure over time and come to be presented anew and worked-over many times in a variety of locations. When we come across a picture, we recognize it as a human product of rXe-presentation and may thus attempt to re-invest it with meaning. We tend to do this with pictures because we have conventions for the re-picting of de-picting. Indeed, as was noted earlier, we tend to over-do it, laying readings upon productions whose placement within the discursive arena, in which they originated, is outwith recovery.

> *Interrupter: This sounds like another variation on your early enigmatic theme – that rXe-presentations have a life of their own, they stand apart from discourse.*

Beryl: Yes, indeed. A bit like us in that, my friend.

Although rXe-presentations can be discursively located they can also be dislocated – there is no one-to-one concordance of any rXe-presentation onto a single discourse. The same rXe-presentation may be drawn upon within a number of discourses. Of course, the objects of discourse and discourses themselves are intimately related in that they emerge in the same process (Foucault 1972). RXe-presentations of the mad, for example, can inform discourses about madness, and in turn, folk theories and beliefs about madness can feed into images of the mad. However, there is no necessary or inevitable contingency between the two – a culture's systems of rXe-presentations of the mad will at times be ontologically quite separate from that culture's discourses about madness.

Consider, for example, the Jekyll and Hyde (Stevenson 1886) character. While it can, in one reading, be seen as anchored within the discursive tension between the rational and irrational which dominated discourses about madness in the latter part of the nineteenth century; in another reading it can be seen as a contemporaneous recasting of an older rXe-presentation which draws upon the lyncanthropic myth. And so it has been re-written in its many filmic metamorphoses (Showatter 1985). Thus we can see rXe-presentations as distinct social products which can be studied in their own right, although it would make no sense (ever were it possible) to discuss them other than as discursively located. When they are committed to a permanent medium in a graphic form rather than in language, we can see them as the traces left behind by the processes of cultural tectonics – a record of enfossilization, but not one that can be causally decoded (Gleeson 1991). This is much as happens to blocks of text that experience the 'cut and paste' facilities of the word processors which made this book possible: 'any representation consists of a spatialisation, a cutting out, an immobilisation' (Game 1991: 97).

How tectonics allow us to circumvent a teleological theory of representations

Our writerly experience is that some text changes shape but not place, and other text (the 'cut and pasted') changes place but not shape. This gives a metaphoric handle on the representation–understanding distinction we are seeking to drive through the texted. It is, of course, 'only' an analytic incision. But even so, we need to spell out what it implies for the analytic of tectonics. What we are hazarding is the possibility of a 'two-track' tectonics, for it would seem that what we are otherwise calling discourses and rXe-presentations differ in their modes of mutability. RXe-presentations, once constituted, appear to us to acquire a high degree of functional autonomy. They may then be addressed by 'new' discourses. New stories may be told about the old characters, and new characters may be formed discursively on the bones of the old – but the old characters still remain to a large extent accessible in the archive. In contrast, discourses are not so much constituted and then archived as discursively relayed – and in the process, added to and taken from, moulded and changed, created and extinguished. They are linked synchronically in a way in which objects of discourses are not.

> *Interrupter: Now just hang on a minute. Some rXe-presentations both endure and are discursively located in the same way for centuries at a time. What about Mary, the Mother of Christ, for example.*

> *Beryl* [after a significant pause]: I could say Her non-answer is your answer. She doesn't know which Mariolatrous icon to personate – or none of them!

We would not deny the ability of knowledge-power synarchies to story into being the appearance of representation-discourse cogency: from the old Soviet Kremlin's identikit Lenins, to the Vatican's Madonna clones. However, any appearance of an historic 'fixedness' enduring over relatively long periods of social time is dependent upon the power structures that support it (e.g. the Catholic Church, the guild of art historians, the Communist Party, or the Union of Soviet Artists). Equally, transformations in power relationships can affect representations (e.g. of Trotsky) but not discourses – as Stalin showed. Or they can affect discourses (e.g. of the temporal jurisdiction of the Prince of Rome) but not representations – as happened in the English Reformation. Furthermore, as we argued over mammary imagery, representational conventions can variously fuel the many oppositional discourses that co-exist sympatrically in any plural system.

Be that as it may, it is the textuality and tectonics of madness which we have chosen to provide a paradigm instance for our argument. In that location it is most easy to argue that the same cast of 'peculiars' endure, albeit differently understood, alongside newly constituted concretions expressive of their times (over the latter we can think of the madness of 'inversion' [homosexuality] constructed under High Modernism only to be muted under Late Modernism).

> Although professional hegemonies may throw a spotlight on those representations of the mad which fit their current theory or which justify their current practice, the other characters remain present 'in the wings' to be drawn into the drama as required. (Gleeson 1991: 121).

> *Interrupter: So rXe-presentations are the characters which images (constructed either in words or pictures) bring to mind?*

Beryl: Remember, I said madness was a chosen paradigm case. RXe-presentation as characters makes for a user-friendly explication – but they can equally refer to any other relatively concretized or imaged understanding. We could be talking about a car like the VW 'beetle', a kind of music like 'blues' or the concept of piety. The term rXe-presentation gives us a way of thinking and talking about the expressing or exhibiting of the characteristics of something: exemplifying, typifying, portraying, presenting an image of . . . you get the picture? It's an analytic, a tool, a means for talking about pattern, nothing less, nothing more.

> *Interrupter: Ah ha! Isn't that just what Moscovici would say about his Theory of Social Representations?*

Beryl: Well, yes and no. Social Representations, as described by Moscovici, works very well as an analytic. It allows us to talk about images as well as understanding, it concedes the socially constructed nature of social knowledge and it allows such social products an existence outside of the individual cognitorium. But as you pointed out, rather gleefully if I may say so, earlier in the chapter, it has its problems. To our way of thinking, Moscovici couldn't leave well alone. On the one hand, he has unreflexively imposed a very particular kind of theory of the social (cf. Parker 1989). On the other hand, he couldn't resist being a psychologist, he had to attempt the 'splitting of the representation' and so he got caught up in cognitive speculation about social representations as intra-psychic phenomena.

But there is no reason why we cannot use this very useful term as an analytic without carrying Moscovici's excess conceptual luggage with us. Certainly we would not wish to claim, as Moscovici does, that all thought and understanding is based upon social representations. As critical poly-textualists we would wish to avoid this 'singularizing discourse' and allow for a variety of kinds and forms of social knowledge, including, of course, discourses. We recognize a discursive flux around rXe-presentations, including rXe-presentations of social presentations. In reading the work of Social Representation theorists such as Herzlich (1973) and De Rosa (1987), and their critics such as Parker (1989) and Ibañez (1993), we detect the possibilities for a play of multiples, none of which is, for us, foundational. We can therefore take a role in constructing another re-presentation of rXe-presentations.

The empirical presencing of the mad

The importance of rXe-presentations becomes apparent as soon as we enter into an empirical investigation of social knowledge. If we are, for example, to explore social knowledge about mental illness, a focus on discourse over madness would allow us to explore ideas about and understandings of topics such as social policy over mental health, knowledges about the assumed causes and cures of madness, and the institutions and institutionalized knowledges of madness. However, even a cursory glance through the literature of our collectivity reveals that many of the ideas that we have about madness are informed by, and inform, a rich and varied collection of presentations of the mad – in painting, photography, film, popular fiction, theatre and song. We cannot escape these images of the mad, and we cannot escape the idea that they may have some linkage with the things that we say about the mad.

Of course we need some way of talking about these images, and their commonality and diversity. The work on discourse has provided us with a range of terms which we can use to talk about pattern in texted forms of understandings, explanations and policies. When we find oft-repeated ideas we can talk about the apocryphal discourses from which they seem drawn. We avoid apotheosis by emphasizing the notion that discourse, account, voice and the other terms we use are mere descriptors evoked in the service of talking about pattern. By parity, we can afford rXe-presentation this same status. It is a mere analytic used in the service of discoursing pattern in description and depiction.

Approaching rXe-presentations with Q-methodology, it is possible to take a 'wide-angle snap-shot' of the range of rXe-presentations of the mad which are centre stage at any moment in time – that is, those offered to us by people when we ask them to tell us about the mad. Thus we are able to view the *dramatis personae* of madness a-discursively, outside of the morality play in which they typically comport themselves.

Gleeson (1991) identified fifteen mad characters in this way. She used the text of 'reason' as an organizing structure in sub-scribing this set of rXe-presentations – grouping the characters according to whether they were 'deficient in reason', 'beyond reason', 'lacking in reason' or 'unreasonable'. The Unreasonables, for example, were '. . . the depressives, who demonstrate unreasonable behaviour – they weep, they fail and, basically, can't "get their acts together"' (Gleeson 1991: 291). Six of the characters displayed this unreasonable condition, and were described variously as post-natally 'oppressed', self-destructive, emotionally labile, having low personal control, withdrawn, passive, and even 'odd looking' and 'twitchy'.

Two rXe-presentations were 'lacking in reason' in that they were seen to be disorganized, inconsistent and unpredictable, oscillating between passivity and volatility. Three characters were 'deficient in reason', in the Piagetian sense. They were described as immature in their thinking and ill-equipped to cope with everyday life, and in other situations might have been dubbed as characters who had 'learning disabilities' rather than being mad. Four characters were 'beyond all reason'. These were the more floridly mad characters with whom one simply cannot reason. They were variously portrayed as deluded and paranoid, manic, psychopathic and megalomanic.

Gleeson's work provides not just categories or dimensions of madness but fully fleshed out and holistic descriptions of the mad. Some of the characters map neatly on to descriptions in the fairly comprehensive catalogue of rXe-presentations provided by medical psychological diagnostic manuals such as the US DSM III. Others are more easily linked to fictive accounts of mad characters as provided in, for example, Iain Banks' *The Wasp Factory* (1985).

Interrupter: Can we pause there? This sounds very interesting but people like to know a bit of the nitty-gritty behind data – even with your post-empirical scrutinies. Like where do these descriptions come from? Who or what were they describing?

Beryl: Well, basically, Gleeson gave eighty-one people packs of ninety statements which described aspects, features or characteristics which might be used to describe a mad character, such as: 'Is emotionally withdrawn and apathetic', 'Comes over as extremely tense and uptight' and 'Stares fixedly at people', and asked each participant to use them to describe someone who was mad. Some participants selected people they knew or had met, some described historic or fictive characters, and some described themselves. From these eighty-one descriptions, the factor analysis found the commonalities between Q-sorts and yielded fifteen exemplary factors, identifying, thereby, fifteen alternative descriptions of mad characters. We talk about these shared or exemplary characters as rXe-presentations of the mad because they are communally drawn and socially owned images of the mad.

Interrupter: Not to be nosey but just to satisfy my scientific curiosity, perhaps you could introduce me to some of these mad characters?

Beryl [after consulting the cast]: With pleasure – figments prepare to meet figment. We just need a little more explanation first. [Figments line up and wait impatiently in the wings.]

One of the interesting things that happens when you ask both medical psychological professionals and lay people to provide descriptions of the various manifestations of madness which have currency in our culture, is that you get an odd sort of mixing which wouldn't be found in psychiatric discourse alone. Some of the rXe-presentations which emerge can be surprising. Of course, Gleeson did have some ideas about the kinds of mad characters which she might be able to get to appear – after all, she is a member of her culture just like anybody else. In putting the Q-pack together, she strove to include items which would permit the description of all the personifications of madness which she had come across in her earlier trawl through the professional and popular literatures, films, theatre, and so on. However, she obviously had no control whatever over which mad characters would actually appear in the study. This was entirely up to the participants, and the way they sorted the statements she gave them.

It was therefore informative about notions of 'who is mad' that accounts of those who are 'deficient-in-reason' appeared in the study. Admittedly, such characters (along with the psychically troubled) are described and defined within DSM III – for example, as having disorders of mental retardation – and are therefore presumably included within the remit of medical psychology generally. However, individuals so described tend not to be regarded as mentally ill by the wider population, and are more typically referred to as mentally handicapped, mentally challenged or having learning disabilities.

Interrupter: Or as 'severely euphemized'.

Beryl: Quite, but it may be an improvement on being 'severely pathologized' as they used to be by psychiatry as 'idiots, imbeciles and morons'! Or being 'dumb' and 'thick' (or worse) as they may be called in school playgrounds.

Three factors in the Q-study presented rXe-presentations of those deficient-in-reason. These depicted the kinds of characters who are regarded as 'deficient' in the medical psychology, in that they are seen as immature in their thinking – they reason like 'children' and are ill-equipped to cope with the complexities of adult life.

The stigmatized/victimized fool

One of these epitomizations, dubbed by Gleeson the 'stigmatized/victimized fool', presents as a naive and dependent character, trusting of others, lacking social perception, with low intellectual ability, and having difficulty in adapting their behaviour to the specific demands of any situation. They are warm and compassionate, and although they have the potential to form close relationships, as one participant says, 'this character is seldom given the opportunity to develop close relationships despite his best intentions' (Gleeson 1991: 277). In keeping with previous research which describes the denial of the sexuality of the mentally handicapped (e.g. Giami 1986), this character is presented as asexual and as also failing to conform to gender stereotypes. In fact this kind of person is portrayed as a moral innocent. There is nothing in the least bit evil about such characters; they are warm, trusting and show 'puppy-like' devotion and adoration for their loved ones. But this is not a happy innocence. This is not an image of the 'happy fool' (such as the characters played by Norman Wisdom in the 1950s Ealing comedies) which is at times, in our culture, associated with this child-like state. This character has no real capacity for enjoying life and for experiencing happiness. They are aware of their own incompetence, and feel inadequate. They are described as 'exploited and abused' – 'affection is often met with repulsion'.

This character looks different from others, acts differently from others and is described as frequently behaving in a way which upsets or offends others. They are not integrated into their social world – they are rejected and neglected. As Townsend (1969: xxi) says:

> If a person behaves towards others invariably with trusting obedience, makes gestures or noises inappropriate to the context, repeats statements or instructions, touches and embraces others with embarrassing familiarity or affection, he [sic] is liable to be assigned to a social category of 'simple fool', or 'mentally subnormal'. He runs the risk of becoming a deviant with inferior status.

To the psychiatrist and those informed by liberal mental health education, this kind of person may not be mad. But not all of those in ordinary society will necessarily make this fine distinction between one kind of 'mental' deviance and another, for:

> There is a tendency for society to separate people into strictly distinct categories of deviant and non-deviant, incapacitated and non-incapacitated, subnormal and normal, irrespective of the graded differences of degree revealed in any objective study of behaviour. (Townsend 1969: xxii)

> *Interrupter: I'm impressed, I'd always thought that 'case book examples' were made-up composites. Here the composition of the character is made explicit.*

Beryl: And moved out of being created by authorial whim into being produced by a method designed and used for tapping shared knowledges. I'll make a Q-researcher out of you yet. Do you want to meet some more?

'Storm and strife'

Some of the typifications of madness are particularly interesting in that they do not adequately fit any of the psychiatric diagnostic categories available, although they do fit with characterizations which are recognizable within our culture. One example is the storm and strife persona, which clearly coincides with characters commonly represented both in fictive and 'factual' accounts of adolescent or youthful crisis, such as the character played by James Dean in the film *Rebel Without a Cause*.

The storm and strife manifestation is presented as someone who mistrusts others, is impulsive and has a tendency to 'fly off the handle'. They are lethargic, unable to cope with day-to-day living, are irresponsible, do not eat properly, are unmotivated and find it difficult to make decisions. Furthermore, this character is negative, discontented, pessimistic, self-destructive and aggressive. They shout a lot and tend to lash out at others both physically and emotionally. They don't get on with their family and tend to feel alienated from the rest of the world.

> *Virgin Mary*: Sounds just like my boy at thirteen.

> *Interrupter: Or 'Treasure', the all-purpose adolescent in* **The Guardian** *column.*

> *Beryl:* Well yes it does seem to be an account of adolescent 'sturm und drang' some of me know only too well. But, you may ask, is it an image of madness?

Although this character is presumably regarded as pathological by those participants who provided it as a description of madness, it is not generally treated as such in psychiatry's scheme of things. As an integrated whole, it simply has no place in the diagnostic structure. Looking at how 'storm and strife' is textualized in culture, it seems to be treated as a kind of temporary madness – a 'peculiar-arity' which comes and goes and whose episodes can usually (if painfully) be 'worked out' or 'worked through' and which itself should be 'grown out of'. It is therefore a condition very different from the permanently marking and integrally changing madnesses (even cyclical ones) that psychiatry usually deals with. It has more of a handle on and home in the books of developmental or educational psychologists, among the stock 'horrors' of right-wing tabloids or the annals of delinquency (cf. Stainton Rogers and Stainton Rogers 1992a). It is very difficult to treat the condition of 'adolescence', but because it pains the adult world we are, it seems, well able to see it as a 'pathology'.

> *Interrupter: Mmmm. And with the health service being what it is today, somebody is likely to have grown out of it before they got to the top of the waiting list anyway.*

This characterization makes the point that youthful turmoil is pathologized in our culture despite of (or perhaps because of) the way that the 'craziness' of the adolescent is so much in flux that it would be a major challenge to pin down the 'sufferer' diagnostically. Adolescence becomes a time of culturally sanctioned madness – a local equivalent of such exotic dis-eases as running 'amok' in Malaya or going 'wild pig' in New Guinea:

> ... the upholding of a steady equilibrium during the adolescent process is in itself abnormal ... adolescence resembles in appearance a variety of other emotional upsets and structural upheavals. The adolescent manifestations come close to symptom formation of the neurotic, psychotic or dissocial order and merge almost imperceptibly into ... almost all mental illnesses. (Freud 1958: 273)

> Personally I would feel greater concern for the adolescent who causes no trouble and feels no disturbance. (Geleerd 1961: 17)

> *Interrupter: OK. All very interesting. But what about someone I would risk calling the 'really' mad? Can't I meet them too?*

The 'mad-bad' persona

Some of the characters which emerged in Gleeson's study were re-scribed as 'beyond-all-reason'. These are the 'really mad', the floridly insane characters beloved by Hollywood film producers and hack writers. The description of one of these, dubbed a 'mad-bad' character by Gleeson, is dominated by statements which reflect a cold and uncaring nature. This remote character has no close personal relationships, and is described by one participant as 'a malicious computer – estranged, alienated and affectionless' (Gleeson 1991: 249). This character is egocentric, ambitious, ruthless and completely without guilt, conscience or morality. They are also described as positively evil, even though there appear to be very few rXe-presentations of madness for which ascriptions of evil are considered to be appropriate. In this description, we find a clear account of an extreme and anti-social character, prone to violence and cruelty and having an obsessional and ruthless drive for personal power.

Of the seven participants whose Q-sorts loaded significantly on the factor which provided this account, six said they were drawing upon fictive characters from novels, film and TV, the other described an escapee from Broadmoor Hospital (an institution for the 'criminally insane') who had been discussed in the news media at some length. It therefore seems unsurprising that this character is very much a mad persona writ large. We can easily trace this figure through our culture's literature and find it (as did some participants), for example, in the character played by Marlon Brando in the film *Apocalypse Now*, and in the character of Hart in Martha Randall's science fiction novel *Journey* (1978).

This 'mad-bad' persona does in many respects fit with the description of the psychopath based, for example, on Cleckley's (1964) criteria. That is, it describes a character who does not have a strongly developed moral sense, and is free from feelings of guilt. Furthermore, this character displays the stimulus-seeking behaviour which the clinician would expect of a psychopath, as well as a lack of emotional ties, and a tendency to be 'irresponsible'. However, although one of the participants who provided an exemplar for this factor explicitly described the character as psychopathic, there are features which are said to be characteristic of the psychopath which are noticeable by their absence. For example, there is no indication of either impulsivity or the renowned ability of the psychopath to make a good impression on others. Participants who provided exemplars for this factor say, rather, that this persona 'has no desire to be seen as kind hearted or caring by others; [is] generally thought of as an evil and nasty person; [and] tends to arouse apprehension and fear' (Gleeson 1991: 248–9). Therefore, this factor does not provide a complete portrait of the psychopath as presented in the professional literature, although it does seem to capture adequately a rXe-presentation which has wide currency in the culture and is drawn upon as a contemporary image of madness. It is this bad-mad image which is used to such effect by the tabloids – in their salacious accounts of the so-called 'serial killers' Sutcliffe and Nilssen – rather than the sad-mad characters which psychiatrists would more frequently recognize and manage.

Popular interest and concern with the bad-mad has a long history. Certainly the Victorian novel is characterized by a fascination with the tension between good and evil of the kind epitomized in Stevenson's (1886) novel *The Strange Case of Dr Jekyll and Mr Hyde*. From this book, one of the screen's most popular characters emerged (more than twenty film versions of the story have been made to date) when Dr Jekyll, by tinkering with the darker side of his mind, allowed himself to be possessed by his psychopathic alterego. In the early filmic presentation of this rXe-presentation, the mad man was physically transformed – his eyes bulging, his skin swarthy, his hair wild, in order that his pathology be physically manifest. Such 'wild man' images of madness are among the earliest sedimented of all – a case in point is the Biblical Nebuchadnezzar (II Kings 24–5). However, as we move closer towards the present day, mad-bad characters have become less animal-like in appearance. In fact, one of the most sinister aspects of the modern-day filmic psychopath is their ability to pass for normal (e.g. Anthony Perkin's character Norman Bates in Hitchcock's *Psycho*). Our present-day mad-bad characters are more deliberate, organized and systematic in the cruelties which they inflict:

> Thus we see Fowles' (1963) butterfly collector systematically observing, trapping and eventually killing a woman, and planning his second acquisition in order to make scientific comparisons. Rhinehart (1972) presents the character of Frank Osterflood (a wealthy socialite who rapes and kills young girls) asking an analyst to help him either by providing an alternative outlet for his tension, or by helping him not to worry about getting caught. Banks (1985) presents the character

of Frank, a sixteen year old with a penchant for ritually killing animals and for murdering his younger relatives. (Gleeson 1991: 98)

A currently contemporary popular case study of this rXe-presentation is to be found in Dr Hannibal Lecter ('Hannibal the Cannibal') in Thomas Harris's novel (and the film) *The Silence of the Lambs*. Lecter is only ever shown as calm, even super-controlled. He is a cool and calculating genius of perfectly ordinary appearance. And yet we are told, that he is intrinsically 'other' in both thought and action. Lecter is given to us as animal-like, savage and brutal – a modern-day cannibal with an insatiable appetite. He invokes such fear in those given the task of containing him that he is bound and muzzled like a mad dog. Yet he is also highly intelligent, sophisticated, urbane – and in a neatly reflexive irony, a psychiatrist! Lecter contains both Dr Jekyll and Mr Hyde and thereby is both ideal-typical and 'other'. His 'otherness' is not itself so different in kind from previous filmic 'horrors'; there is casting continuity to the rXe-presentation of the mad-bad character. But in being both ideal-typical and 'other' rather than alternating identities, he carries a changed narrative possibility. While Jekyll must die so that Hyde shall die, Lecter lives – self-destruction is not on his (read our as audience's) agenda.

Depression-through-oppression

Another instantly recognizable character that emerged in Gleeson's study, one could almost call it a cultural icon, is that of the oppressed and de-pressed woman, trapped inside a 'caring' role within the family. This persona is perhaps the gendered antithesis of the mad-bad character described above, in that she is more a disturbed/troubled creature than a disturbing/troubling one. All three exemplar Q-sorts for this factor described women who were defined in terms of their family commitment. This typification of madness is described as warm and nurturing but feeling inadequate and lacking self-esteem. She is a worrier, prone to feeling guilty, unhappy, pessimistic, iso-lated and unable to cope. This character seems to be drawn within a particular emergent discursive frame which emphasizes the negative and undermining experience of being a woman and mother. It does not present an image of a person who is in any sense removed from what is generally taken to be reality. Rather, their madness lies in the reality they are reacting to and against. As one participant put it: 'Depression seems to me to be a reasonable reaction to their circumstances' (Gleeson 1991: 247).

This character, beloved by 1960s kitchen-sink dramatic 'realists' (acquiring the then current appellation 'Poor Cow'; cf. Dunn 1967), was well-shaped for appropriation within the nascent ideologized discourses that first coalesced under the rubric 'women's liberation'. Certainly the oppressed/depressed woman is an image commonly found within the writings of such feminist-informed novelists as Fay Weldon (cf. *Down Among the Women*, 1971). Such novels typically centre around the unfair, unceasing and unmeetable de-mands made upon women and the unequal treatment which they receive.

As Chesler (1972) said, it is almost as if women are, by definition, created to be mad. If they take on the feminine role prescribed by a patriarchal society, they will find it very hard not to crumble under its pressure. If they resist the role and fail to perform their womanly and wifely duties, they will be condemned and perhaps confined (Warren, 1987). Either way, they run the risk of 'going crazy' – the woman's role is immanent with craziness.

French's (1978) *The Women's Room* provides a typical example of a feminist appropriation of this rXe-presentation. In this novel, the hero(ine), Mira, is forced by her husband's cruelty into drinking and depression and an attempt at suicide. Similarly, Mortimer's (1962) *The Pumpkin Eater* describes a woman seeking treatment for depression when she becomes unable to make sense out of her role as wife and mother, and unable to cope with the manipulation of her 'unfaithful' husband.

However, a feminist appropriation is not inevitable. We argued earlier that rXe-presentations are not ideological in themselves and can be 'worked-over' within many different discursive locations. Non-feminist utilizations of this rXe-presentation can be seen in Zelda Fitzgerald's semi-autobiographical novel *Save Me The Waltz* (1932) as well as in a number of television soaps and dramas, such as 'Sue Ellen' in *Dallas*, and 'Rita Fairclough' when abused by her partner 'Alan Bradley' in *Coronation Street*.

Besides being a twentieth-century literary motif (and the adjacency is powerfully intertextual), the depressed-oppressed woman is a mad character recognized by Psychiatry, and prescribed for and treated by counsellor, psychiatrist and general practitioner. Of course, for the feminist, a prescription for such a character would include resistance and relocation rather than Valium. French feminists such as Cixous and Gauthier (cf. Showatter 1985) describe madness as the label applied to female protest and revolution. Other feminists, Showalter included, would, however, claim it to be the desperate communication of the powerless rather than a serious challenge to the *status quo*. Thus even within feminist discourse, this rXe-presentation is open to a variety of different uses.

> *Interrupter: Okay, you've got me hooked. As material I find this compelling but, is it really that new? Haven't other researchers been over this ground before?*

> *Beryl:* Amazingly to me, much less than you'd imagine and not in anything like this detail.

Social representations and the mad

As we have hinted above, there is no shortage of feminist literature which reads representations (particularly of mad women) against an ideological deciphering agenda. But, for all their merits, they are not concerned with popular nosology *per se*. From within medical history, Gilman (1982) has produced a superbly researched, Foucaultian-inspired visual archive of icons of madness but again without a specific focus on rXe-presentational analytics. Others have, of course, looked at rXe-presentations of the mad, but within very different frameworks from that used by Gleeson. De Rosa (1987), for example, was also interested in images of madness but she worked quite specifically within Moscovici's Social Representations framework. She looked at children's drawings of the mentally ill, picking out common themes, emblems and signs in order to demonstrate that social representations of the mad change, or rather, 'progress' from a criminalized conception based on images associated with deviance, to a medicalized conception based on illness, and more resonant with the scientific or 'liberal-orthodox' rXe-presentation of the mad. But, of course, in keeping with the Social Representations Theory approach, De Rosa was not looking for diversity in the representing of the mad but its opposite. She sought out consensus and employed a convergent structural analysis with which to carve up the 'representational field' – what Potter and Wetherell term the 'ironing out' of diversity.

Bearing this in mind, it should not surprise us that metaphors such as the singularizing tale of progress from deviance to illness should have been read out from the presentations of madness constructed by De Rosa's participants. We, on the other hand, might suppose, contrarily, that images of the mad are drawn from a manifold of sources beyond and outwith the scientific and medical, rejecting Moscovici's contention that all such contemporary social representations are of more or less scientific origin (Moscovici 1988). The very different (and we would argue far fuller and less theoretically pre-set) results that Gleeson reports not only reflect upon the contrasted projects of the two approaches to (social) representations, but indicate that the latter does far more justice to the richness that is popular imaging.

The authorship of rXe-presentations

A concern with notions of the origins or, indeed, authorship of representations is, in general, a fascinating field. Foucault (1969) talked about the author function with which certain discourses are endowed, whereby socially negotiated and culturally mediated discourses are personalized into biographic units. The interesting thing here is that the author function doesn't seem to work in the same way for rXe-presentations, especially (but not exclusively) when we talk about rXe-presentations in pictorial rather than textual form. You can talk about a particular presentation of a rXe-presentation in terms of an originator or at least a crafter. That is, an individual can put brush to canvas and paint a Madonna. But this would not make them the author of this rXe-presentation as much as the author of the canvas. To put this in crude economic terms, it is not Leonardo's rXe-presentation of 'The Virgin of the Rocks' which is valued, but the objectified, authored canvas he painted. The rXe-presentation adorns everything from trinket boxes to T-shirts, but only the original canvas gets guarded by bullet-proof glass and placed in the Louvre (or the National Gallery, London).

Consider now a painting of a mad person. We can question its provenance (was it really painted by X?). We can question its quality (is it technically well-done?). But we cannot deny its rXe-presentation, any more than we can deny the rXe-presentations in Gleeson's study. No one can argue with them in the way that they can argue with an understanding of madness laid upon such images, for example. It is only when specifically discursively located that an image can be said to be in moral or factual 'error'. The image *qua* image cannot be refuted.

Interrupter: Because the artist can say 'That is simply how I see it'?

Beryl: No, that gets us back into the representation trap again. It is not 'a mapping some reality' argument. There is no capturing, no project of striving for a truer representation implied in what I am saying.

All intercourse with images is a presencing practice. 'Screaming heads' (à la Munch) have, via their juxtaposition with text in medical psychology books, become themselves texted – the informed viewer sees in the skull-like heads what is specifically a representation of desperation, torture, madness, not an image of the pre-represented reality of a mad person. The 'art' of the mad themselves is similarly employed, whether by accepted artists (such as Dadd) or by 'mere' patients. Indeed, as De Rosa has shown, in this game anyone can be the artist – we can all present what others (or indeed ourselves) may take as rXe-presentations. The hierarchies which operate to organize other kinds of knowledge in society, from orthodox to heterodox, professional to lay, don't apply themselves to images in the same way.

Interrupter: What about, say, applying tests of socialist realism?

Beryl: Remember, I am not talking about Art here but image. But yes, perhaps I should have said 'in our kind of society'.

Perhaps because power/knowledge synarchy encompasses the power to 'cut out' and 'paste in' imaginal social representations from or into thick texted knowledge, hegemonies directly vie for power over the latter more than the former. But it was not the essential Madonna that the Catholic Church 'pastes in' so catholicly, or the Puritans 'cut out' so vigorously, but her multitudinous simulacra. No-one claims ownership over the 'true' Madonna.

The Virgin Mary: I can.

Beryl: Sorry but the copyright rests with the image maker not the imaged.

No one can claim ownership over a rXe-presentation because the relationship between rXe-presentations and power is different from that of the relation between discourse and power – not least because of the way in which knowledge is mongered. Knowledge is a market of at least claimed expertise; rXe-presentations are promiscuously given away.

Interrupter: Except where captured and mounted, which is what I think you are doing.

Beryl: Nasty, sounds a bit like 'The Rape of the Sabine Mad' or what my Aunt Matilda had done to her cat when it died. But it does help to develop the question as to why there hasn't been the same trade as with knowledge.

This is not because images are considered to be unimportant or lacking in power. We can dislike them. We can actively seek to ignore them. They can be censored and hidden, they can be ideologized and worked over within various discursive locations. What seems to be the key to their position is, as previously noted, that we cannot refute them. They have, therefore, little exchange value in a regime of 'Truth' (such as received science or, more generally, a scientized society). And, as we say, they are promiscuous, their iterative and sometimes concrete properties mean that they have a habit of popping up opportunistically.

We would also note that rXe-presentations do not necessarily have the same conditions of inscription and transcription as a discourse. Thick texts have a clearly extensive temporal dimension (Martinez 1992). Any text, beyond a slogan, cannot usually be crafted out or apperceived in all its aspects at once. We can experience a text as a whole only when we have finished experiencing it. A rXe-presentation can be presented visually in such a way that a viewer can experience it as a whole in an instant. Even when a rXe-presentation is described in a text, it is typically revealed quickly, as a whole, rather than built up over time through the narrative.

Take a discourse about madness (e.g. *One Flew Over the Cuckoo's Nest*) in its filmic form. Here we can literally freeze the frame in the flow of images over and over again – we can 'cut out', for instant access, its images of the mad. And indeed pastiche them or 'paste in' them elsewhere (as film-makers have long done). By contrast, the discourse, the story, takes time to emerge. We can only extract it by further narrative effort (e.g. in precis).

To summarize this chapter overall we can see several reasons why we might want to act upon rXe-presentations as if they were a separate kind of social knowledging. RXe-presentations

- are immanent with meaning-making, but have no fixed or inherent meaning.
- are not imbued with ideology in the way that discourses usually are, although they can be ideologized.
- are functionally independent of discourse, although within the social knowledge systems we inhabit they are nomically positioned to be appropriated within discourses.
- stand in a very different relation to power compared to discourses – there is no orthodoxy in rXe-presentation.
- do not have the same conditions of inscription and transcription as do discourses.

Beryl: Does that do enough to justify this chapter Interrupter, dear?

Interrupter [expletive deleted to 'dump']: No textualization without representation.

7

Topologies of understanding

This chapter will use the analytics of textuality and tectonics to tackle the issue of 'understanding'. An exploration of the ways in which things – phenomena, issues, problems, and so on – are 'understood' is clearly of central importance to any human endeavour. Before we can address this directly, however, it will be helpful to recapitulate some of the arguments set out in previous chapters, with specific reference to 'understanding' itself.

Understanding understanding

To understand something is to grasp its meaning. However, if (as we have argued in Chapter 2) a thing has no inherent or essential meaning and, further to this, if a thing's meaning is provided for it by its having been gathered into an understanding, then what can 'to grasp its meaning' mean? In other words, if meaning is the *effect* of an understanding, then how can understanding be the grasping of a previously unheld meaning? This paradox is brought out when we talk in the same breath of understanding as both 'revealing' *and* 'constructing'. 'Understanding' and 'meaning' seem, in this sense, to gain their being in the relationship between a person and a thing or issue, or in a person's involved engagement with a thing or issue.

Understanding is local and contingent

The reason why understanding can both reveal and construct is that we only ever 'understand' within the specific setting of a concerned engagement with a thing or issue at a particular time and in a particular place. Understanding is always local and contingent – we can only 'understand' with regard to specific circumstances, specific local conditions, at a specific point in time. However, the analytic of textuality moves us away from viewing 'understanding' as *simply* a relationship between independent subjects and objects. From the subject/object perspective (discussed in Chapter 2), we are led to think of 'understanding' as some 'spark of insight' which occurs in a subject when he or she relates appropriately to an object. The 'meaning' of something is then thought to be either an inherent property of the thing-in-itself which is grasped by the knowing subject (revelation), or a cognitive 'projection' on the part of the subject onto an object (construction). These conceptions ignore both the passage of time and the always-already of textuality and they lead, inevitably, towards a positivistic (and hence limited) conception of knowledge. It is this limited conception of understanding as simply a *mental process* which has been repeatedly challenged by philosophers such as Wittgenstein (1958), Heidegger (1962) and Ryle (1973). Ryle argued that it is more useful to think of understanding as an achievement than a mental process, and Wittgenstein states that:

> Try not to think of understanding as a 'mental process' at all – For that is the expression which confuses you. But ask yourself: in what sort of case, in what kind of circumstances, do we say, 'Now I know how to go on,' . . . In the sense in which there are processes (including mental processes) which are characteristic of understanding, understanding is not a mental process. (Wittgenstein 1958: 154)

Understanding has an 'aboutness'

To assert that 'understanding is always local and contingent' is based on the assumption that we are only usually called upon to understand something when that something is a problem it matters, or, at least, it is at issue (a matter which *requires* understanding). And things only become 'an issue' or 'a problem' for us in specific concrete circumstances. We cannot 'understand' in some kind of conceptual limbo – we never 'understand' in abstract. Understanding has an 'aboutness' in the sense that it requires a particular issue-to-be-understood. As Heidegger (1962: 88) says regarding 'knowing': 'If knowing is to be possible as a way of determining the nature of the occurrent by observing it, then there must first be a *deficiency* in our having-to-do with the world concernfully' (emphasis in the original). 'Knowing', in this Heideggerian sense, is neither detached nor abstract, but intimately intwined with the particularities of our engagement with the world. To give a simple example, if we 'know' that a tool we are using is too heavy, then this knowing is inseparable from the problems we are having in using it. The same tool used by a stronger person, or for a more appropriate job, would no longer be understood as 'too heavy' because it would no longer 'stand out' as an issue-to-be-understood.

The problem with limiting our analysis of understanding to the proximal relationship between subject (understander) and object (understood) is that this can ignore the constitutive importance of the background context against which something stands out as requiring understanding. For example, we can ask (as does Foucault 1979a) why it is that the life-style of the 'homosexual' has been delivered to us during the nineteenth and twentieth centuries *as demanding scientific understanding*? How is this modern understanding of sexuality different from that of the Ancient Greeks? Such a focus upon the tectonic conditions of plausibility for certain understandings led Foucault to his concern with the inseparability of 'power/knowledge'.

Having an understanding

'Knowing', however, does not capture all that can be meant by 'understanding'. Certainly, if something is understood, then it can be said to be known. But, like almost any word, 'understanding' is polysemic. We can be said to have 'an understanding' when we have formed an agreement (as in, 'Yes, I am married, but my husband and I have an understanding'); we can be an 'understanding type of person' who is empathetic, sympathetic and considerate; we can have 'different understandings' about an issue where those understandings are recognized to be personal judgements and perceptions. Also, there is a common use of understanding which requires that the matter was not previously known or understood. To understand in this sense is to grasp the meaning of something which had previously been unclear and which now falls into place.

Interrupter: Ah, now I understand

Beryl: Precisely!

Box 7.1 An understanding box

Sue and Ian, for example, may understand (know) what the word 'argument' means and what an argument is. However, Sue may suddenly understand (grasp) why Ian has been acting stand-offish with her (a matter which Sue had noticed as an issue-to-be-understood) when she learns that Ian had attended a public school and that, consequently, all of the snide anti-public school jokes and comments that Sue had recently been making will not have been well received. On arguing the matter out, Sue and Ian may find that they have very different understandings (viewpoints or perceptions) about public schools. Yet – being understanding (empathetic) people – they may reach an understanding (agreement) not to bring the matter up again.

We should not be surprised at this complexity, however, as it simply reflects the complexity of everyday life. Some of the 'understandings', for example, are separated by time (something we understand in a present grasping-at-understanding act will hopefully still be understood tomorrow), and once we have an understanding, then this can be pitted against that of another person and hence emerge as a 'viewpoint'. Likewise, 'understanding' can name a type of person who is inclined towards understanding another's viewpoint. Or, finally, it can name a kind of 'meta-understanding' whereby we mutually understand and tolerate our different viewpoints.

All of these usages, however, point to the crucial importance of the locatedness of understanding within a background of concerned engagement with (and in) a world of lived time and lived space. In this sense, to 'understand' is to know your way around this life-world (Gadamer 1975). It is interesting that the original meaning of one of the German words for 'understanding' (*verstehen*) came from the legal context of representing a case before a court (Gadamer 1975: note 173). Not only does this highlight the sense of knowing your way around the arguments (defence and prosecution) of the court room, it also points towards Heidegger's usage of *verstehen* or under-standing as 'standing up for'. If we limit our conception of under-standing to the subject/object dichotomy and restrict 'understanding' to a matter of mental representation, then – despite (quite rightfully) focusing upon the relationship between person and issue or thing which is proximal to understanding – we obscure the textuality and tectonics within which issues are delivered to our understanding and within which our understanding is directed towards issues.

Understanding both reveals and constructs

We are now in a better position to grasp how an understanding may simultaneously reveal and construct. Things are revealed through understanding, in the sense that we confront issues that *require* understanding, we do not simply 'invent' them or 'will them into being', but rather they 'stand out' for us because of the particular forms of our engagement with an always-already meaning-full world. In this sense, the significance of any thing-to-be-understood (i.e. how and what it matters) extends well beyond the significance with which we (as proximally independent 'subjects') imbue it. Hence certain understanding will always be more appropriately applied to certain concerns – such as an understanding of car mechanics to the mending of cars but not, say, to the mending of broken hearts.

> *Interrupter: Where, presumably, the understanding required is of cardiac mechanics?*

Beryl: Yes, sometimes, though at others an understanding of jealousy might be more appropriate.

Nevertheless, any given understanding is also a construction, not only because understanding must always be partial, directed and located, but, more basically, because the significance of any issue is always-already a matter of textuality (though this point may matter somewhat less when a person is mending cars than when they are, say, seeking to understand an emotion like jealousy). The idea that an understanding can both reveal and construct only reveals itself as a problem when constructed within a 'subject/object' understanding limited to a choice between 'either' and 'or'. Thus to explore the ways in which various issues are understood is to explore their issuance within and through various situated understandings. This reframing of the concept of 'understanding' moves us away from viewing it as simply a cognitive activity or a subjective achievement, and moves us towards a recognition of the socio-practical locatedness of the various modes or styles through which issues become revealed.

Interrupter: Translation into plain English please?

Beryl: The time and place of the action, the particular practice in question, what else is going on at the time, that sort of thing.

Hence in this chapter we constitute 'understandings' as always located within a socio-cultural terrain. The empirical work which will be described, then, must be read as located in late twentieth-century Britain, among, in general, its modal culture.

Interrupter: I get the feeling you are saying something rather obliquely.

Beryl: I suppose I am, in part in an effort to be politically correct – I want to avoid the accusation of being ethno-centric. Having said that, there are always going to be problems seeking to understand understanding outside of one's own socio-practical location. I suppose what I'm trying to do is to warn that my work is inevitably localized culturally and socially, and time-limited in its applicability, but to stress that this is done reflexively, in an awareness that I can *only* address understanding in a strictly localized sphere. I'm perfectly aware there are other local systems. But I simply cannot address them.

Understanding jealousy

In order to emphasize the inapplicability of a modernist split between abstract 'thought' and embodied 'feeling' (where 'understanding' might be immediately consigned to the status of 'thought'), we will here take a human emotion (jealousy) and demonstrate its interpenetration with 'understanding'. This will add empirical substance to one of the central arguments of Chapter 2: that 'experience' is not a separate thing from textuality.

As with understanding, the way we use the various concepts implied by the term 'jealousy' reflect the complexity of our everyday lives. As Wittgenstein (1981: para. 488) observed, emotion words tend to be coupled with the word 'feeling' in a way which beguiles us into equating emotions with sensations. We can say we 'feel jealous' or 'feel sad' just as we can say we 'feel cold' or 'feel pain'. This, Wittgenstein noted, especially inclines us towards reifying or objectifying emotions, and therefore mistakenly thinking of emotions *as if they were* merely internal bodily responses with not only no 'cognitive' corollaries (cf. the James/Lange theory of emotion in psychology), but indeed, no engagement with the textual at all. In this analysis, emotions just 'are' 'natural' sensations over which we have no control.

The observation that things are more complicated than this with regard to the emotions is indicated by drawing attention to at least three different conventional ways of combining an emotion word with 'feel' or 'feeling'. First, we can feel jealous or sad or angry; second, we can feel jealously or sadly or angrily; and, third, we can feel jealousy or sadness or anger. These three usages roughly correspond to the distinction between adjective, adverb and noun, respectively. To 'feel jealous*ly*' directs our attention to the style or manner through which one experiences or approaches the world. To do something jealous*ly* is to do it in a particular way, which is perhaps possessive or guarding, just as to do something sadly or quickly is to do it in a particular manner. This is very different from 'feeling jealousy'. Here jealousy-as-noun seems, as discussed above, to name a particular internal feeling, just as the word 'red' names a particular colour. In this sense, we are led to think of jealousy as a particular set of sensations. Finally, when we say we are 'feeling jealous' we seem to be describing not simply an internal feeling, but *the manner* in which we relate to something or someone. To 'feel jealous' is not simply to report a feeling, but to feel *through* jealousy. Likewise, if I say I feel angry or sad, I am telling of my present way of relating to the world, and not merely of some independent sensation I am currently experiencing.

> *Interrupter: So you would, in a case like this, expect a concerned friend to ask 'what about?' or 'why?', and not 'how does it feel?' or 'where?'*

Beryl: Yes, that's right. It's this extra complexity that Wittgenstein is getting at when he remarks that he would 'almost like to say: One no more feels sorrow in one's body than one feels seeing in one's eyes' (Wittgenstein 1981: para. 495).

These observations indicate that things are too complex for a simple distinction between thought and feeling or between narrative and experience. To add a further complication, however, not only can we feel jealous, jealously and jealousy, but we can also *be* jealous (although it makes less sense to 'be jealousy' or to say that 'I am jealousy'). In a sense, to be jealous is to own one's jealousy: you don't just feel jealous, you *are* jealous. Hence to 'own' one's jealousy is not 'have' it (we might as well say that it 'has' us), but to be it – we are jealous. As Armon-Jones (1985) points out, we tend to use the word 'feel' in front of an emotion word when, for whatever reason, we either lack the justification or reason to 'be' that emotion, or we want to draw attention to our 'selves' rather than to the situation that is 'making us' [feel] it. However, if, as this observation indicates, 'being' is more 'basic' than 'feeling', this is not because it is any the less a matter of textuality. Quite to the contrary.

Interrupter: Are you saying that it is impossible to conceive of jealousy in its full complexity without the notion of 'understanding'?

Beryl: That's right. To be jealous is to 'understand' jealously or through jealousy. It is always-already to be enmeshed within a meaningful system of relationships.

Interrupter: But what is the understanding and meaningful system of relationships which is jealousy?

Beryl: Well, we always have to be wary of attempting to delimit precisely a concept or a way of being which is in itself fuzzy and somewhat imprecise. But at the same time this fuzziness should not lead us to the premature conclusion that jealousy is meaningless: if someone were to say that they woke up with a jealousy ache in their mouth, for example, we would assume that they were mistaken about the meaning of jealousy!

Interrupter: Or that they were being poetic.

Beryl: Yes, that's another possibility, though I think getting into poetry could bog us down in this discussion, so I suggest we leave it aside.

Let us look at it this way. The following brief account should be taken as a sketch, or perhaps a 'brass-rubbing', of the contours of jealousy. The word 'jealousy' is elliptical for a diversity of particular situations or experiences, which nevertheless share a definitive form or organization.

Making jealousy (locally) meaningful

In the textuality of twentieth-century Western thought, jealousy is seen typically (though not exclusively) to have a core cast of three people. For person X to feel jealous, he or she usually has a (real or imagined) relationship (broadly understood) with person Y which confers attention, affection, privilege or whatever onto X. Here X can be held to be jealous when they believe themselves (rightfully or not) to have been unwantedly displaced (or when they perceive the threat of displacement) from their location in this attention, affection or privilege. Usually this displacement involves a third party, person Z, who could be called a 'rival'.

*Interrupter: As in, say, Maggie (X), Joel (Y) and Joel's ex-fianceé, Evelyn (Z) in **Northern Exposure**?*

Beryl: Yes, those names might help us to make the argument more comprehensible, though I prefer to use the letters so we don't get bogged
down in one particular story.

From this definitional organization, various productions may ensue. On
the one hand, X may voice bodily references such as 'it chews me up inside
to see them together' but engage in no further production. On the other
hand, for a full melodrama, a number of 'ingredients' are usually in play,
such as interlocution (and other activity) focused on the claimed infraction,
its denial, acceptance or reconstruction, followed by resolution, which may
be the breakdown of the relationship, or something more of a 'muddle-
through'. Such a description of the typical lineament of jealousy-as-
melodramatized does not, of course, constitute *a definition* of jealousy.
Rather, it serves to reveal something of the ways in which we ordinarily use
the concept. This avoids the trap of reifying or 'thingifying' jealousy. We do
not need to assume that there is some essence to which the word 'refers'.

> *Interrupter: Are you saying that the concept of jealousy is somehow 'pre-
> packaged' out of always-already social knowledge and a particular configur-
> ation of textuality?*

Beryl: Yes, that's a good way of expressing it. The point is that these relationships do not somehow inevitably 'accompany' jealousy (and still less
are they 'causes' or 'effects' of jealousy – we might just as well say that
the container-shape of a cup causes it to be a cup). Rather, they are
what we *mean* by it: they are criterial to its ascription.

Hence it makes little sense to be jealous of a spoon (although it is perfectly
possible to be angry at one if, for example, it breaks as we are trying to use
it) because a spoon cannot enter into the relationships which are criterial for
jealousy (we can be jealous of the spoon owner, of course). Likewise, we can
easily describe a film as 'sad' or 'angry', but much less easily as 'jealous'.

> *Interrupter: Well my friend is jealous of her husband's car.*

Beryl: It's always possible, within textuality and with a little hard work, to
create new scenarios to express previously 'unthinkable' ideas. But yes,
in our present popular understanding of jealousy, while cars and films
cannot credibly be regarded *as* jealous, people can be jealous *of them*.
I suspect that in the case of your friend, she sees that the car has been
presenced as 'a rival' for the time and even affections of her loved-one.
I bet he spends every waking moment tuning and polishing it.

> *Interrupter: You're right – not helped by the fact he's recently taken to calling
> his car 'Boopsie'!*

Beryl: Quite!

Within the confines of this analysis, it should be clear that there will
always exist considerable scope for multiple understandings of the nature,

meaning and significance of jealousy. The point is that we come to recognize ourselves and others as jealous (and all that this can be made to imply) only through discursive practices. For this reason, by studying the different discursive frameworks through which jealousy comes to show itself – through which jealousy is presenced – we stand to learn not merely about different ways of understanding this emotion, but also about the means by which jealousy is storied into being as an emotional experience.

The point of focus for the empirical work in the remainder of this chapter, then, is on jealousy as a site for multiple, competing and contrasting understandings of jealousy. In gaining access to the organization of textuality around jealousy, we aim to show how insight into the tectonics of its construction may be gained.

Understandings of jealousy

The empirical material discussed below is selectively derived from a number of studies using a variety of methods which are outlined more completely elsewhere (Stenner 1992). The methods include Q-methodology, thematic decomposition of interviews about jealousy, cultural analysis and seeded thematics (cf. Chapter 5). In the Q-study in question, participants were asked to sort a pack of 55 items according to a scenario they had previously constructed outlining what they considered to be a typical scene of jealousy (in which the jealous character was designated with an 'X'). The understandings un-covered in this way were as follows.

Jealousy as natural

> The man who has not been jealous, beaten his mistress, torn her clothes – he has yet to be in love. (Lucian, 'Scenes of Courtesans', as quoted in Gonzalez-Crussi 1988)

One distinct way in which Stenner found jealousy to be understood is as a natural phenomenon. This understanding usually gets brought to bear on 'sexual' or, if you prefer, 'romantic' jealousy. Through this discursive framework, jealousy is revealed as a sign of true love, and is thought of as if it were the 'emotional glue' which holds a loving relationship together. A 20-year-old male interviewee from North London, for example, stated that jealousy is:

> ... healthy in small doses I reckon. Because jealousy can keep something between you two that you always respect someone because there is that bit of jealousy inside ... it always keeps you on your toes about somebody.

Likewise, an 82-year-old female interviewee recounted the following scene of jealousy involving her late husband:

> *Interviewer:* But was he [participant's husband] ever jealous of you?
> *Participant:* No. Oh, I don't know, he punched two violinists on the nose!

Interviewer: Why, what was that about?

Participant: Well I'd gone to play for one at a concert and he saw me home, and we were saying goodnight on the corner – it was quite an amiable . . . just a friendly good night, and George came up, and didn't say a word – but knocked him down. And . . .

Interviewer: Did he say why he'd done it?

Participant: No. Oh I did say to him, I said, 'I can go out with who I like, we're not engaged'. He said, 'well let's be engaged then'. Wasn't that a romantic proposal! Wasn't it the essence of romance! And the other one, he said if he didn't keep away, he'd break his bowing arm.

This is an historically well-sedimented understanding of jealousy. The God of the *Old Testament*, for example, described Himself as a 'jealous God'. Moreover, he made no bones about authorizing jealous husbands to interrogate their wives (sometimes by use of the 'water of bitterness and cursing') on the slightest suspicion of adultery (Numbers 5: 11–22). Within this understanding, the etymological links between jealousy and zeal become particularly clear, and jealousy takes on positive connotations of 'watchfulness' and concern.

Within such a discursive framework, jealousy is acceptably seen as underpinning 'established coupled' relationships and as providing the extra motivation or zeal necessary to keep the relationship in order – it is regulatory in function. Hence it makes sense that this particular understanding of jealousy tends to be predominantly (though not exclusively) associated with men (in a heterosexual discourse the fidelity of the husband is usually less of an issue than that of the wife or daughter) and largely condoned, expected and even demanded as a matter of duty and honour (White and Mullen 1989; Baumgart 1990). In societies where this understanding is influential, it will tend to be legitimated by powerful institutions such as the Church and the legal system. In the USA in 1859, for example, one Daniel Sickles was excused for murdering his wife's lover on the basis of the following eloquent law-defense (taken from Stearns', 1989, excellent historical analysis of jealousy);

> [H]e would have been false to the instincts of humanity if that rage of jealousy had not taken possession of him . . . 'Jealousy is the rage of a man'; it takes possession of his whole nature; no occupation or pursuit in life, no literary culture or enjoyment, no sweet society of friends in the brilliancy of sunlight, no whispers of hope or promises of the future, can for one moment keep out of his mind, his heart or his soul, the deep, ineffaceable consuming fire of jealousy. When once it has entered within his breast, he has yielded to an instinct which the almighty has implanted in every animal or creature that crawls the earth . . . 'Jealousy is the rage of man' and although all the arguments that my learned opponents can bring, or that can be suggested, that a man must be cool and collected when he finds before him in full view, the adulterer of his wife, to the contrary notwithstanding, yet

jealousy will be the rage of that man, he will not spare in the day of vengeance. (Stearns 1989: 20–30)

At some level it is easy to acknowledge the textuality of accounts wholly located in books and legal discourse. However, it is worth observing that this same account of jealousy has been legitimated by scientists, who offer scientized justifications for its 'naturalness' (i.e. that jealousy is a naturally occurring 'thing'). Sociobiologists such as Trivers (1972) and Wilson (1975), for example, argue that jealousy is a genetically programmed response which arose through evolution in an economy of 'parental investment', whereby sexual monogamy (supposedly) proved the most effective means of safely reproducing the species.

For such writers, human societies are organized the way they are in part *because* jealousy operates to make them so. In a variation on this theme, Daly, Wilson and Weghorst (1982) argue that 'male sexual jealousy', or 'the dogged inclination of men to possess and control women, and the use or threat of violence to achieve sexual exclusivity and control' is a direct, genetically determined consequence of males requiring 'paternity confidence' (i.e. the sure and certain knowledge that one's offspring are their 'own'). From this perspective, a range of regulatory activities – from chastity belts to the mutilation of female genitals and the forced imprisonment of 'wives', not to mention the murder of women suspected by their husbands or fathers of infidelity – are passed off as natural and instinctive behaviours.

Interrupter: You wrote in Chapter 1 of stories warranting or justifying conduct. This strikes me as an all too easy excuse by men to justify absolutely unjustifiable behaviour.

Beryl: I agree – it's an excellent example of the way discursive praxis can take a justificatory function, which is precisely why I want to challenge such notions.

This understanding of jealousy-as-natural also emerged as a factor in the Q-study. Here are two examples of 'jealousy scenarios' provided by the various participants exemplifying this factor:

There was this young married couple called Scott (person X) and Charlene (person Y) who went on holiday. While on holiday they became friends with a man called Steve (person Z) who was from the same town as them. Unfortunately, after a couple of days Scott became ill so he couldn't go out or enjoy the holiday, but not wishing for his wife's holiday to be spoilt insisted that she go around with Steve to keep her company. So seeing what it meant to him that she was happy, she spent a lot of time with Steve sight-seeing. But as the week went on and Scott saw so little of his wife, he became very bad tempered and resentful of Steve because he was seeing more of her than he was, and she was his wife!

Susan (person X) went to a party with long-standing boyfriend John (person Y). After half an hour he went to get her another drink. When some time lapsed and he had not returned, she went to look for him and discovered him talking to another female (person Z). He was obviously very interested in her. This made Susan very jealous.

These scenarios (and various others) were understood as indicating that X's problem is that they have 'fallen in love with' somebody who they believe is less dependent on X that X is on them. This, the argument goes, has set X up to be jealous at the slightest sign because they can never be sure of the intentions of their partner; they are helpless and insecure. In this situation, jealousy is understood as being natural, normal and powerful enough to place X in a situation where their emotions are beyond their control. The jealousy X feels causes X to act in a way which is destructively stifling to their partner, and in the cold light of reflection X will come to regret being so possessive, even though at the time they were utterly powerless to stop themselves. It is made clear that these reactions do not indicate that there is something wrong with X's personality. They are not resentful, immature, consciously possessive or competitive. If they are at fault in any way it is simply in allowing themselves to get into this situation in the first place.

Jealousy as psychological immaturity

In contrast to the understanding of jealousy-as-natural which insists that this emotion does not normally indicate anything unusual or pathological about the jealous person, there is a second broad understanding which does just that. Again, this is an understanding promulgated as much by scientific specialists in the production and circulation of understandings (mainly by psychologists), as it is to be found in ordinary, everyday understanding.

The understanding of jealousy-as-psychological-immaturity first entered into significant issuance during the early part of the twentieth century, alongside other medicalized notions siting people as 'psychologically disturbed'. Psychological narratives constituted the scientific category of the 'jealous type' as a person who has experienced problems during their upbringing, who is insecure because of lack of mother-love, and who was not trained properly as a young child to resist such emotion. It is important to note that this understanding was not restricted to 'extreme' instances of jealousy, but came to apply to *any* activity which was recognized as being 'jealous'.

In fact, much early attention was directed to jealousy among children, and through this concern the category of 'sibling rivalry' was born (i.e. storied into being as a psychological phenomenon). Stearns (1989) lists a rash of papers, articles and advice manuals which appeared in the USA between 1920 and 1940, with titles such as *Some Causes of Jealousy in Young Children, The Influence of Differences in Age, Sex and Intelligence in Determining the Attitudes of Siblings Toward Each Other, Studies in Sibling Rivalry, Rivalry Between Children of the Same Family, Characteristics of the First, Second and Third Child,* and so on. Stearns argues that such a proliferation of concern about 'the problem' can be understood as being part of a wider 'campaign against jealousy'.

Box 7.2 The psychological problematization of sibling jealousy

The following quotations from promulgators of 'specialist knowledge' on jealousy are all taken from Stearns (1989: 88–113):

Thom, in a widely cited government publication of child-rearing published in 1925 said 'few emotions are experienced by man which from a social point of view are more important than jealousy'. Parents are warned to be watchful of their young children and to ensure that jealousy does not take root because 'the jealous person becomes an object of dislike . . . and all too often this . . . causes uncontrolled resentment and disastrous results'. Dorothy Fisher warned parents in 1932 that 'in inciting their children to rivalry . . . parents may be wrecking their chance of present and future happiness'.

Jealousy, as told in these publications, is natural and normal in young children, but it is dangerous and parents and other carers must be vigilant. They must prepare themselves for its appearance and cut it off at its roots before it insinuates itself permanently in the delicate and impressionable young personalities of our children: 'Unless parents recognise that jealousy will normally appear, and are prepared for it, strong feelings of hostility often develop which continue to make life miserable for both children over many years' (Fromme 1956).

Also, in conformity with Freudian theory, the absence of jealousy is presented as even more suspicious than its presence: 'The child whose jealousy is not as easy to recognise suffers more and has greater need for help' (Barauch, 1940). Montgomery states in his 'baby book' (1955) that 'if he [sic, the child] does not have the right kind of help, his personality may be damaged. Unfriendly, disagreeable, self-conscious adults show these traits because of unsolved jealousy problems in their childhoods.' Sibling rivalry 'indelibly stamps personality and distorts character'. 'A prolonged state of jealousy is a symptom of retardation in emotional development and shows itself along with other evidences of emotional immaturity.' 'We only have to read the daily paper to see the results of ungoverned jealousy in adult life.' 'Jealousy flourishes in souls where affection and response are wanting' (Thompson 1953).

Finally, The Child Study Association of America [sic] in 1926 warned that unchecked jealousy can be:

. . . so intense that little but harm can come from rousing it in its more primitive forms, and that even in the higher form of rivalry and emulation greatest caution must be used . . . there is [sic] no limits to the depths to which he [the jealous child] may sink . . . Children who quarrel because of jealousy . . . are in a serious state. This type of quarrelling should be treated at once by getting at and doing away with the cause of it. (p. 100)

The shift in discursion on jealousy reflects a general growth of individualizing discourse – where a chief concern is to respect the 'rights' and autonomy of people, and their entitlement to achieve psychological 'growth' *as individuals*. Jealousy, under this discursive practice, becomes increasingly revealed as a loss of control (leading to a 'possessive' compromising of individuality), rather than as a righteous and necessary reclaiming of control. The conditions of plausibility have thus been laid for an understanding of any experience of jealousy as indicating not only weakness, but pathology:

> Jealousy is a mental illness which should not be dismissed lightly, as it is at present, but which should be given a serious consideration by physicians before it may reach an uncontrollable state impregnated with the danger of a complete destruction of the sufferer's mental integrity; it should be treated before a crime is committed ... We believe, and we intend to prove that jealousy is autonomous to a great degree, an independent psychological unit of enormously variable manifestation and of unusual complexity due to the numerous factors involved in this emotion. (Sokoloff 1948: 9)

In the naturalistic narrative, jealousy was 'the rage of man'. In this account, by contrast, it is an 'autonomous ... independent psychological unit' which 'manifests itself' in complex ways.

> *Interrupter: Hold it. What does that imply? The King James version of the Bible warns 'For thou shalt worship no other God: for the Lord, whose name is Jealous, is a Jealous God'. Does that mean God has a serious personality defect?*

Beryl: No, under critical polytextualism it means you will shoot yourself in the foot (so to speak) if you try to apply an understanding from one discourse directly to another discourse.

According to extreme versions of this psychological-immaturity understanding, whenever we are jealous it is never to do with the person we are jealous of or the situation we are in. It is never reasonable, never communicative, never perceptive, but always *our* doing, *our* problem, *our* insecurity. Our jealousy, from this perspective, speaks only of us. 'It' speaks through our mouths and works through our bodies, displaying the lamentably immature state of our 'inner worlds' and nothing more. Hauck (1981: 35) is clear on this point:

> Jealousy is always the same no matter where you find it: a) a neurotic need for approval, and b) an intense feeling of inferiority. If you conquer those two conditions, nothing, not even having someone sleep with your partner, can make you jealous. In fact, you could have several people sleep with your partner on a regular basis and still not feel jealous if you did not have problems with inferiority feelings and a neurotic need for approval.

Although the influence of 'specialist' knowledges on this understanding of jealousy is central, it should also be pointed out that this understanding is prevalent among 'non-specialists' too. A variation on it also emerged as a factor in the Q-study. Two jealousy scenarios from this factor are as follows:

This is a scene between two friends, one of whom is describing her feelings for her boyfriend's ex-girlfriend:

Person X: I don't know why Fred (X's boyfriend) wants me when he's had Wilma (X's boy friend's ex). She's got a beautiful face, lovely skin, straight teeth and a perfect figure, I think he is just with me because he can't have her any more.

Friend: If Fred didn't want you he wouldn't be with you now, I don't know why you worry. You've got a lot to give.

Person X: But if I was more pretty and had a better figure he might want me more than he wanted her.

Friend: I think you should just get on with living in the present and forget what's happened in the past.

Person X: I'm not living in the past, it's just, I've always wanted good skin and I've put on weight and I'm not as tall as Wilma and I've always wanted longer legs – it's just so unfair that some people have got what I've always wanted.

Friend: Nice weather we've been having lately, would you like a coffee?

Gertrude (X) and Boris who had been married for about ten years, decided to have a dinner party, which was a great success and everyone was enjoying themselves. After they had finished they lounged about in the lounge (where else?) chatting. Gertrude was talking to someone and when she turned around, saw Boris kissing her best friend. Gerty flew into a rage, yelled and screamed at everyone, and stormed out of the house.

Although these representations of jealousy are not markedly different from those of jealousy-as-natural, the understanding of jealousy conveyed in the associated Q-sorts is clearly and distinctly different. X is understood as acting in this jealous way because of various flaws in their personality. It is stated that it is certainly not natural to be jealous in this situation, as most people would not be affected in this way. The reason that X reacts so strongly is that they feel inadequate, inferior and insecure as a person. They cannot accept themselves as they are, and this makes them over-react in a confused and possessively jealous way to trivial incidents (and this is of course very counter-productive and destructive). The argument continues by locating the reasons for X's insecurity 'deep in their childhood'. They have an immature personality and must learn to look deeply at themselves, to accept themselves, and to stop and think about what they are doing. Then they will be better able to deal with their jealousy.

Note that in this understanding jealousy is presented with the help of such standard psychological discursive themes and motifs as 'developmentalism', 'personalization' and 'pathologization' through which jealousy is located within an agenda of psychological 'health' which assumes as a basic tenet – but never needs to state directly – that the jealousy is never justified.

The tectonics of understandings of jealousy

To comprehend the strong differences between the understanding of jealousy-as-natural and that of jealousy-as-psychological-immaturity it must be pointed out that they tend to be directed towards, and to grow up within, different concerns. These different concerns must themselves be located in the context of different tectonic topographies. The understanding of jealousy-as-psychological-problem, for example, can be viewed as making sense within a broader cultural setting within which growing importance is accorded to individuality. A growing valorization of individuality is, of course, inextricably bound up with modernization, urbanization and bureaucratization. These processes brought into being, among other things, heightened demands for bureaucratic and service skills which placed emphasis on 'emotion work' (Hochschild 1983) and, in particular, the containment of anger (Stearns and Stearns 1988). They were also associated with a 'loosening up' of sexual mores (as in the 'roaring twenties', for example); a move in the direction of more equitable gender relations; and a general decline in family size which no doubt influenced the significance of sibling rivalry (Stearns 1989). Also, the related concept of love underwent significant changes in meaning whereby jealousy came to signify less its 'proof' than its antithesis.

Cancian (1987; see also Gillis 1988) narrates the recent historical development of love (particularly in the USA) in terms of prevailing 'blueprints', i.e. what we otherwise have called stories or accounts. The first 'blueprint', which Cancian calls 'Family Duty', supposedly arose in the mid-nineteenth century (particularly among the middle classes) at a time when love became 'feminized' – that is, constructed as an internal feeling divorced from action and placed mainly in the care of women. This newly feminized love was predominantly played out within a marriage governed according to 'duty' where 'the key relation was an intense, emotional tie between mothers and children, and raising moral, respectable, healthy children was a woman's major task' (Cancian 1987). 'Feminized' love can thus be understood as developing along with the intensification of the gendered private/public dichotomy mentioned earlier where 'an ideal woman centred her life on love of husband and children, a love expressed mostly through emotions and piety, not practical action'.

The end of the nineteenth century and the beginning of the twentieth, according to Cancian, saw the gradual erosion of this 'blueprint' and its gradual replacement with the 'Companionship blueprint' which 'identified the family with marriage, not parenthood, and emphasized emotional and sexual intimacy between husband and wife' (Cancian 1987: 34). Self-fulfilment through intimacy in marriage replaced the concept of duty 'but love was still feminized, and wives were still expected to be economically dependent and submissive to their husbands . . . marriage was to be all of a woman's life but only part of a man's' (p. 34). According to this 'blueprint', it was not so much the wife's duty to 'lighten his cares, to sooth his sorrows, and to augment his joys' (Welter 1966, quoted in Cancian 1987: 34) as, rather, an opportunity for her own self-fulfilment and personal happiness. As one Mrs Duffy wrote for women in 1873, the 'truest, purest highest form' of love is a 'strong, unselfish affection blended with desire' (from Stearns 1989: 211). This second valorization of love is clearly related to the problematization of jealousy charted earlier. When love is defined in terms of selfless devotion to another, jealousy, with its unattractive connotations of selfishness and possessiveness, comes to represent its antithesis – not a sign of true love, but an enemy of love.

Just as it is possible to talk of representations of love as stereotypically 'gendered', so too with jealousy. Thus we could view jealousy-as-natural as a predominantly 'masculine' discourse because of the association of jealousy in this understanding with action, honour and protectiveness (this could be symbolized with the figure of the 'duel of honour' – the man who does *not* act jeopardizes his manhood), and jealousy-as-psychological-immaturity as a 'feminine' discourse because of its associations with passivity, reactivity and internal emotionality (this could be symbolized in the 'problem pages' in women's magazines).

> *Interrupter: Ouch! Talk about sexism – a real case of a male=good, female=bad argument that!*

Beryl: Not at all. I am not proposing these as the way such things *should* be understood, but suggesting that this is how they often *are* understood. If you would hang on a moment you would see I am going to go on to develop an argument about why this may be so, and what the effect of this is.

Jealousy as an ideological construction

At the turn of the twentieth century, anarchist feminist Emma Goldman wrote:

> The most prevalent evil of our mutilated love-life is jealousy, often described as the 'green eyed monster' who lies, cheats, betrays and kills. The popular notion is that jealousy is inborn and therefore can never be eradicated from the human heart. This idea is a convenient excuse for those who lack ability and willingness to delve into cause and effect . . . Jealousy is the very reverse of understanding, of sympathy, and of generous feeling. Never has jealousy added to character, never does it make the individual big and fine. What it really does is to make him blind with fury, petty with suspicion, and harsh with envy . . . Jealousy is invariably a one-sided, bigoted accuser, convinced of his own righteousness and the meanness, cruelty, and guilt of his victim. Jealousy does not even attempt to understand. It's one desire is to punish, and to punish as severely as possible. (Shulman 1979: 170)

Through this commentary, jealousy – defined as the 'reverse of understanding' – is subjected to a relentless critique. Notice that the understanding of jealousy-as-natural is explicitly challenged and reframed as a 'poor excuse'. It is replaced, however, not with the calm, scientific 'description' of the 'faulty personality' of the jealous person discussed in the previous section, but with a hot and highly moralistic and political (or anyway, strongly evaluative) diatribe on 'right and wrong'. From the position of this understanding, placing jealousy into the neutrality of the discursive arena of 'health' misses the political and moral essence of the matter.

In our culture, such politicized anti-jealousy themes reached their popular peak after the 1960s. This development can be related to wider social changes such as the development of new 'permissive' legislation in Britain and the USA during the 1960s regarding such issues as divorce, homosexuality, abortion and censorship. The arguments used in the legal debates surrounding these changes demonstrate a marked shift towards individualistic and consequentialist modes of thought (cf. Davies 1975). This growing liberalism and individualism is also reflected in contemporary times in an increased incidence of cohabitation, and 'serial monogamy'; a decreasing popularity of marriage (Clark and Haldane 1990); an increase in 'extra-marital sexual liaisons' (and a decreased likelihood of reference to these as 'adultery') (Lawson 1988); a massive increase in divorce (Burgoyne, Omrod and Richards 1987; Clark and Haldane 1990); and a decrease in fertility (Cancian 1987).

These socio-practical events, combined with an increase in women's autonomy and a general weakening of religious warrants against pre-marital sex, multiple relationships, infidelity, divorce and so forth, represent a massive change in the tectonic conditions for the textualization of what were seen as appropriate feelings about and expression of jealousy. Compared to the nineteenth and early twentieth centuries, the grounds and opportunities for jealousy today are manifold. And yet a 'melodramatic', 'florid' jealous 'scene' today is considered inopportune, unsophisticated or distinctly 'uncool'. This again is related to a growing emphasis on both 'independence' and 'interdependence' in loving relationships, which was influenced both by the 1960s counterculture – including sexual experimentalists such as the 'swingers' (Gilmartin 1977) and alternative life-styles such as the 'hippies' or the 'Kerista' villagers (Pines and Aronson 1981), all of whom attempted to 'outlaw' jealousy – and by the Women's Movement (Cancian 1987). As put by Durbin in a 1973 Village Voice:

> To be jealous is to be the capitalist pig of the heart: you're being possessive . . . being politically incorrect . . . [jealousy is] well on the way to becoming the New Sin of the liberated generation. (Clanton and Smith 1977: 38)

These tectonic conditions, then, provided the discursive arena for the popular expression of the understanding of jealousy-as-ideological-construction. A male interviewee in his mind-twenties expresses this neatly:

> *Interviewer:* So how do you feel about jealousy then, do you see it as a kind of weakness?

Participant: Uh . . . it's one of the many things I don't understand about people. Why do they go around chopping each other up with axes and stuff? Why do they go around shooting each other when it's patently not necessary to do so? How do the very rich people feel about the grinding poverty surrounding them? Why do people get sexually jealous? . . . You know, I don't understand the mass of humanity at all.

As expressed in the Q-study, this understanding of jealousy was concerned with the ideological domination of men over women. Each of the participants whose sorting patterns loaded onto this factor chose as their exemplification of jealousy a scene in which person X is male. In all but one case, this male responds in either an outrightly or potentially aggressive way towards a perceived threat. In each case, this perceived threat is directed towards another male who is considered to be a rival. The rival is seen to be a threat to a relationship that this male is having with a female. A typical example is the scenario given below:

> Beryl [*authors' note*: this character is purely fictional, and any resemblances to real people are purely accidental] and her husband Stan had decided to throw a party and everything was going swimmingly until . . . Beryl who had become a little over-excited and drunk a bit too much, felt slightly under the weather and had to retire to the bathroom. Neville, a local GP, found that he required to use the bathroom and, on discovering Beryl, decided to stay and make sure she was allright. He made what would prove to be the mistake of locking the door, for when Stan found the two of them shut in the bathroom together jealousy reared its ugly head and he planted one on Neville, removing one of his teeth and sending the unfortunate general practitioner tumbling down the stairs.

In this account, X is viewed as acting in a thoroughly unreasonable way – as attempting to control others with their possessive activities. This is seen to be a particularly male way of behaving and X is assumed to feel totally justified in acting this way. They are not justified, however, and by no means should their jealousy be excused on the grounds of 'naturalness' – this behaviour is by no means instinctive. Rather, the argument goes, it has everything to do with the ways in which men view – and seek to regulate and dominate – women. The other people in this setting have done nothing to provoke this situation, and X's behaviour is likely to do a lot more harm than good.

Jealousy as an insight-into-the-self to be expressed-and-learned-from

The previously described two understandings are thoroughly condemning of jealousy. It is almost as if, paradoxically, they prescribe that we should 'jealously' guard against being jealous! The fourth understanding of jealousy Stenner described has a more positive side to it. This positivity does not flow from jealousy itself, however (and in this sense can be viewed as accepting many of the criticisms levelled at 'jealousy' by the previous two). Rather, jealousy can be positive when used to 'develop' one's self in a direction away from jealousy and towards 'self-contained individuality' (cf. Sampson 1989). In this sense, this understanding can be considered as part of a 'technology of the self' (Foucault 1988). That is, in a cultural setting where self-development, self-actualization and self-exploration are constantly valorized and required in all aspects of life, jealousy can be appropriated as an index of one's success on these terms or as a 'material' to be worked on in order to attain 'success'. As Mazur (1977: 187), psychologist and self-valorized jealousy-expert, proclaims: 'Let your lover look at you with all of your blemishes and shortcomings and let your relationship be a dynamic exploration in living and becoming rather than a wedding exchange of personality packages.'

In order to achieve this 'dynamic exploration', jealousy must not be repressed; on the contrary, it must be discovered, owned up to and expressed. Of course, the incitement to express, far from being borne of a wish to condone jealous actions, is part of a technology for working on the self so as to craft a more self-contained ethical/aesthetic identity:

> All too often most of us permit jealousy to deteriorate into feelings of guilt or self-pity or helplessness. What jealousy says then is, 'poor me!' But jealousy can be used to motivate us to constructive action: to examine our emotional needs more intelligently; to do something positive about shortcomings... When allowed to go unquestioned, jealousy remains malevolent. Examined in the light of reason, it can be a stimulus for growth. (Lobsenz 1977: 34)

According to this understanding, the attitude we adopt towards our jealousy is crucial:

> If all jealousy is simply rejected as undesirable or immature, the affect goes underground and interferes with group functioning and the exchange of other feelings. If jealousy is lauded or facilely accepted, growth in important dimensions can be hindered... Jealousy must be recognized, admitted, and worked with if it is to lead to personal growth and relational enrichment. (Mazur 1977: 182)

To institute such self-technologies, it is important to develop a detailed knowledge of jealousy so as to better learn from it. Thus Mazur (1977), in running his 'jealousy workshops', identifies 'possessive', 'exclusive', 'competitive', 'egotistic' and 'fearful' types of jealousy, and contrasts each with a form of being which is sanctioned, approved and striven for. The 'ideal self' in this scheme is 'autonomous', 'sharing', cognizant of 'specialness', 'free' and 'secure'. Likewise, the production of such characteristics must be encouraged in childhood. On the one hand, measures must be taken by parents to avoid jealousy in their children:

> [J]ealousy in a child... can be prevented by proper planning. A child should be prepared for the arrival of a new baby. If changes in his [sic]

routine become necessary, they should never coincide with the arrival of the new child. Unavoidable changes of the room or the bed, or being sent to kindergarten are easily taken as displacement and punishment unless they are properly timed. Too much attention to the new baby in the presence of the older child should be avoided in favour of demonstration of continued attention and reassuring affection to the older child. (Vollmer 1977: 64)

And, on the other hand, when it does arise, 'he should be encouraged to express his jealousy instead of being compelled to hide and repress it', so that he 'gains a proper self-evaluation and self-confidence [where] . . . the experience of jealousy is no longer detrimental' (Vollmer 1977).

Nowadays, it is difficult to escape the incitement to talk about feelings in general and jealousy in particular represented by numerous television programmes, self-help psychology texts, counselling services and the countless articles, particularly in women's magazines, asking us to assess just how jealous we are on a scale from 1 to 10, or how jealous we would feel in a list of hypothetical social scenarios. The first step in controlling our jealousy, we are told, is to recognize its existence, to accept it and own up to it – to confess it. Only then can we 'work through' it and 'deal with it' in a 'psychologically healthy' way.

Discussion

The four understandings of jealousy identified in this research indicated something of the rich complexity involved in what might otherwise be construed as the simple 'animal passion' of jealousy. Not only is there a diversity of experiences which can be gathered together under the heading of 'jealousy' (although ideally more attention would have been dedicated to this matter), but also it should be clear that the 'same' rXe-presentation can be understood in multiple ways. The ensemble of discursively organized positions or understanding represents a partial (and necessarily incomplete) glimpse at the range of cultural resources presently available for the construal of our own and others' jealous experiences. These understandings are culturally and historically contingent. Their specificity is derived from an enmeshment within the tectonics of local discourses and practices with attendant negotiable rights, duties and obligations.

A further point, that can be no more than sign-posted here, is the notion that our experiences of jealousy form out of the 'fault lines' of our valued identifications, and hence reveal and re-structure the tectonics of our local culture and of our personhood. To talk of the 'textuality' of emotion in general and jealousy in particular, however, seems often to provoke indignant defensive responses. We sometimes seem to have an 'emotional investment' in the idea that our emotions have the status of singular truths and hence to associate jealousy with stories, narratives and texts may appear somehow to either devalue or to deny such experiences.

In fact, in this case, the analytics may be useful precisely because of the challenge they present to the claim that we can unequivocally ground experience in the certainty of feelings. The aim in applying these analytics, then, is not to deny the often extreme 'bodily feelings' which may accompany an experience of jealousy, but rather to insist that, regardless of phenomenological intensity, we are still dealing with the enactment and use of a cultural resource. Meaning and textuality work their influence at each 'layer of the onion', and any claim of access to the 'real nature' of jealousy must be viewed as yet another aspect of textuality: another text on text.

It is not the 'reality' of the jealous experience that is called into question through these analytics, then, but the *nature* of that reality. Arguably, there is nothing more 'real' than to be 'tortured by jealousy' (provided we can reach an agreement on which experience of jealousy we are dealing with). But what is interesting from a critical polytextualist perspective is the question of how the reality of a social construction comes about: How is it that we have come to so involve ourselves in the narrative in question? Who must we be that we are so moved? How have we constructed ourselves, and been constructed, that this 'fiction' can, for us, be a singularly and pressingly real 'fact'? These questions of the 'fictioning' of 'fact' or the construction of reality are at the core of the analytics of textuality and tectonics.

8

Topologies of conduct

One of the major legacies of modernism (although its roots lie much deeper) is the notion that what people or collectivities *do* is, if not always simple or straightforward to account for, at least obvious in its rXe-presentation – *they behave*. Indeed, a whole branch of psychology – behaviourism – is grounded upon this naive view that what people 'do' (including their talk) is 'simply' their observable behaviour. Within a climate of problematization, of course, things can never be that simple. Behaviour, like anything else, is a text that can be read and re-written in a diversity of ways. 'Doing' is textualized into being as much as any other endeavour, whether that 'doing' involves language or not. Some consideration of how that has operated in much modernistic human science and fictive expressive accounting is a necessary precursor to the empirical work we will report later in this chapter.

Conduct under modernism

The claim both to be able to explain human conduct and to offer a technology of its troubles and its deviances is a key feature of the post-Enlightenment project of the human sciences. That project (and the modern 'climate of governance' in which it was located, cf. Parton 1992) was disciplined around received explanatory tensions or oppositions. Conduct and its vicissitudes were viewed, for example, as either personal or social in origin. In its turn, in various theoretically problematic ways, the personal was itself seen as compounded; for instance, as out of biological and environmental oppositional foundations, arrived at via some process of development or socialization (cf. Morss 1990; Stainton Rogers and Stainton Rogers 1992a, for specific critiques).

It is equally possible to cast the modern novel and other forms of popular fiction as part of the same sort of project. Novels, soaps and movies account (within the theoretics culturally available to the author) the lives and the life-worlds of individuals in terms of their rebellions and their conformities, their triumphs and their sorrows.

Modernism has made us all 'popular scientists' (cf. Moscovici and Hewstone 1983), 'social representations' providing us with access to (albeit naive versions of) science's cause-and-effect canons which enable us to interpret and predict the world 'rationally'. Whether one's oppositional investment is in the 'person' or the 'situation' as an explanatory foundation, claims of consistency and predictability can be used to adduce evidence for an operating causality in whichever of these one chooses.

Thus notions of consistency and predictability are critical both to a very considerable range of human science treatments and to fictive accounts of conduct (we are using the received distinction not endorsing it, of course). Both hold that we can (in a probabilistic sense) rely upon particular social locations, circumstances or milieux to elicit particular kinds of behaviour – people tend to 'behave' sociably at parties, devoutly in church, and in a scholarly manner in libraries. Equally, both the world of science and fiction hold that we can (again in a probabilistic sense) rely upon particular persons (or categories of persons) to evince particular kinds of 'behaviour' – Texan 'good ol' boys' tend to be brash, nuns devout, and academics scholarly. Such ideas in psychology go back at least as far as the work of Heider (1944). In fiction, of course, they go back as far as fiction itself.

There is to all this a pressing taken-for-granted constitution of reality. It is a grammar of attributive explanation which is remarkably theory-tolerant. 'Person' explanations of consistency and predictability hold good, irrespective of whether they are seen to result from unconscious motives, inherited character or conditioning. Equally, 'situation' explanations about consistency and predictability hold good whether they are seen to arise from role expectations, patriarchal power arrangements or the weather. To have (and hence to find plausible) a culture of soap operas, social work, selfhood and psychometric assessment means being competent to work with this taken-for-granted grammar. But for those 'scientists' who study 'human behaviour', behind such order there must be some essential substance – some causal mechanism – and it is this 'essentialism' which we now need to consider.

The essence of behaviour?

The key site of scientized explanations of behaviour is the psy-complex (Ingleby 1985; Rose 1985, 1990), centred upon psychology but incorporating a range of practitioner crafts from psychotherapy to social work. In its most blatant reworking of the grammar of consistency, psychology has made the assumption that verbal behaviour (such as expressing opinions) is the making operant of inner, causal essences (such as attitudes). Such verbal behaviour is seen to make possible the prediction of 'actual' behaviour (i.e. conduct). In other words, it is assumed that there are direct, causal links between 'essences in the head' (such as attitudes or personality) and expressed behaviour.

> *Interrupter: Isn't that just what is going on in current popular idiom when someone showing troublesome behaviour is said to have an 'attitude problem'?*

> Beryl: Pretty much, yes. The notion of 'attitude' has woven in and out of professional and popular discourse for much of the last century. But idiomatic 'turns of phrase' don't always imply direct representation – think about 'a bit under the weather'. My point about essentialism is that many psychologists proceed as though there is some real mapping of the word onto the world (to borrow Mulkay's 1985, phrase).

> *Interrupter: But surely there is a pragmatic case to be made – expressed attitudes do predict behaviour, and they must have come from somewhere.*

> Beryl: That's just what I'm about to question.

Despite a research history of the most limited success in seeking empirical support for this meta-model (see McGuire 1986, for a thoroughgoing critique), there seems to be little dampening of the commitment that mainstream psychologists have to it. Rather than resulting in a questioning of the venture itself, its problems have been taken as a challenge to the conceptual and methodological machismo of the researchers. The consequence has been the generation of ever more psychometrically sophisticated models, such as Ajzen and Fishbein's model of 'reasoned action' (cf. Ajzen and Fishbein 1973), which expresses (and claims to reveal in research) the supposed links between attitudes, social forces and behaviour. This they do by way of seemingly complex mathematical equations – we say seemingly, because this use of 'the sacred language of science, the mythic script known only to those few who have undergone the dreaded rites of initiation' (Klein 1988: 24) can be just as well understood as a variety of scientistic window-dressing that attempts to make the really rather banal, commonsense musings of scholars appear to be profound statements of psychological theory.

Stripped of its mathematical pretensions, the theory of 'reasoned action' proposes that you can predict fairly accurately whether or not people will or will not do something if you ask them just beforehand if they think doing it is a good idea, whether they think others will approve, and whether they care about what other people think. Even true-believing psychologists can sometimes see through that! For example, Leventhal and Hirshman (1982: 199) argue that 'it is questionable that we greatly advance our under-standing . . . by concentrating on the measurement of factors so proximate to action that we are practically using measures at the beginning of the act to predict the action itself'.

> *Interrupter [yawning, slightly]: Does this recounting of bickering between psychologists really matter? Haven't you forgotten your reader and slipped back into 'tutorial mode'?*

Beryl [irritably]: Yes it does and no I haven't. If you care at all about what is going on out there in the 'real world', then you ought to be aware of the way that this kind of pseudo-science touches all of our lives.

> *Interrupter: It does?*

Beryl: You bet! This kind of psychometrics adds up to big bucks and big business, and not just in terms of public opinion polls. These power-seeking forms of textuality are entered into by psychologists (these days, of course, chartered into 'experts') in the pursuit not only of academic credibility, but increasingly in professional hegemony over activities like the selection of staff (Warner 1992, is a good example – a government report arguing for the need to make staff selection more 'scientific' by greater use of psychological scales).

> *Interrupter: Thanks for the party political broadcast, but how does this link back to the 'grammar of behaviour prediction' you were talking about? That sounded pretty reasonable to me.*

Beryl: Listen and I'll tell you.

Troubling transformations

One of the transformational pay-offs of the climate of criticism, as so-called 'interpretative' social psychologists began to sense from the 1970s (cf. Rogers 1974), is that once commitment to the discipline is loosened, it becomes possible to entertain all sorts of readings of experimentation as a form of social life in its own right. Seen outwith an ethos of hypothesis testing, being able to 'predict' using the 'reasoned action' or any other attitude model does not formally establish *any* 'causal' links between expressed opinions and action. One could just as easily say that it demonstrates the workings of a 'grammar of behaviour prediction'; in other words, that the researchers and subjects in a study appear to have shared and to have ex-pressed a common understanding of what contingencies exist between ex-pressing opinions and action, in the particularities of that form of social life. What we would argue is that this kind of common agreement about contin-gency is *all* that is needed to make such experiments 'work' empirically.

Interrupter: Can I ask a terribly obvious question? Why is it, then, that psychologists (who, I would assume, are no different from other folk in their stock of native wit or social competence) usually (except in these very constrained situations) find it so very hard to empirically establish links between what people say and what they do? Surely the ability to predict the actions of others is a basic, essential social competence required for the smooth running of interpersonal relationships and common endeavours. If you are arguing for there being a grammar of behavioural predication, isn't that crucial to any sociality, whether that is working together, living together or simply, say, making a journey?

Beryl: Yes, indeed. Without a fair level of confidence that people will do predictable things, in predictable ways at predictable times, life as we know it would soon come to a grinding halt.

Our assumptions of a high level of consistency between the promises and social contracts people make (explicitly and implicitly) and their fulfilment comprise much of the 'doxa' on which social life depends. Yet it does seem that in study after study, psychologists have lamentably – even, according to attitude research's major historian, McGuire (1986), scandalously – failed to capture this doxa in empirical studies. We would argue that a lot of the problem lies not so much in the models themselves (which, as we have argued, are frequently no more than codified commonsense) but in a critically unreflexive belief in the possibility of objectively defining and measuring the elements in those models as the means to prediction.

Interrupter: Hold it right there! Beyond your ritual attack on 'positivist methods', where is this taking us?

Beryl: You bet it's more than a ritual attack. Our point is that it's not social life which lacks predictability. It is *psychologists' attempts to model it* in terms of nomothetic (applicable to everybody) measures that's the problem.

Interrupter: But when I look at studies into, say, racist attitudes and racist behaviour, they do look as if they are measuring what they say they are measuring.

Beryl: Of course they do, they're meant to – it's called 'face validity', and that is a lot of the problem. They are so blatant and so over-drawn, that they are a dead-giveaway. They locate the subject in the study in the position of being asked: 'Are you a racist or not?'

Interrupter: But sometimes, perhaps because of that, they do actually work, don't they?

Beryl: Yes, true, but only through imposing a contract (which gets called the 'demand characteristics' of the study). But as often as not they don't work, sometimes because there are so-called problems of 'social desirability' (because people see through the attempts to malign them), and sometimes because the subjects in the study object to what they are being asked to do (that's called 'reactance').

Interrupter: But you're no more keen on individual, so-called ipsative approaches are you?

Beryl: That's right, we're not. Predictability, as we see it, is not a result of good modelling, nomothetic or ipsative. It's not a *result* at all, but an intrinsic feature of certain social narratives that are contractual. We have mischievously defined psychology as the study of things that don't exist (outside of textuality that is). The study of attitudes is a prime example. We are not in the least surprised that if you go round trying to measure things that do not exist (other than as textuality, itself inherently multiple and fluxional), it will not get you much further than making cameo appearances in the pages of psychological journals!

Interrupter: And you think you can do better?

Beryl: Well, yes we do. Once you get into critical polytextualism then the difficulty that psychologists have in predicting behaviour (despite their capacities, as persons-in-culture like everybody else to draw on doxa) becomes less para-doxical.

Within polytextuality, we view people as always drawing, in whatever they do, upon multiple texts; as being, if you like, always 'in two minds' (and indeed, often more than two!). Such texts often (but not always) contain mandates to justify or prescribe conduct. Indeed, as was noted in Chapter 1, we would argue that one of the most important questions to be asked about a text is what conduct it warrants.

Interrupter: So what's better about that?

Beryl: Well, if nothing else, it does begin to explain why, outside of the constraints of soap opera scripts or promissory contracts with heavy penalties, conduct is, in fact, not all that predictable. If, as we would argue, people themselves often do not know which one of the textualized, multiply-transitive mandates for action that are available to them they will make substantive in action until they actually 'do' something, how on earth could anybody else possibly predict what they will do?

Interrupter: So where does that get us?

Beryl: Don't you see, it changes completely what you are trying to do?

The task as we see it is not to try to predict action, but to explore the ways that textuality can mandate and warrant action. In this we are not pretending, in our empirical studies, to 'measure' either attitudes or behaviour. But we do accept that there are potential links between what is ordinarily meant by 'what people think and say' and 'what they do'. These links, however, are not causal, but matters of textualized contingency (i.e. the contingency is textualized into being).

For example, the notion of 'a promise' can be seen as an assumed or interpreted contingency, where verbalization (whether oral, written or merely thought) implies a certain form of conduct. It is also the case that what an account often means is the giving of verbal expression to an explanation for past conduct. Such textualized contingencies comprise the taken-for-granted doxa which underpin cultural competence in predicting conduct – it is what makes conduct appear to be causally linked to, say, expressed opinions or beliefs or the making of promises. The ability to make sense of and use notions such as 'keeping a promise' are predicated upon having the necessary cultural competence in verbalization/conduct contingency.

However, cultural competence in 'reading' contingency is not, of course, a sufficient (though it may well be a necessary) basis on which to bring about an outcome. For example, knowing that writing a 'best seller' is contingent with getting rich does not do a lot for those who lack the skills to write one! Similarly, expressing the opinion that were society differently organized, women would not be oppressed by patriarchy, does not bring about that state of affairs.

> *Interrupter: I say again, so you think you can do better?*

Beryl [with a sigh of frustration]: Yes! Though I really am getting fed up with the way you seem to want to turn this conversation into a game of 'tit for tat' all the time. You make me look like an arrogant egotist. This isn't fair (I have my doubts whether I even have an ego). I am really not into that game. In arguing that we 'can do better' I'm not trying to score points off others, but genuinely searching for ways to tackle a difficult problem. How about we call a truce for a while, and move on to look at the empirical work, which, I hope, will show we are on to something. All right?

> *Interrupter: You mean you think you can tell a good story?*

Beryl: Yes, and if you are sitting comfortably, I'll begin.

Approaching the empirical study of accounts of conduct-prescription

In this section, we seek to illustrate some of the ways that conduct can, within textuality, be prescribed, mandated or warranted; and their reverse, how conduct can be proscribed, prohibited or regulated. In other words, here we aim to show how (via textuality in relation to conduct) people can be read as variously positioned as enabled or disenabled over what they may do, or how they may account for what they have done.

Although one-shot studies remain the norm in the North American dialect of Q-methodological research (see Stainton Rogers and Stainton Rogers 1990a for a review of some of the differences between the UK and USA), our own use of Q-methodology under a climate of problematization has a different, more analytic, agenda. Whenever we as researchers have looked at the ways individual action or public policy are textualized, this has been in order to explore empirically links and disjunctions between how an issue or phenomenon is explained or debated, and what people think should be done about it – what, in other words, the tectonics of conduct warrant. We have explored such contingency in the studies of madness (Gleeson 1991) and jealousy (Stenner 1992) described in previous chapters (each of which contained a conduct/policy-prescriptive Q-sort), and studies of energy policy (Stainton Rogers and Stainton Rogers, Lowe and Kitzinger 1986) and addiction (Stainton Rogers 1986; Stainton Rogers and Stainton Rogers 1990a).

Exploring textualized contingency between explanation and conduct

To reiterate what was said in Chapter 5, what this means in practical terms is that we devise two (or, in some cases, more) Q-sets around the same topic, one sampled from its concourse of explanatory propositions (usually, though, we sometimes look at other concourses) and the other from its concourse of conduct/policy-prescriptive propositions. In such studies, we ask the same people to Q-sort both sets, as well as providing us with open-ended comments on both sets of items. We then Q-analyse each data set independently, and interpret the factors in the usual way. This gives us two sets of account-descriptions: one on explanation (or whatever) and one on social policy/conduct prescription. We can explore links and disjunctions by observing where, say, certain individuals' sorts are exemplificatory in both sets. The illustrative studies we will describe in this chapter were concerned with the textualization of the issue of 'child abuse'.

Child abuse: explanations and social policy

In these studies, the textualities addressed were to do with the different ways people think we ought to respond to, and how, as a society, we should organize social policy with respect to the 'abuse of children'; and the ways in which these are contingently textualized by alternative understandings of the 'causes' of child abuse.

Study 1: Explanatory and conduct-prescriptive accounts in relation to child abuse in general

In the first study, the research was conducted for a distance learning pack on Child Abuse and Neglect (Open University 1989). As a contribution to the overall course, Stainton Rogers and Stainton Rogers (1989) carried out a

Q-study using two Q-sets: one on understandings of and explanations for child abuse, and one on social policies and actions in respect to what should be done to 'tackle the problem'. Two eighty-item packs were devised which were sorted by fifty-six participants. These were all people with an interest in the subject (i.e. medical, legal, social work and police staff and academics working in the field).

Items from the Q-sets used show the differences between the two samples. Explanatory propositions used included:

> A lot of times child abuse is not deliberate cruelty, but something that happens when an adult loses control and 'cannot stop themself'.

> All oppressed groups are at risk of being treated as sexual objects of those in power – children are no exception to this rule.

> Some forms of child abuse are the product of a biological drive to promote the 'survival of the fittest'.

Social policy/conduct-prescriptive propositions used included:

> Children will continue to be abused in large numbers until the fundamental injustices in society are tackled.

> The oppression of children by men needs to be tackled by feminist social policies.

> Increasing the likelihood of detection and the imposition of the severest punishment on conviction are the surest means to stamp out child abuse.

From interpretation of the factors three main explanatory accounts were identified, each of which was fairly directly linked to one of three accounts on policy. Here, then, were found straightforward correspondence between explanations and prescriptions for conduct (see Fig. 8.1).

> *Interrupter: Does it always come out cleanly and simply like that?*

> *Beryl:* Not at all, but this one did. Um, well, actually, to be honest, like most Q-studies it was rather more messy than the story we are about to tell. But we decided to keep it simple to make the task of illustrating simpler. Can you live with that?

> *Interrupter: I suppose so.*

Explanatory accounts

Family dysfunction explanation This was primarily concerned with the physical abuse and neglect of children by their parents, viewing these as largely a consequence of parenting under stress, often by parents who themselves had had few opportunities to learn how to care for children. The 'problem' of child abuse was seen as largely restricted to disorganized,

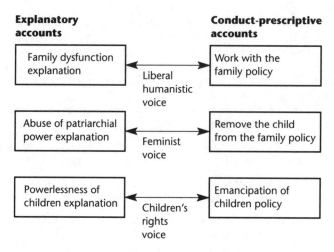

Explanatory accounts

Conduct-prescriptive accounts

Family dysfunction explanation

Liberal humanistic voice

Work with the family policy

Abuse of patriarchial power explanation

Feminist voice

Remove the child from the family policy

Powerlessness of children explanation

Children's rights voice

Emancipation of children policy

Figure 8.1 Links between explanatory and conduct-prescriptive accounts in the first study (Stainton Rogers and Stainton Rogers 1989).

inadequate and disadvantaged families with a history of family violence. This viewpoint tended to be exemplified by the Q-sorts of older and more orthodox, non-specialist social workers, by GPs and by health visitors.

Patriarchal oppression explanation This was more concerned with sexual than physical abuse, and attributed the sexual abuse of children to patriarchal male socialization, reinforced by cultural expectations of male sexual domin-ance and 'uncontrollable' male sexuality. Its manifestations were seen in all kinds of families, with abusers almost exclusively male but coming from all walks of life. This viewpoint tended to be exemplified by the Q-sorts of younger, specialist social workers and doctors working at the 'sharp end' of child protection, often with an expressed commitment to feminism.

Non-emancipation of children explanation This was concerned with all forms of mistreatment of children, including abuse by professionals in the way they ride roughshod over children's rights in their practice, institutionalized abuse in terms of things like inadequate provision for children's welfare (e.g. allowing them to be brought up in bed-and-breakfast accommodation) and the exploitation and oppression of child workers in the Third World. It explained such mistreatment as the consequence of children being both powerless and constituted as non-citizens, whose entitlements – indeed, full humanity – are denied. This viewpoint tended to be exemplified by the Q-sorts of academics (including Stainton Rogers and Stainton Rogers them-selves) and children's rights activists, including some radical lawyers.

Exegesis was both formal (e.g. via analysis of mass media and professional sources) and informal (i.e. as participants in teaching, policy making and research in the area). Narratives were, for example, sampled by engaging in conversations with professionals working in the field, with civil servants involved, at the time, in drafting new legislation (notably the England and Wales Children Act, 1989) and with members of pressure groups (e.g. PAIN: Parents Against Injustice).

Linked conduct-prescribing accounts

This research was conducted during the 'Cleveland crisis', a time of major discursive tectonic activity in the field of child abuse in the UK. The sexual abuse of young children was hitting the headlines, with much press reporting and public debate around competing arguments about, for instance, whether or not child sexual abuse on such a scale was 'really happening' or just a 'moral panic' (see, for example, Jenkins 1992). At that time, physical abuse was still generally viewed as the most serious and the more ubiquitous problem, and hence 'family dysfunction' was the dominant explanatory account, both within professional ortho-doxy (exemplified by the NSPCC's notion of 'dangerous families'; cf. Dale, Davies, Morrison and Waters 1986) and in the eyes of the general public. This understanding had been promoted by the doyens of the field, notably Henry Kempe and his colleagues working in Denver in the USA (e.g. Kempe, Silverman, Steele, Droegmuller and Silver 1962). It was Kempe and his associates who had coined the term 'the battered child' and it was an image of the bruised and battered child that the NSPCC was using at that time in its advertising and the covers of its books (see Kitzinger 1990, for a more detailed analysis).

Not surprisingly, the linked conduct-prescribing account was one of 'working with the family'. Both were clearly sited within the discourse of protectionism and welfarism, where 'the problem of child abuse' (i.e violence towards and neglect of children) is viewed as treatable by a strategy which combines ameliorating (via welfare provision) the poor living conditions and poverty of the families concerned, and by intensive therapeutic work with inadequate parents, offering advice about child-rearing and compensatory 'parenting' to the parents. Prevention was seen as a more effective longer-term strategy than crisis intervention, including screening for 'at-risk' babies at birth, in order to focus support on those families where abuse and neglect were most likely to happen (see, for example, Browne, Davies and Stratton 1988).

The feminist explanatory account epitomized a growing concern about the sexual abuse of children. Its origins, we suggest, arose particularly from feminist critiques, of systems theory approaches to family dysfunction, seen as failing to attribute responsibility to the perpetrator (see, for example, Nelson 1987) and a flourishing of women 'speaking out' against their sexual exploitation by men. At that time, it was noticeable that professional discourse was beginning to undergo change. We can surmize that one of the reasons for this was the training of social workers within a psychodynamic tradition, which emphasizes the harm-potential of traumatic experiences in childhood. This, and its 'harm warrant' (see, for example, O'Dell 1993) for intervention, provided, we would suggest, fertile ground in which a challenge to 'working with the family' could flourish. Such an analysis was bolstered by the work of people like Alice Miller, whose books (e.g. 1986, 1987a) were rapidly becoming the 'bibles' of social work radical chic. It was also receptive to ideas coming out of the USA (e.g. the work of Finkelhor 1984).

The linked conduct-prescribing feminist-informed account directly challenged the policy of 'working with the family' and argued instead for 'removing the child'. Since it was at that time virtually impossible to enforce the removal of the putative abuser from the home, the action prescribed was taking children from their parents to 'a place of safety', both to stop the abuse from happening any more, and to prevent children from being coerced to retract their allegations. There was among the participants' open-ended responses an evident recognition that while bedrock, feminist-inspired changes in social policy were unlikely to be possible in the short term, what could – and should – be done was to change professional practice and the law in ways which directly challenged parental (i.e. paternal) power and authority.

The 'non-emancipation of children' explanatory account was informed by books such as Parton's *The Politics of Child Abuse* (1985) arguing for a more broadly based understanding of the mistreatment of children, and Hoyles's *Changing Childhood* (1979) arguing for the emancipation and enfranchisement of children. The legal world was beginning to raise questions about children involved in legal proceedings being denied a voice in decisions made about them. The topicality of this view is demonstrated by the way it found explicit expression in the Cleveland Report itself (published just after the research was completed) in Butler-Sloss' now well-known phrase: 'Children must be treated as people, not objects of professional concern' (Butler-Sloss 1988).

Its linked conduct-prescribing account argued for according children greater citizenship rights and, especially, giving them a greater say in decisions made about their own upbringing and welfare. It supported the notion of codifying children's rights (as in the UN *Declaration of the Rights of the Child*). It stressed that parental rights should yield to children's rights, once a child is capable of making an informed decision and acting autonomously. This principle was clearly influential, for example, upon the Gillick Appeal Ruling (*Gillick vs West Norfolk and Wisbech Area Health Authority*, 1986), which was also in the news and subject to public debate at the time.

> *Interrupter: So let me see if I've got this right. Stainton Rogers and Stainton Rogers found three linked explanatory/social policy accounts: a family dysfunction explanation linked to a policy of 'working with the family'; a feminist-inspired 'misuse of male power to sexually exploit children' explanation linked to a policy of removing children from their families; and a 'child abuse as a consequence of children's powerlessness' explanation linked to a policy of promoting children's emancipation. Is that right?*

Beryl: Yes, in a nutshell, you have got it nicely summarized there.

> *Interrupter: Though you admit the actual data were a lot more messy, don't you?*

Beryl: Yes, they were, I-as-them admit it.

> *Interrupter: I can live with that. Now, if I've got it right, what you're saying is that the links are not causal (adopting one does not impel you to propose the other) but narrative, they are tectonically contingent, right?*

Beryl: Right! Our concern is with textuality and tectonics – the topological qualities of narrative contingency, not of causal links between 'essences in the head' and action.

> *Interrupter: Well, how come then you are basing your interpretation of links on the observation of contingency between individual people's responses? Isn't that just like saying they are evincing consistent attitudes?*

Beryl: No, I'm not saying that at all. All I'm suggesting is that there is contingency of expression (i.e. Q-sorting). In other words, we see it as happening because particular individuals are voicing certain texts-on-texts. We could call these 'liberal-humanist', 'feminist' and 'rights-analysis' voices, which people weave in and out of the different domains of explanation and social policy.

> *Interrupter: Well, I'm still not terribly convinced, it seems a very subtle distinction to me.*

Beryl: Yes the distinction is subtle, but crucial. It comes down to viewing the people in the study as not so much the sites of 'attitudes' or 'beliefs', but as the vehicles through which textuality and tectonics get expressed, the sites through which they are presenced.

Engaging in Q-sorting produces narrative 'snapshots' which freeze (i.e. make substantive) expression at a particular point in time. But it is perfectly feasible for people to endorse all three of the sets of ideas Stainton Rogers and Stainton Rogers identified: to argue, for example, that the physical abuse and neglect of children has a different 'cause' from sexual abuse, and that these each require a different response; and that there are indeed other forms of mistreatment (such as dispensing with children as if they were mere 'objects of professional concern') which require yet other ways of dealing with them. Which one gets expressed will depend not on any 'essence' like a person's 'attitudes', but what is salient at a particular moment.

> *Interrupter: I think I begin to understand. You're interested, really, in the accounts themselves, and how they inter-act with each other, where they come from, what moulds and changes them, and so on. Your participants are acting as Polaroid 'cameras', taking instant 'snap-shots', from which you can begin to build up a picture of a larger whole*

Beryl: Yes, or perhaps more like the cameras on satellites taking pictures of different parts of the earth.

> *Interrupter: Which, I assume, is why you can only get the bare bones of your analysis from interpreting the Q-sort data alone.*

Beryl: That's right. In a Q-study, the really instructive 'data' at our disposal are the cultural knowledge which comes from working in the field, talking to lots of people, attending conferences and sitting at the kitchen table cutting bits out of newspapers.

Interrupter: So the interesting stuff tends to come not from the number crunching that produces the factor scores – that's only really a device to get you thinking – but the skill (and access to what people are writing and saying) with which you devise the Q-samples, and the access you then have to the cultural marketplace of ideas in order to be able to do a cultural analysis on the factors you uncover. In fact you are doing textual analysis, just like discourse analysts or, say, filmic theorists. It's just that instead of using, say, movies or interview data as the texts upon which you work, you use the factor patterns as texts.

Beryl: Sort of – there is a difference, which is that the Q-sorting is itself a form of analysis, so that we share the task with our participants.

Study 2: Explanatory, rhetorical and conduct-prescriptive accounts in relation to child sexual abuse

Three years after this first study, Marcia Worrell carried out a further study on accounts of and for, this time, specifically the *sexual* abuse of children (Worrell and Stainton Rogers 1992). This study comprised three linked 69-item Q-sorts dealing with three concourses: one on definitions, explanations and understandings of child sexual abuse; one on debates, rhetorical arguments and moral analysis surrounding the subject of adult–child sexual activity; and one on social policy towards child sexual abuse. These were undertaken by 82 participants, who included a diversity of professionals working in the field and a proportion of 'ordinary folks'. Adults who reported having been sexually abused in childhood also took part in the study, together with adults who reported having engaged in sexual activity with children (who were serving prison sentences following conviction) and adults who were recruited because they expressed a willingness to argue for the acceptability of consensual sexual activity between adults and children.

Explanatory accounts

The family dysfunction and feminist explanatory accounts were re-discovered. However, the account identified (by cultural analysis) as the dominant professional orthodoxy in this field was based on a psychodynamic explanation of harm, and an assumption of a 'cycle of abuse' whereby sexually abusive experiences in childhood were seen to make men susceptible to becoming abusers and women unable to protect their children. The 'seeds' of both of these had been evident in the feminist account in the previous study, and it could be argued that this indicates a fracturing of the original

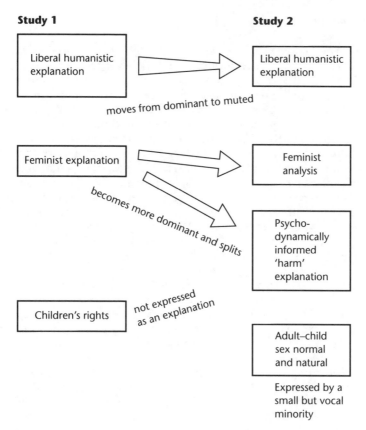

Figure 8.2 Shifts in explanatory accounts between the first study (Stainton Rogers and Stainton Rogers 1989) and the second study (Worrell and Stainton Rogers 1992).

into one focusing on a feminist analytic (but psychodynamically informed) and one focusing on the psychodynamic notion of harm (but informed, still, by feminism). Figure 8.2. sets out the changes (over time and because of the differences in the two studies) in the ecology of explanatory discourses.

A further three explanatory accounts were also found: one drawing on a bio-medical model of sexual drives; one centred around notions of cultural relativity; and one viewing consensual adult–child sex as a 'perfectly normal' manifestation of child sexuality. This was expressed by five men who saw themselves as explicitly advocating 'boy-love' (their terminology). The child enfranchisement account was not expressed in terms of an explanation, but in the parallel Q-set on ideologizations, alongside two others – one broadly psychodynamic in flavour and the other a scientized discourse of individual, biologically caused pathology (i.e. a medical model).

Conduct prescription

So far as conduct prescription was concerned, three main accounts emerged once more. The first argued for action and policy directed to 'punishment, control and protection'. There were clear commonalities with the interventionist 'remove the child' conduct-prescriptive account found in the previous study, but the emphasis appears to have shifted to a focus on longer-term outcomes – arguing for imprisonment of perpetrators and therapy for abused children. This was articulated by those expressing both the specifically feminist and the psychodynamic explanatory accounts (i.e. it reconstitutes the split which we have speculated had arisen in respect to explanation). As well as being evinced by a number of specialist professionals working in the field, it was also, interestingly, expressed by a number of adult 'survivors' of child sexual abuse. It stressed the need to treat abusers as criminals, punishing them both for the wrong they have done and as a means to protect children from the risk they pose. Resources were seen to be needed to be directed to providing therapeutic intervention to help sexually abused children overcome the harm they have suffered.

The second conduct-prescriptive account also echoed one found earlier. Although this new study had shifted the focus onto sexual abuse, this account nonetheless (as before in relation to physical abuse) argued for 'working with the family', here in the form of treating (rather than punishing) perpetrators, and for a balance to be made between protecting the rights of vulnerable children and meeting the needs and civil rights of alleged offenders. This conduct-prescriptive account was articulated by a number of professionals (who tended not to be specialists in child protection work) offering a family dysfunction explanation of child abuse, which viewed sexual abusers as 'damaged individuals' rather than evil people. Not surprisingly, it was also articulated by convicted offenders serving prison sentences for sexual assaults against children.

The third conduct-prescriptive account identified, however, was new: an explicitly paedophilic account, expressed by the participants who had provided a 'boy-love' explanation. It argued for decriminalizing consensual adult–child sex, making a clear distinction between loving relationships between adults and children, and sexual 'crimes' (i.e. where violence or coercion was used). In other words, this account argued for the sexual 'emancipation' of children, such that a child's sexual conduct (including sex between child and adult) should be sanctioned – no more a criminal offence than adult sexual conduct of the same kind. From this perspective, the notion of criminality should be reserved – as it is for adults – for cases of assault (i.e. non-consensual sex).

Links between the children's emancipation account (expressed in the debates, rhetorical arguments and moral analysis Q-sort) and this paedophilic conduct-prescriptive account were found. In other words, the expression of the argument for decriminalizing consensual adult–child sex was linked to the expression of an overall child-emancipatory argument. This rhetorical account on 'children's rights' was also expressed by Worrell, Stainton Rogers and Stainton Rogers and indeed, some others of Beryl Curt's amanuenses.

Interrupter: Didn't those bits of you find that rather uncomfortable?

Beryl: Yes and no. It did not surprise them that the rhetoric of 'children's rights', used by us to mandate promoting children's broad entitlements to citizenship, will also be expressed by those who wish to justify promoting children's sexual rights. A consistent narrative can be woven around such a set of ideas, and certainly they themselves were concerned about the way, say, that law intended to promote children's rights to make decisions for themselves (such as the Gillick ruling) seems to have become constrained to allowing them to consent to contraception but not to sex! This seems to be operating more broadly, in that a legal minor is now seen as capable of consenting to life-saving medical treatment but incapable of refusing it.

The researchers in this study were concerned, nevertheless, when they observed that children's rights arguments were being used to rationalize the sexual exploitation of children. This they saw as an undesirable conduct-warranting potential of the children's rights argument, if one is naive to the power imbalance between children and adults.

Study 3: Cross-cultural tectonics

Additional insight into this whole problematic area is offered by a further study conducted by Beryl Curt with colleagues in Catalunya which explored understandings of childhood, childrearing and child welfare policy between our two countries.

Interrupter: Beryl got to do this one in her entirety, I see!

Beryl: That's another long story. Fantastic place, Barcelona. I had a great time.

In both communities, an old-style 'traditional' popular understanding was expressed, in both cases by 'ordinary people' with strong religious beliefs. This centred on a perception of the child's immaturity, children's need for discipline, love and 'family life', and the rights of parents to bring up their children as they saw fit. In both communities, we also discovered a 'children's rights' discourse, although its exposition was more clearly and more frequently articulated in Catalunya, with an explicit argument in their accounts focusing on children's sexual emancipation. There it was expressed not only by academics, but by professionals working in the field and by feminists. Here in the UK, these latter groups expressed, instead, a much more cautious 'protectionist' account, more alive to the dangers of the sexual exploitation of children if 'children's rights' are extended into the area of sexuality.

> *Interrupter: What do you think these differences are due to?*

Beryl: Well, I want to avoid the rather dodgy story that people in the UK are more 'advanced' or 'sophisticated' than Catalunya in their 'understanding of the issues'. I think there are probably a number of factors, but possibly the most obvious one is the greater permeability of the UK to ideas from the USA (given, to some degree, a common language and a history of cross-talk between professionals and academics in this field). But I also think that the political scenes in the two places makes a difference. The UK is still very much in the grip of post-Thatcherism, while Catalunya seemed to me to be still celebrating and enjoying the emergence of democracy, and its freedoms (including, in Barcelona, a very considerable amount of sexual freedom). Also, I suspect that religious differences played a part. I definitely think more research will need to be done to tease this out further.

> *Interrupter: And you're volunteering? I see, you want another excuse to drink beer in the Ramblas, go rapping with Thomas Ibañez, joy-riding with Joan, living it up with Lupi, making hay with Miguel and Margot . . .*

Beryl: Perish the thought, it never crossed my mind. But to get back (again) to the overall story about these data, this issue they raise about the 'hidden dangers' in the 'children's rights' discourse provides a good example of the kind of 'horror' analysts like Parker and Burman argue will be let loose by according epistemological equivalence to all texts. Our counter-argument is that it is better to expose such horrors, and thus to be able to learn from their exposition about the ways in which a particular account may be used to justify actions which we, certainly, would not intend.

We nevertheless regard it as critically important for it to be possible to consider issues of children's sexual rights, without being immediately accused of being apologists for the paedophile lobby. Elsewhere Stainton Rogers and Stainton Rogers have argued, in relation to the overall issue of child concern:

> What this boils down to is a recognition that heroic 'child saving' or 'child protection' and villainous 'child mistreatment' are not two different kinds of action, with opposing mandates (to work for the good or for the bad of children). They are two alternative facets, or readings, of virtually any kind of conduct towards children. Similarly children themselves are not either innocent victims of adult mistreatment, or culpable delinquents whose anti-social behaviour must be controlled. Rather these (and many more in between) are alternative placements that the adult world creates for children, into which individual children are located at different times, in different circumstances,

according to the adult gaze adopted. All childhoods are oppressive, if by that we mean power unequal . . .

Once we address a critical polytextualist analysis to concern, we have to transcend the limits of a singularising discourse, in which the 'goodies' and the 'baddies' in the plot are so universally and uniquely identified, both in terms of the adults and children concerned. What must be explored (and all that can ever be at issue) are prospective (and hence speculative) or *post hoc* moral cost–benefit analyses of the alternative readings of actions and conduct towards children, and of locating children themselves in different discourses of responsibility and blame. It is this perturbating doubt within an arena of plural textuality which must be the basis of child concern. (Stainton Rogers and Stainton Rogers 1992a: 191–2)

The warranting of conduct

Examining what happens when Q-sorts are linked in this way enables us to see how one conduct-prescriptive account may be predicated on two rather different explanatory accounts (see Fig. 8.3). We were fortunate that because there were data available from an earlier study, and the researchers had a strong engagement with the discourses involved via the work they do, it was possible to make sense of contingencies by looking at their common epistemological roots. In this study, the 'punish, control and protect' conduct-prescriptive account seems to have been predicated upon both the newly dominant psychoanalytic professional explanatory discourse and upon the feminist explanatory account, both drawing on a psychodynamically informed rhetorical set of arguments. These offer a 'harm warrant' which justifies punishing abusers and treating abuse victims, which in itself justifies strong intervention. (See O'Dell 1993, for a more detailed treatment of the 'harm warrant'.)

The decriminalization of the adult–child sex conduct-prescriptive account is warranted by the rhetoric of 'children's rights' and a story which tells that consensual adult–child sex is 'normal and natural'. It is the latter, however, which is specifically conduct-prescriptive, and that can be used to justify the sexual exploitation (rather than emancipation) of children. As before, 'family dysfunction' prescribes 'working with the family', here by treating the abuser.

Conclusions

In this chapter, we have shown that contingency between, say, explanation and conduct can be empirically explored, without recourse to any causal model. Rather, what is proposed is that textuality not merely describes or accounts for re-presentations and understandings, but can be used to warrant or prescribe conduct. Understandings, we suspect, always imply conduct (i.e. contain elements from which appropriate conduct may be inferred). We

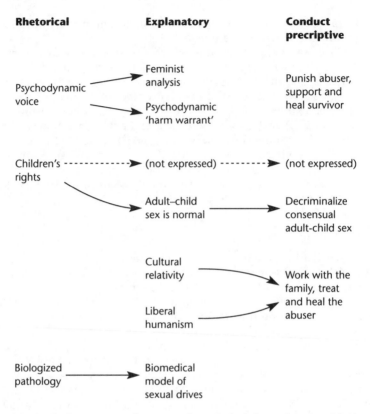

Figure 8.3 Links between explanatory, rhetorical and conduct-prescriptive accounts in the second study (Worrell and Stainton Rogers 1992).

could say, then, that understanding 'contains' within its textuality a transitive prescience *of* conduct, which, when made substantive, can actively warrant conduct – conduct is always immanent within understanding. We identified an example of this, where an understanding centred on ideas about the emancipation of children (which implies emancipation of children's sexual rights) can be used either exploitatively, to warrant adult–child sexual activity, or (as we see it) non-exploitatively, to warrant, say, giving children greater rights in law to self-determination.

In this chapter, we have also been able to show that sampling over time and between closely related concourses allows us an *entré* into tectonics. To do this requires not just Q-method (or something like it) but, crucially, exegesis and cultural analysis, as it is only the latter which allows us to speculate about, for example, the shifting sands of discursive activity. We were able to get some clues about the way in which ideas about 'child sexual abuse' have undergone rapid change, within professional circles at least. To uncover longer-term shifting of the tectons of textuality requires another approach.

Elsewhere Stainton Rogers and Stainton Rogers (1992a) have examined professional literature to explore the ways in which concern over childhood sexuality has moved over the last hundred years from a preoccupation with 'self-abuse' (i.e. masturbation) to a preoccupation with 'child abuse' (i.e. an analysis and a conclusion paralleling Foucault's well-known genealogy of sexuality more generally, cf. Foucault 1979a). At the turn of the century, 'experts' like Walling (1909) raised concern about the harm caused by 'self-abuse'. Symptoms were listed, cautionary tales told, and the 'fact' that children were taught this vice (usually, according to Walling, by governesses and servants) was no more than a throw-away line. In the 1980s, 'experts' (e.g. Vizard and Tranter 1988) told a startlingly similar tale, listing much the same symptoms, exhorting much the same cautions, but here it is the 'fact' that sexually abused children tend to masturbate which is virtually dismissed.

We are not suggesting that because we can now view Walling's obsession with 'self-abuse' as risible, we can dismiss current concern about child sexual abuse as similarly ludicrous. To do so would be to side-step legitimate concerns over the sexual exploitation of children. But we do find the resonances instructive. Both, we would argue, indicate that when knowledge is textualized into being, its production is purposeful – whether to warrant paedophilia, professional power, or the regulation of child conduct and child power. Focusing on the conduct-potential of what is textualized is, therefore, a critical and essential task. If we turn our backs on it, then we deserve to be accused of hiding in ivory towers. How we make sure we do not is one of the main agendas of our last chapter, where towards the end we will specifically examine how issues of child abduction, rape and murder may be addressed within a climate of problematization.

9

Inconclusion

Beryl Curt (1969–1993)
Ms Curt, now widely hailed as the meteorologist of the 'climate of problematization', gained that reputation primarily through one work – the
posthumously published *Textuality and Tectonics*. Known to aficionados and
critics alike as 'T 'n' T', it exploded into the nineties to become 'the bible
of a generation struggling against the tyranny of meaning' (Hewett Stall,
New Statesperson and Collectivity). From graffiti to gymnosophy, tee-shirts
to theses, 'T 'n' T' became a pro-text (one of the many neologisms Beryl
insinuated into our language) that signalled disturbance and trouble. Yet
it is typical of the Beryline phenomenon that little is known of Ms Curt
herself, even her birth has been hotly contested . . .

Beryl: Hold it, hold it right there! That isn't funny! There's plenty of life in
me yet. I resist closure, even in the narrative form of writing my own
epitaph.

*Interrupter: Revenge at last! I've been doing a little reading myself, and I
was much taken by Ann Game's final words to the reader 'if there is any
truth, it is the truth of the body' (1991: 192).*

Beryl: 'A *little* reading' is right. Ann Game uses the notion of body not because she wants us to think on death, but on disturbing pleasure – the way that what she calls 'open texts' can be used to joyfully perturbate the given, and to move us without destination. Mine is such a story, and hence without any need for closure. So there!

Interrupter: But this is the last chapter, so how can you avoid it being **a fin de Berylennium?**

Beryl: Well I could begin writing another book or planning a performance for the Edinburgh Festival . . .

Senior Editor: Hey you lot, stop squabbling. The manuscript for this one is now well overdue. I respectfully suggest you get it finished before you start contemplating the next.

[Beryl and the Interrupter, duly chastened, go into a huddle, to decide what to do with the last chapter].

We have decided, for once, to approach the last chapter relatively traditionally – to extract some of the general themes we have identified as pertinent to the 'climate of problematization', and to bring these together as a broad overview of the position we are seeking to promote.

Going critical?

We begin our review with a project which pervades the book – that of 'going critical'. This draws upon one of the most compelling icons of our times – nuclear fission. Unstable isotopes, bombarded with neutrons, split into fragments giving off further neutrons, which promotes further fragmentation leading to a chain reaction. Implode together fragments to make a critical mass and you have a first-generation atomic bomb. Control the disintegration, and you have a nuclear reactor. It offers, we think, a nice metaphor for what we have been trying to do in this book.

By now it goes without saying that the notion of 'going critical', can be read in a variety of ways. One way of reading it, which we would obviously want to avoid, is too literally, as if it were a causal proposition derived from the covering laws of textuality and tectonics. Beryl has no ambitions to survive in the form of an ephemeral oracle, spouting pre-recorded utterings at regular intervals about the crises she has predicted.

Interrupter: Yuk! Swallowed a dictionary have we?

Beryl: No, I'm just showing off that I have read Asimov's *Foundation* which has a psycho-historian, Hari Seldon, doing precisely that – coming back as a hologram-like image to taunt future generations, long after his death – having predicted what will happen to them.

We are more interested in the possibility that people will find the ideas we have suggested useful, and use them, than in 'becoming famous' as their originators (though some of us think that would be rather cool). But what really interests us is trying to get to a 'critical mass' – of reaching and then convincing enough people of the need to work under a climate of problematization that the chain-reaction becomes unstoppable (tritunic forces notwithstanding). We have (perhaps too optimistically) a hunch that so long as certain criterion conditions are met, it will happen, if nothing else in the realm of science fiction, where, perhaps, such myths belong.

A second reading of 'going critical', which also gives us grief, is any recourse to the grand theme of 'endism' – the present-valorizing arrogance which says that we live in interesting, millennial times. We are very aware here of the bones of Asimov's *Foundation* myth:

> The Old Empire is crumbling into barbarism and Hari Seldon and his band of psychologists see before them only the despair of thousands of years of anarchy, unless they can create a new force – the Foundation dedicated to art, science and technology – the foundation of a new empire. [Dust cover of the Grafton edition, 1960]

Imperialism has never been our aim, and this is a future we distinctly would *not* want to seed! A third reading, which causes us some concern as well, is 'going critical' as a political description or, indeed, prescription. Here we feel a need for a careful clarification. Beryl is tempted to suggest:

Text in
Tecton
Drop out.

But another psychologist (Timothy Leary), in another time-warp, seems to have pre-plagiarized her. 'Going critical' is not a mantra set to release an outbreak of peace, love and understanding. Just because we can envision the dystopias we might wish to disenable does not mean we have a utopia we wish to enable. We are not about to set up a commune so that Beryl can live 'happily ever after'.

What then is the reading we are employing? Is it 'going critical?' as a continuous questioning – a questioning which can be made to perpetually surf along the flux of possibilities that are opened up by the notion of criticality, but a questioning which also does not assume any antonymous answer and that is always and ever reflexive. Taking reflexivity not as a 'thing' but as a box of tools, among its implements is surely a device that positions such efforts as both objects within and subjects for our operations. Expand that notion, and we would be in a universe of reflexion, infinite in its ultimate possibilities but bounded by the lineaments of knowledging (power-knowledge synarchy if you prefer) at each time and place and space of action.

If the boundedness of discursion points to a condition of discursivity (or as we call it, textuality), the boundarying dynamics of discourse point to a condition of constructivity (or as we call it, tectonics). Further, if discursivity is taken not as singular but as multiple (i.e. a polytextuality) and we are not talking of discourse but discourses, then reflexions within and between that polytextuality and those tectonics are radical (i.e. thoroughgoing) and potentially critical. We have a quest without a quested in which even that new concern, 'the text', can be doubted.

Interrupter: Aren't you getting into another tautological loop again?

Beryl: Not with you beside me Tonto. We are starting to make a great duo. Do you know 'The second time around?'

Interrupter: [Taking out his guitar] No, but if you hum it, I'll play along.

The most common concern addressed within the climate of problematization is the pantext. Nevertheless, we (i.e. Beryl) have had problems with the notion of 'text' and we know we are not alone in being worried about it. The term is at least as much troubled as it is troubling, not least because it can be seen to invite an idealist reading, and hence engenders, all too often, a realist reaction. Just as crucially, 'text', like 'discourse', seem to cry out in language-use (at least it does in English language-use) for appropriation as an 'object' of study. This readiness in current language for the easy production of some textual or discursive discipline suggests that, say, 'discourse' and 'analysis' conjoin through more than random contingencies. Such conjunctions appear as though on an established associational chreod.

We are reminded of thoroughly Modern projects like psychoanalysis and content analysis and all the subject/object problems they bring with them. (Here, as elsewhere, we are drawing upon the second of our analytics – that of tectonics – in order to make the space for the first. This condition of motility is deliberate and desired.) If part of the problem with using the notion of 'text' is that of its summonability, just as troublesome is the tension which surfaces when we juxtapose 'text' against that other pandect, 'discourse'. Again, we do not think we are alone in worrying about this problem. 'Text' implies an aura of stasis, requiring qualification to move it. Game (1991) does this by introducing the idea of textual practice; reading and re-writing. Potter and Wetherell (1987) do so by according agency to texts (i.e. emphasizing that they *do* things).

Discourse, however, at least outwith French theory, runs to and fro (like its root), although apparently with (somewhat) more direction than a headless chicken. Wanting an analytic within that network of meanings, but not wanting those troubles, we appropriated the more vacant, less adopted term 'textuality'. Once we had it, we worked it into new possibilities – through its counterpoint with tectonics. What we have sought to achieve through textuality and tectonics is to use them as dialogic analytics in order to make possible (sometimes!) a reflexively moderated, self-sustaining criticality. The Beryline enterprise, with its dislocation of authorship, is part of that – with Joni Mitchell, Beryl would like to say to others that:

part of you flows out through me
in these lines from time to time.

Interrupter: Now I know you care.

Beryl: By now, you are part of my disturbing pleasure.

For us, an important part of that fluxional ambition is what it does to and for notions of empirical work. In our view, 'going critical?' involves the continual reading, and hence re-writing (to borrow Game's terms), of the expressed structurations of textuality. One route we used to this was Q-methodology. We used its formal procedure of pattern analysis to mimic the informal pattern analysis of everyday knowledging, to re-cover some of the manifold of patterns of propositions which are expressed by persons-in-culture and culture-in-persons. However (despite the accusations of others to the contrary), we regard Q-methodology as far from the be-all and end-all of the empirical procedures available for 'going critical?' For a start, in any such study, whatever manifold of positions we were able to abduce, whatever links and disjunctions we were able to observe, Q-method inevitably leaves out any sense of short-term change and flux. In other words, it is only really able to address textuality, except where used sequentially (as, say, in the sequence of studies described in Chapter 8).

One example of our other analytics for scrutiny is that which we have called 'thematic decomposition', by which we mean any improvisory narrative proceeding from a thematic issue (see Chapter 5). How we read the procession that emerges can employ tectonic language. The tectons of knowledge that a Q-study freeze-frames can now be seen in flux and mutual tension intra- and inter-personally. Concurrently, we can attempt a genealogical interrogation of that lithosphere of knowledges. We can consider, for example, what seems to have been sweated out at different depths of any moving text and what that may imply about past tectons of personal or cultural biography now subducted under the present textuality. And at every point, provided we can (with whatever mutual aid we can muster) keep this mass in moderated criticality, we will also know that it could have been told otherwise, that Beryl's subduction can be another reader's 'unconscious', that her analytic counterpoint is just, to others, another text. More broadly still, the whole tectonic treatment is in textuality (just as textuality is 'over' tectonics). Like the snake Ouroboros, we (Beryl) have swallowed our tail.

> *Interrupter: Wow! I'm almost moved myself. Did you have a prior career in sales or religious evangelism by any chance?*

Beryl: Well, I have studied rhetoric and I thought a strong, positive position statement might end that section with 'a bang not a whimper'.

The minimalist agenda

One major feature of 'going critical?' is a thorough-going agnosticism over all God-games (cf. Haraway 1991), academic or otherwise. The stress upon agnosticism rather than atheism is deliberate. Unbelief is also a dogma, a singularization. As Korzybski put it: 'There are two ways to slide easily through life; to believe everything or to doubt everything; both ways save us from thinking' (quoted in Peter 1980). The moving, fluxional 'affirmative doubt' and 'doubtful affirmation' of critical polytextualism is our attempt to avoid just such a slide. In discarding absolute doubt along with absolute certainty, we have sought to minimalize the fixed baggage we carry. There is, of course, a price. Like itinerant jongleurs we have a lot 'in the air' compared to the little in our hands at any one point. Indeed, we would argue that a minimal craft (in terms of its materiel) is not to be taken thereby as a *simple* craft.

In Chapter 2, we made use of the topological metaphor of the Möbius strip and the Klein bottle to challenge notions of interiority. Like critical polytextualism, topology (or analysis situs) is an analysis of situation or position. Topological geometry is a minimalized discipline compared to plane and solid geometry. Quantitative considerations (such as lengths, areas and volumes) are removed – rather as they are in our own work. But because it challenges the taken-for-granteds of both popular and formal, Euclidian geometry, it is not at all simple to use. In fact, it directly confronts the very term 'simple'. In topology, if we draw a circle on a sheet of rubber and then stretch or squeeze that sheet, the form remains a 'simple closed curve' whatever the convolutions, the fiords and isthmuses we give to it.

Minimalism, as a situated worrying of positioned assumptions is a means to challenge the 'natural attitude'. If one can trust nothing, then the best way to start travelling is to travel light, and each episodic transformation should leave behind yet another discarded veil of Maya.

Interrupter: Maya the Great Goddess of Illusion, I presume – Beryl as a PoMo stripper. This I have got to see!

Beryl: Not if I can help it, sunshine. My first target is going to be your unreconstructed scopophilia.

Salomeic phantasies aside, we are arguing that the climate of problematization is, for now at least, the best condition of minimalization around. The term 'the climate of problematization' is itself thoroughly minimalist. We have adopted it rather than some of the better known buzz-words (like social constructionism and postmodernism) to describe our endeavour because it makes only the most minimal of claims about what we are up to. It is more 'true' to the principles we have embraced (in disturbing pleasure) and hence avoids a number of problems which have beset those other formulations. For a start, it gets us out of what Graham (1992) identifies as the three paradoxes of postmodernist social science: fragmentation, periodization and grand narrative.

The fragmentation paradox, according to Graham, arises from the criticism that postmodernism is no more than modernism which has reached a stage of crumbling dilapidation. Postmodernism, in this analysis, is a thin pastiche used to paper over the cracks of all that is falling to bits underneath. As applied to social science, ever increasing disciplinary specialism and a proliferation of local 'crises' have resulted not in anything genuinely new or different from what went before, but merely something which has the chimeral appearance of novelty simply because it *is* so fragmentated. But the

real problem about fragmentation, Graham argues, is not a matter of nomen-
clature, but that the postmodernism is seen to lack direction, to be bereft of
any critical power, and thus lead to an intellectual stale-mate.

> The problem for the social sciences lies in the possibility that the
> messages of postmodernism are imported in a simplistic form with
> 'many voices' becoming 'any voices' and critical analysis forgotten.
> This would not only be politically disenabling, . . . but also intellectu-
> ally disenabling. (Graham 1992: 202)

The periodization paradox arises predominantly out of the reading that for
a movement to be 'post-' something (be it modernism, structuralism or
whatever) implies that what is going on is a sequential process, an idea
which elides all too easily into the triumphant story of progress – a story
totally inimical to postmodernist thought (hence the paradox). The 'grand
narrative' paradox is in similar vein. One of postmodernism's central tenets
is its rejection of the imperialist pretension of modernism and its refutation
of the quest for explain-all 'grand theories'. The paradox arises because:

> . . . having removed the metanarratives of truth and rationality, the
> postmodernist has no ground or transcendent standpoint from which
> to convince the sceptic of the rightness or truth of any postmodern
> view. The self-referential quality of local language games denies any
> such broader foundations which could establish the truth of claims
> outside the rules of particular language games. (Graham 1992: 208)

Adopting a minimal agenda – one which claims to be no more than working under a 'climate' and to do no more than 'problematize' – means such
problems can be neatly ox-bowed (as we described in Chapter 4). Viewing
the endeavour in which we are engaged in minimalist terms is entirely consistent with renouncing 'meta-narratives of truth', and avoids altogether the
singularized tale of the victorious overthrow of an old order. At the same
time, it celebrates what Game has called the 'disturbing pleasure' of problematizing. We have argued the need for affirmative doubt (i.e. doubt that
is purposeful and functional) and doubtful affirmation (i.e. having the courage to let go of the hand-rail of truth and external validation). These to us
are the basic tenets of a 'climate of problematization', which, in their minimalism, seek to encourage 'disturbing pleasure' without bogging ourselves
down with a load of cumbersome and unnecessary conceptual baggage.

Embracing the minimalist agenda of a 'climate of problematization' also
avoids all the wranglings about what 'kind' of social constructionism, or
what variant of postmodernism, we are into. We can 'get into' (i.e. make use
of the ideas) of any or none of them, at particular points in time, the choice
being one of pragmatics rather than doctrine or affiliation. In this sense, to
be into minimalism is to become a kind of conceptual scavenger (a term
which is these days becoming more positive in its eco-friendly credentials).

A second important feature of minimalism is the transcendence of discipline boundaries. Such transdisciplinarity needs, we have argued, not only
to encompass the conventional disciplines of the 'social sciences' (most

notably psychology, sociology and anthropology), but also some of the new emergent disciplines (e.g. cultural studies, film studies) and those of the humanities which have been re-formulated under the climate of problematization (such as art history and literature). Transdisciplinarity is minimalist in that it makes no claims about what should, in any specific sense, be the focus of study – the individual, the group, the society or the culture. Indeed, such markers, under problematization, lose their concretized 'thinghood', and come to be treated as no more than particular forms of language practice. Hence they can no longer act as seed-crystals around which either conceptual or empirical work can accrete. What remain are minimalist concerns – concerns solely with the way texts are told and re-told, read and re-written, how knowledge is storied into being, and what these activities can be used to achieve, unfettered by demarcation disputes and 'open' to all, irrespective of their biography or affiliation (under erasure to avoid its sexist connotations).

A third and critical aspect of our minimalism is when it is applied to the empirical. It includes dissolving the assumed chain-of-events in which theory predicates method, which predicates inquiry, by which hypothesized 'facts' are established or refuted (or, to put it more bluntly, data get published or thrown in the bin) as a result of empirical investigation. In its place we have suggested using the analytics of textuality and tectonics, together with methods which seek to do no more than elucidate patterns of constituted re-presentation, sense-making and connation. Such methods, used in conjunction with abduction (see Chapter 4), seek only to illuminate local and contingent 'truths' rather than engaging in meta-theoretical 'Truth Games', and make no claims other than to make possible 'readings' and 're-writings'.

Disenchantment

A major theme orchestrated into our book, and another critical part of 'going critical?', is that of 'dis-enchantment'. Like a number of the words we have homed in on, we find its ambiguity both mildly amusing and helpful in drawing attention to what we are up to. The origin of the word 'enchantment' is to do with the use, in magic, of songs or spells to beguile, impel or charm another into a state in which they will believe what the sorcerer wants them to believe, or are prevented from seeing what the sorcerer wants them not to see, in order that they do what the sorcerer wants them to do. Thus dis-enchantment, in this sense, is to do with the breaking of such spells – re-gaining the ability to resist the beguiling of taken-for-granted 'realities' and hence to re-gain the ability for self-directed action. A more recent reading of 'disenchantment' carries a strong sense of cynicism, disillusionment and doubt: a regretful feeling of becoming worldly wise; the scepticism spawned by discovering things are not so bright and shiny new as they had seemed.

The climate of problematization has perturbated both the certainties of the liberal disciplines and our sense of the enduring nature and invulnerability of the social worlds (from anthropology to art) that they address. The ways in which those social worlds were individually held together and corporately kept apart stands recast, under problematization, as a 'grand illusion' from which we have become dis-illusioned. In saying this, we are not suggesting that such 'grand illusions' were deceits (i.e. deliberate, conspiratorial hidings or maskings), but enchantments which glamoured and will continue to glamour pressing realities into being because, in a sense, that is an inevitable consequence of the synarchy of power/knowledge. It is an enchantment, specifically, which had fixed us (as scholars as much as ordinary, every-day people) into positions of seeming competent-knowingness without our knowing it.

The climate of problematization has, we believe, given us the words and ideas with which to break that spell, with which to become disenchanted. It has enabled us to doubt not only the experiences we structure and the structures we experience, but also the phenomenology/structuralism, ontology/epistemology distinctions upon which they are grounded.

Indeed, it has brought into possibility a troubling of the notion of grounding itself. This is brought into the field of plausibility, not by mere magic but by speculative fiction – specifically, by producing an imaginary future (and future-in-the-present) dubbed 'the postmodern'. From this constituted, conditional condition one can worry the two hundred years past and the past-in-the-present as if it were an era of social history and the history of ideas – the Modern. In so far as the present is posed as though it contained both the part and the future, the climate of problematization can also be a highly politicized forum. But it can also deconstruct notions of history and of politics away from a story of triumphant progress. The climate of problematization can, so to speak, act as a metaphor for the conditions it discourses upon, and those conditions are critically polytextualized. In other words, once again it contains the conditions for swallowing its own tail. As its reflexive possibilities are realized (and/or their inter-textuality with other reflexive orientations recognized), a stark reading of the climate of problematization is produced. It, too, is 'socially constructed' like everything else. 'Socially constructed' itself now has to appear in warning marks because the term social (like the term psychological) is no longer felt to be safe within the minimalism of transdisciplinarity.

The social is challenged not just as a representation masquerading as the represented, but also for representing its purported product – the subject as a political in-valid. Furthermore, it is an invalid whose only basis for resistance is extra-social, its essential biologicality (e.g. its gender or its unconscious). Of course, this re-reading is only possible because every story is now critically polytextualized against every other story. And with the re-reading comes the possibility of re-writing.

This heavily textual way of putting things itself is not, of course, accidental, the climate of problematization being deeply discursive. If we can discourse ourselves into a problematic, we can discourse ourselves out of it again, rather like the man of Thessaly:

He jumped into a bramble bush
And scratched out both his eyes.
And when he saw his eyes were out
With all his might and main
He jumped into another bush
And scratched them in again.
                (Traditional nursery rhyme taken from I. and P. Opie 1955: 140)

Worldliness

When talking of enchantment, we noted that its more recent imputation has
to do with a sense of worldly cynicism – the end-state of a process where
prior illusions (of grandeur, of human betterment, of finding the Holy Grail
of Truth) have been crushed, because 'it just isn't that simple in the real
world'.

Perhaps this notion of 'worldliness' has been the most troublesome theme
we have had to grapple with in this book. On the one hand, we have sought
to tackle the predictable criticism that all we have to offer is a naive relativism, in which not only 'anything goes' but which is incapable of addressing
the 'real problems' which beset humankind and the world we have created.
On the other hand, we have resisted being positioned in the same camp with
critical realists such as Bhaskar (1978) and, to a certain extent, Burman
(1992), Parker (1992a) and Reicher (1993), who, for all their engagement in
problematization, nonetheless are convinced that some 'realities' need to be
inviolate to dissolution. In other words, we can be seen as wanting to have
our cake and eat it (just to get that in before the Interrupter throws it in our
face again).

Under the climate of problematization much has been done to trouble
received understandings of human conduct. Targets have included such reified
essences as attitudes, personality or motivation and their application to
categories such as crime, deviance and psychotic behaviour. Equally, it has
been active in challenging the singularizing (mis)use of such constructs by
practitioners such as social workers, the police, psychotherapists, behaviour
therapists, psychiatrists, personnel officers and management consultants –
and the warranting of their technologies of regulation. Yet worrying the
(taken-for-granted) real does not prevent us – as if anything could – from
reading the (texted) real. And, when we do, that presented condition of
things offers far more in sources of concerned discomfiture than it does in
opportunities for perturbating joy. However, by and large, the climate of
problematization literature has steered clear of tackling issues of transform-
ing human conduct itself, except in highly abstract and/or overtly ideologized terms.

Minimalism and disenchantment do not, as we have said already, have to
imply an empirical nihilism. In asserting this, we seek to avoid the all too
common 'intellectual cold feet' (Graham 1992: 201) which finds the empirical so troubling and troublesome that the only way out seems to be to avoid

the problem altogether. That route, we maintain, leads to the inertia of analysis to the point of paralysis. That is great if all you want to engage in is *salon* gossip (*pour épater les scientistes*, which seems, sometimes, the limit of ambition to which some 'French theorists' aspire). But it is no good if you have any desire to engage with the troubles and suffering which beset humankind and the world it has created.

When we are not beings snide, we are saying that if we are to have any claim to be doing other than, say, dabbling in aesthetics or philosophy, we must be prepared to devise and apply the craft skills of empirical enquiry that will allow us to do considerably more than speculate about how persons-in-culture make sense of and make the world in which we live. In other words, we have in this book argued that there is a place, albeit not a discipline-bound one, for the activity of 'empirical research', and made some suggestions about how this might be pursued. This, we believe, is absolutely necessary, in order to put up a challenge to the welter of 'scientifically proved facts' by which the majority of 'social scientists' currently knowledge so much of our modern world and its troubles and concerns into being. In other words, it is not enough to trouble the received *understandings* of human conduct and the technologies of regulation they warrant. We need to engage directly in knowledge-mongering ourselves, if we are to have any impact on what goes on in the world.

Put bluntly, the climate of problematization will remain a small and local squall, for most people lost somewhere off the edge of the conceptual weather-map, unless and until its winds of change can be seen as having any impact at all on those troubles and concerns. This will not happen out of *salon* gossip or chat-show sound-bights dispensed by a few gurus of postmodernist theorizing. It will only happen when the climate of problematization can be seen to offer a knowledging of its own. To do this means having, however difficult, to address those troubles and concerns empirically.

At the same time, for the ideologized critical polytextualist, just as for utopians down the centuries, transformation of conduct can be prescribed from political analysis. What the climate of problematization is seen as adding is a quantum leap in political analysis (e.g. via Foucault). In this respect, utopians are open to the same criticism as theologians, that every development in philosophy is used as a way of re-packaging the same old stale goods. Nevertheless, at least they have been concerned. One of the most disturbing features of the climate of problematization to some is that it can ironize all concern. While we would argue that the proactive troubling power of open analysis is crucial to any serious addressing of conduct, we would also worry the possibilities of a re-writing of conduct so long as it is reified – strategically or otherwise – around such notions as 'resistance'.

The traditional academic has a worldly 'life' outside of academe. If we take the notions of textuality and tectonics seriously, then there is for us no point at which we cross over from the academic life into real life. All is on the same textual surface, all is moved by common tectonics. Of course, this doesn't mean that we are unaware that there are various stories and practices in which we find ourselves. One marker of that flux of our lives is a shift in local language that we notice as we transit between the discourse of the Beryline collective in academic mode and other (sometimes equally convoluted, sometimes more mundane) discourses.

> *Interrupter: You've lost me. Surely everybody, not just your aristoi, 'changes role' in this way, talks differently at home and at work, differently to their child than to their doctor.*

Beryl: I don't like thinking about this as 'switching roles' as though there was an independent actor hiding away behind the scenes. But, yes, you're absolutely right. If we are all on the same textual surface, how could that experience be unique to a few of us? All that can be distinct comes from transformation – how we re-work it and thereby what it enables for us.

Being analytically unbounded puts a different gloss upon our formal and autobiographical locations in the 'real worlds' of human distress (cf. Chapter 8). If transdisciplinarity is to be used to unbind concern, then it must do so over the manifold. To be critically polytexualized is not just to be concerned with the undoing of the ordinary, the taken-for-granted; it is also to reflect back from that deconstruction to the transformed possibilities of addressing just those ordinary, taken-for-granted concerns that we have recast.

> *Interrupter: I think I see where your argument is leading. You want morality without foundational moral authority, a polis without a foundational political policing. I sense the black flag and quotations from Proudhon and Kropotkin.*

Beryl: If it is an 'anarchy' is it an anarchy under erasure, deconstructed and re-written. But you could just as easily gloss such 'liberation analytics' via Heidegger's notion of concern. Rather than tracing lines of influence, I'd prefer to show what critical polytextualism does: how it fruitfully relocates (rather than rhetorically dodges out of facing) the all too grim 'real'.

> *Interrupter: All right. If you are so certain you can deal with the 'grim real' I think I can offer you what would be many people's worst-case scenario: What does your approach have to say about a man who abducts, rapes and then murders a child? Do you have any insights into what can be done about such horrors?*

Beryl: Well, I can but try.

Tackling a problem in the 'real world'

We are *not*, of course, going to offer particular expertise as 'psychologists', with some special, privileged entré into the 'mind' of the perpetrator. By now, that should not need saying. True to our minimalist principles, all we lay claim to is craft competence in transdisciplinary scrutiny. Moreover, at this late stage, we can only give some hints as to how such a scrutiny might proceed.

The first point to make is that critical polytextual scrutiny does not seek to 'solve problems' but to engage critically with them. This is not, we would stress, a cop-out. As Stainton Rogers and Stainton Rogers (1992a) have noted elsewhere, modernist approaches to issues like the mistreatment of children 'adopt a naive pathology model, [which] assume there is a problem to be solved – that there are self-evident, concrete and particular issues to be tackled' (p. 190). This leads to child concern becoming reconstituted as a moral crusade, in which we are urged to embark on a crusading quest for 'the culprits', either the 'fiends and monsters' who actually commit the crimes, or the vicarious villains, such as those who allow violence to be portrayed in films and television, the patriarchy which promotes hetero-sexual predation, or the lilly-livered liberals who refuse to mete out the punishments which will deter such crimes. This, Stainton Rogers and Stainton Rogers argue 'is to operate within a chimerical fairy-tale world in which, once the brave knight has slain the dragon, children can all live "happily ever after"' (1992a: 190).

Critical polytextualism specifically denies that there are any such simple solutions to problems 'in the real world'. The things which make possible the abduction, rape and murder of children are so deeply enmeshed within our life-world that they cannot, in any meaningful sense, be 'solved'. At the same time we are not arguing for 'reducing' the problem to a mere 'social construction'. Such actions, we would argue, have to be seen as having a compelling *practical* reality in local and contingent terms.

It is perfectly feasible to address such horrors in affirmative doubt over their reified status, and to question the way they have been singularized by totalizing discourses, while still accepting their local and contingent 'reality' *as* horrors. No less is true for any of the other 'climate of problematization' analyses of, say, the 'Gulf War' or the 'Holocaust'. To seek to deny the essential, objective reality of such dreadful incidents is not to dismiss them as 'not having happened', trivialize them, or to in any way dishonour those who were murdered, raped and tortured. It is not, at any level, to condone those who perpetrated these brutal crimes.

However risky, however much it exposes us to misinterpretation, it is none the less critical, we would argue, to be prepared to ask disturbing and troublesome questions about *the ways* these kinds of events are knowledged into being as 'a war', as 'the holocaust', and how child abduction, rape and murder come to be constituted as 'paedophile crime'. To trouble these labels is *not* to deny that they describe horrific, indefensible forms of conduct. It is to positively assert that labelling them can have the effect of sanitizing them, distancing ourselves from them, and thus absolving us as 'ordinary, well-meaning people' from any guilt, responsibility or engagement in mak-ing them possible. We would argue that, in opening up such horrors to critical scrutiny, we are demonstrating *more* not less concern than those who are content to treat them as unproblematic realities. To do the latter, we suggest, allows forms of conduct-warranting knowledge-mongering and world-making to remain uncovered and uncontested. It is these 'cover-ups' that, we believe, it is the job of critical polytextualism to address, and that is what we intend to pursue here.

We would therefore begin our scrutiny of 'the problem' we have been given by asserting our approach is one of *practical realism*, which acknowledges and assumes that, in local and contingent terms, we need have no doubts about the 'evidence' for this set of crimes, *qua* evidence. We will accept that all the terms used – abduction, rape and murder – carry their ordinary meanings and implications; that there is no doubt the man is 'guilty as charged' – that he did all those things, and that he did them knowingly.

In accepting all those ordinary meanings, we can and do also acknowledge and 'own' their ordinary implications – that we feel anger, outrage, and sadness that such a thing could happen. We could not, and would not, then, stand aside, lost in linguistic analysis over, for example, whether death is a social or biological reality. As Berger and Luckmann (1967) pointed out over twenty years ago, 'objective reality' is no less real for us by being socially constructed. In this situation doing nothing is not an option for any 'feeling' person.

This taken as said, the first important thing we can observe is that, in terms of our local and contingent practical reality, cases of child abduction, rape and murder are, thankfully, extremely rare occurrences (see, for example, Jenkins 1992). When men and children are together in the same social space, this only exceedingly rarely leads to this particular chain of events. It is far more probable, for instance, to end in a child's death through a traffic accident, or, even more likely, by an accident in the home. In other countries and at other times, children in the company of men die far more often through famine, warfare, terrorism, illness due to an inadequate supply of clean water, and so on.

So why, we can ask, does child abduction, rape and murder happen so rarely and yet upset us so much? Why does this child death call out for action in a way that, say, the death of a child in a traffic accident does not? Why do child murders hit the headlines, and hence enter public consciousness, in ways that the far more frequent deaths of children on the roads do not, seldom meriting more than a few lines in the local rag? It is not unreasonable to suggest that we could save many more children's lives by introducing a rational and effective public transport system than by *anything* we could do about child murder. Our hunch as to why we do follow such a policy is because child deaths due to traffic accidents do not *matter* so much to us, or, at least, their mattering is not knowledged for us in the same way (cf. Chapter 2).

Thus a conclusion we can derive from our analysis is that to answer the question 'what should be done?' is not a simple matter of evaluating probability and risk. Our concern is not a general one about children suffering and dying, but a particular repugnance towards the abduction, rape and murder of a child. Indeed, we can note that such crimes are so powerfully knowledged as 'unthinkable', so far outside the realms of human acceptability, that our penal system provides special arrangements to protect its perpetrators from persecution by other prisoners. This makes it particularly difficult – but instructive – to consider the explanations offered as to *why* this offence occurred.

At the level of sheer capability, to act in that way, all that are needed are certain basic, locally valid cultural competences. The man may need to be able to 'spin a story' to the child, perhaps to drive a car to a particular destination and so on. These are well within the capabilities of most men, and yet most men, most of the time, do not commit such crimes. We need, therefore, to look to special causes or reasons. As was noted in Chapter 7, locally and contingently we are usually offered primarily individualistic discourses on such conduct, to do with either 'madness' (i.e. individual pathology) or 'badness' (i.e. individual wrongdoing), although situation is often regarded as a factor, where certain events act as 'triggers', dis-inhibitors or what conditions offer the opportunities for offending (see, for example, Finkelhor, Araji, Baron, Doyle Peters and Doyle Peters 1986, for an illustration of this kind of model).

So far as pathology is concerned, the exact form of the susceptibility is hotly contested (e.g. among psychoanalytic, behaviourist, socio-biological and feminist theory). A common current theory is that sexual assault is an 'addiction', not unlike alcoholism or gambling. A great deal of money and effort has therefore been spent on trying to establish evidence for the different kinds of vulnerability, determine ways of identifying those with a proneness to offend, and to regulate them. Projects of this kind include personality testing, treatment programmes for offenders, and child protection policies devised to 'catch the problem' before it becomes acute (by, say, working with adolescents who evince 'lesser' sexually abusive behaviour).

The notion of criminality is less concerned with 'cause' (i.e. explanation) than with conduct (i.e. what we should do about it). The solution here is seen to be deterrence – increase the chance of detection and make the punishment harsh enough (e.g. catch 'em all and then hang 'em all) and, it is argued, the conduct will diminish. Sadly for this view (even in a capital punishment culture, like the USA), murdering one's victim (and only witness) actually reduces the subjective probability of detection, and hence makes it the 'rational' thing to do to a child you have raped.

Contrasted with individualistic discourses are those that operate at the level of society. As was noted in Chapter 8, the dominant discourse here is the feminist argument that heterosexuality, under patriarchy, is inherently predatory and regulatory. Taken to its extreme, this argues that *all* men are potential rapists. Far from being rare blemishes on an otherwise 'natural and normal' life-world, incidents of rape are simply the most evident and most repugnant instances of male oppression, and are powerfully motivated means to control women and children. In this analysis the ever-present risk to women and children of rape, molestation and assault acts as a panopticon, by which women and children are continuously under surveillance, and thus their actions are held in control (see, for example, Gavey 1992).

The 'solution' in this analysis is seen to lie, at its most robust, in nothing less than the revolutionary overthrow of patriarchy. In more liberal-humanistic terms it is seen to rest in projects which open up 'safe spaces' for women, provide 'safe transport' and directly address male violence, such as the Edinburgh 'No Tolerance' Campaign, run by Edinburgh District Council Women's Committee in 1993.

We find all three forms of analysis wanting because they are inevitably totalizing. By this we mean they are mongered as singularizing stories which, in seeking to 'uncover' certain truths, cover others. Each locates its own particular villains as *the* cause of 'the problem', and hence offers only singularized (and thus partial) solutions. Modernism, predicated on essentialist 'Truth Games', *demands* the production and analysis of singularized, totalizing stories. We assert the need for critical polytextualism because it offers the means to resist totalization. Only by subjecting *all* stories to scrutiny and by withstanding the enchanting lure of the totalizing explain-all theory, can we remain reflexive to the 'downside costs', the warrants to power, the hegemonical forces each story renders possible, while still remaining open to the insights that different stories may have to offer.

This latter point is important. To critically scrutinize – to deconstruct – a story or a discourse, is not to destroy it, rubbish it, accord it no explanatory force whatsoever. We can and do take from stories the knowledge they have brought into being and to our attention – we learn from them. It is perfectly possible, for example, to draw upon the feminist critique of heterosexuality in order to better understand something about how the abduction, rape and murder of children is made do-able, and especially about why, in probabilistic terms, such crimes are more often perpetrated by men. Similarly, we can draw on dysfunction discourses, in order to better understand, say, what conditions make children vulnerable to opportunistic assault. The point is that we do not, thereby, have to buy into these stories wholesale, and we insist on exposing its warrants to critical inspection.

A critical polytextual analysis (as, indeed, do feminist critiques) would point out, for example, that in fact the most pervasive 'solutions' offered to preventing assaults on children are directed not to the perpetrators but to the potential victims. These include formal programmes such as *Kidscape* (see Elliott 1985) designed to help children to resist assault. Thus the effect is to regulate children, by, for example, limiting their freedom of movement and their contact with men. We think it is worth asking why we seem, for instance, far more prepared to put children under curfew than adults; or why it is only in terms of sex (but not, say, school) that we are encouraged to teach children to 'say no'.

Thus our emphasis is not upon 'why' but 'how' such crimes come to be perpetrated. By doubting the value of seeking to ground the offence in any one of the many competing singularizing discourses, we are reflected back into the open possibilities of a narrative approach. Here we would pick up upon an earlier issue: despite their rarity, child abduction, rape and murder are profoundly meaningful to us – they *matter*.

In this we can observe that as a chain of conduct, it is an old, wide-spread and continuously re-told narrative, deeply sedimented in our cultural archive as melodrama. If we portray in a book or a movie an image of a man and a child located in, say, a park, and this story is one (but just one) of many archived narratives that could follow on from this scene. It is a 'tragic tale' which is continually refreshed for us in both the fact and fiction we consume. Thus in one sense, the abduction, rape and murder of a child is made possible – made do-able – because it has been 'storied into being'.

It is important to stress, however, that we are *not* arguing that simply being told or shown the story is, for some vulnerable individuals, enough to trigger a 'copy-cat' re-enactment of the crime. This would be just as totalizing as the other discourses we have held up for scrutiny. All we would have done is replaced one version of a causal argument for another, and have opened up just another warrant to authoritarian control.

Yet we do see benefit in exploring the textuality and tectonics at work, because doing so does at least offer the prospect for change, and hence at least some new possibilities for 'a solution'. At least it helps us to avoid conceptualizing the abduction, rape and murder of children as an inevitable feature of (hu)man conduct. Under a critical polytextualist analysis it cannot, singularly, be seen to spring from some inescapable 'fact' of the human condition, such as a 'wired-in' biological program (i.e. instinct) or some unchangeable, in practical terms, 'force' in our current society (e.g. patriarchy). Our minimalist stance is that this offence is do-able to the extent (and only to the extent) that it is discursively legitimated in personal subjectivities, and structurally supported by local cultural conditions.

As events in what was once Yugoslavia now make clear as we are writing this book, those conditions of textuality can be subject to dramatic and unpredictable tectonic changes where 'the unthinkable' rapidly becomes sayable. 'Ethnic cleansing', once discoursed into being, warrants (however unacceptably to those outside the legitimating power of its originating discourse) certain conduct that previously had no such mandate, and thus it becomes more do-able. Similar arguments can be made for the way terms like 'freedom fighter' warrant actions prohibited by terms like 'terrorist'.

In this book (notably in Chapter 8) we have argued that conduct changes with changes in cultural texts, and is local in social space and time. For example, hunting 'game' animals like deer is now a relatively rare form of conduct in British culture and 'bear-baiting' is obsolete. For many, deer hunting is 'unthinkable' not so much because they lack the resources to do it, but because it has not the cultural currency it would have had in the past, or continues to have in some other parts of the world. Thus the 'hunter narrative', while still accessible from the archive (e.g. tales of Robin Hood) is, for the majority (perhaps soon for all) accessed only in negation, now over-written with other dis-enabling narratives (e.g. of animal rights).

If we apply this indigenous analysis to our offence, we can now see how a critical polytextualist could proceed to offer 'a solution'. Basically, we need to explore the subjectively and objectively available narratives in which the offence is enabled, albeit only for a small number of people, and thus come to consider what needs to be done to disenable it. In particular, we need to find out how warrants to conduct differ between those who perpetrate such crimes and those who do not.

This should not proceed (and cannot effectively proceed) at the individual level alone, nor can it assume statis or fixedness – another problem with totalizing accounts. Just as 'ethnic cleansing' is a political invention enacted through individual subjectivities, so too is, say, the Lolita-ization of the pubescent young woman. Working with narratives needs to develop alongside a careful deconstructive analysis of the changing lineaments of the 'tragic narrative' itself. Until we have done this goundwork, we cannot have the specific texts involved in this particular tale opened for us to work upon.

Certainly our analysis would want to question the current policy of incarcerating convicted offenders together in an atmosphere that encourages shared reality maintenance and mutual narrative plausibility enhancement. It might be thought that our critical polytextual position would also lead us to hail the emergence of programmes of 'discursive therapy' (cf. McNamee and Gergen 1992). These are treatment programmes in which offenders are placed under strong 'therapeutic' and peer pressure to replace their assault-enabling warrants with the institutionally-legitimated discourse required to evidence their 'cure' (and hence, return to the community and, potentially, their families). However, we are cautious because such schemes seem to be more informed by notions of the individualized site of text than by textuality.

These concerns have also been voiced by others. Jervis (1993), for example, criticizes the regime at the Gracewell clinic, and claims that in her conversations with offenders, they were cynically all too aware of what they were expected to articulate in order to 'play along' with the dominant therapeutic discourse. Similarly our own research (as described in Chapter 8) found quite different views being expressed by self-declared apologists for 'boy love' who approached us with the aim of having their views heard, and convicted offenders serving prison sentences for sexual assaults on children.

Such worries are unlikely to go away so long as 'discursive therapy' retains the received problematic over the contingency between text and conduct. Rather, we would suggest, 'discursive interventions' (whether directed at prevention or treatment) need to acknowledge 'thinking', 'saying' and 'doing' as three moments of textuality-moving-to-the-tectonics-of-feasibility. While we acknowledge that such contingency *can* be voiced (i.e. conduct-enabling, conduct-prescriptive or conduct-prohibitive textuality may be narratively linked to, say, particular understandings) such contingency is in no way to be seen as causal. It does not identify a fixed site of intervention. New narratives (and new narrative productions) can, and probably will, make for new forms of conduct (and vice versa). We have access not only to a diverse but also to a diversifying range of narratives – each with its own bounds of constraint and possibility. Conditions of feasibility mediate both whether or not we endorse them, and whether or not we enact them. These shifting tectonics of feasibility act everywhere, and cannot be successfully predicted.

Specifically, a climate of problematization approach argues for extreme caution towards making simplistic and credulous expansions of the 'discursive therapy' approach. In particular, we worry about any singular over-valoriza-tion of the consequences of gaining competence in voicing particular, legit-imated stories. Such skills may (just as they do in mainstream 'cognitive restructuring' therapies) allow a person to 'pass' as 'cured', just as similar skills, more informally gained (in a quite different situation) allow gays to 'pass' as 'straight' when social conditions severely penalize 'not passing' (e.g. as is currently the case in the armed forces in the UK).

> *Interrupter: Watch it! I'm sure you are not wanting to imply that there is any moral equivalent between 'passing' as 'cured' of paedophile tendencies, and 'passing' as 'straight' to cover up being gay, but it's distinctly dodgy to put these two together.*

Beryl: Yes, I worried that one a long time, but I could not find another example that worked as well. I'm glad, though to have the opportun-ity to stress that I am *not* implying any moral equivalence at all.

> *Interrupter: My pleasure. What's an interrupter for but to stop you putting your foot in your mouth?*

[Note that at this point Beryl could not agree whether, having no body, and hence no foot, or mouth to put it in, she was uniquely invulnerable to this fate; *or*, with so many feet and mouths, she was uniquely vulnerable. The frantic attempts by some of her to test this out empirically were deemed not only in distinctly dubious taste, but an unwanted sideshow when others of her were anxious to get the chapter finished!]

Indeed, we could speculate that the kind of proficiency in the skills of persuasion and 'seXduction' (this word VERY much under erasure) required to lure children into sexual activity are *just* the kinds of skills required to hoodwink well-meaning but naive therapists into believing you are 'cured ' because you can smoothly and convincingly articulate the accounts of your motives and behaviour they want to hear. Where their livelihoods, reputa-tions and funding are dependent on demonstrating the 'effectiveness' of the 'cures' they are bringing about, we have all the ingredients for an enchant-ment in the making!

For the abductor, rapist and murderer, then, we are highly sceptical that an other-orchestrated change in language-use is a sufficient (though it may be a necessary) basis for preventing re-offence. To get closer to that we must look to the discursive counter-pole – those conduct-enabling discursions which can warrant such horrors. These, we suspect, have to do with deeply sedimented cultural representations of human sexuality in adults in general (others such as Kitzinger 1992, would argue specifically heterosexuality, for men in particular), the discursive space that 'childhood' and sexuality oc-cupy, and understandings of 'motivation'.

We will hazard that there are, for the 'paedophile', at least two main elements in the cultural calculus. One has to do with what makes children 'desirable' (i.e. what 'motivates' sex-with-children, or indeed any other en-gagement with children which results in their abduction and murder). The other has to do with why a person may risk the severe consequences of committing such offences.

Obviously an analysis of this could take a whole chapter in itself, if not a whole book. Here we only have space to speculate, in outline, on a few of the possibilities. One source of clues we have found informative is thematic decomposition work done on 'paedophile literature' – stories sold in magazines that describe the 'seXduction' of boys and the 'joy of sex' with them (although the latter aspects are, in the texts we have studied, far from explicit). These are not, in the legal sense of the term, child pornography, partly because the law allows far more license over the written word than the visual image. However, they are not on 'general release' and usually have to be ordered from specialist publishers, for example, via Holland.

What is notable about these stories is just how closely they resonate with run-of-the-Mills-and-Boon romantic stories of heterosexual adult 'seduction'. The discourses of 'romantic love' have been subjected to extensive study by others (see, for example, Barthes 1979; Modleski 1982; Wetherell 1991), though in relation to adults. When we examine 'romantic' portrayals of adult–child sex, it is interesting that three thematics appear pervasive in both genres. First the stories are full of descriptions of the desirable *physical* qualities of the to-be-seduced – descriptions of the purity of their unblemished, smooth, honeyed skin; the silkiness of their hair; their doe-like eyes. These re-present the objects of desire as child-like in both kinds of text, though in the one the locus is the child-like woman, and in the other the child-like child.

This revelry in the 'wholesome physical perfection' is juxtaposed against a thematic of power and control – again, just like in conventional 'bodice-rippers', the clichés that trip off the page are couched in a discourse of powerful domination over a willing and acquiescent other: 'his shy *surrender* to my caresses', 'he *yielded* to my passion', 'he fell back in playful *submission*'. The third thematic is an 'adult' sexual 'knowingness' and receptivity to seduction itself, albeit one which must be 'won over', a latent sexuality which is aroused by the seducer.

There are undoubtedly other, much less 'romantic' narratives around (e.g. ones which stress the thrills of defilement, or the perverse pleasures of breaking taboos) which can equally warrant adult–child sex, and, most likely, more warrant rape and murder. But we find these stories of 'romantic seduction' particularly interesting because of the way their social acceptability is so intensely, discomfortingly different from one narrative location to another. Apply them to the discursive domain of adult sexuality and (at least in the normative heterosexuality of popular culture) they are seen as perfectly acceptable – indeed, for many, powerfully legitimating – ways of knowledging (hetero)sexuality (cf. Wetherell 1991). But apply them to the discursive domain of adult–child social relationships, and they are, conventionally, completely unacceptable, and powerfully de-legitimated ways of knowledging paedophile sexuality.

The point being, of course, that the tension between them raises all sorts of questions about sexuality in general. It can be argued that paedophiles are drawing upon the discourse of 'romantic love' to render their predilections 'normal' and hence acceptable. Further, such normalizing arguments can also be found in the academic literature, particularly following the tectonics of feasibility that operated in the 'sexual liberation' discourses of the 1960s and 1970s. Righton (1980), for example, has suggested that a sexual preference for children should be construed as no different from a 'penchant for redheads'.

The reading we prefer, for its critical possibilities, is that such appropriation of the romantic discourse renders visible the power-domination warrant of love-romanticized. This is the argument that writers from a feminist variant of the climate of problematization perspective (such as Dominelli 1989; Kitzinger 1992) put forward to explain child sexual abuse. They argue that such conduct is the consequence of the legitimated, orthodox discourse on heterosexuality, which warrants coercive sexual predation by men on women, simply extended to predation on children.

However, as we have argued already, we see it as important to drive rather than be driven by this analysis. While this analysis is helpful in understanding why the majority of those who sexually abuse children are male, it does not offer any explanation for women sexually abusing children (although, for example, feminists such as Saraga and Macleod 1991, acknowledge it is something that needs to be addressed by feminist theory). Nor does it generally address the ways in which men's and women's conduct is presenced differently with respect to some activities which could be termed 'sexual abuse' (e.g. 'intimate care'). None the less, what it does do (as we have earlier acknowledged) is to stress the possibilities of understanding that come from seeing such offences as a manifestation of the doings of an ordinary, normal person-in-culture rather than the perverted work of a monster or fiend.

Under this analysis, our example of abduction, rape and murder needs to be made sense of not only, as we had previously suggested, as a rare action, but also as a common 'script' immanent with enaction and common in fragmental action. The sexual abuse of children is claimed by some feminist writers (e.g. Bass and Davis 1988) to be commonplace – not something a very few men do, but something most men do, to some degree, and something all are capable of doing. That abduction and murder are rare, in this analysis, is because they are seldom necessary, and for the abuser, not functional. It is only the man who cannot find himself a more secure setting for his predation that needs to resort to abduction, and may thereby get 'forced' into murder.

We do not have to subscribe to this analysis in its entirety to accept some of its implications. These are that if we are to prevent (or at least reduce the incidence of) rapes, abductions and murders perpetrated on children, far from seeking to apply 'sticking plaster' kinds of specific treatments to individuals, we must direct our attention to how these actions currently inhere in the pervasive, legitimated discourses on sexuality that are 'storied into being' in our life-world. And it should be noted that we are deliberately *not* just saying 'heterosexuality', since we acknowledge boys as victims as well as girls, and lesbian sex as certainly not immune to being used predatorily or coercively (however unpopular that may make us).

It is these, seemingly so innocuous (to some) narratives of 'lovable rogues', 'romantic seduction', 'innocence immanent with knowingness', and 'no-that-means-yes resistance' which must be knowledged out of taken-for-grantedness and troubled. And 'troubled' is the right term, in our view, since they neither can nor should be mere targets for exercises in ideological censorship at the cultural level. Concern belongs to their seeming narrative autonomy, their warrant to 'possess us' and their justification of our 'possessing' others. Equally, we must trouble the conduct-warranting potential of discourses on adult authority over children (see, for example, Newell 1989) and those which locate children as vulnerable rather than fostering their empowerment.

Beryl: That, dear Interrupter, is an outline of what a climate of problematization thematic scrutiny might offer in terms of insights on and response to the abduction, rape and murder of a child.

Interrupter: I'm really quite impressed. It made me think in places, but there is still a sense of having to work the ideas out of your language. Any chance (and here I'm trying to speak for the reader as well) of a simple summary?

Beryl: I will, but please bear in mind that I've only been sketching out an approach. These recommendations are tentative and nothing like as solid as they are going to seem by getting put in such a format.

Over the immediate concern over this child:

- Clearly a crime has been committed, and, in the 'real world of the here and now' it will be treated as a criminal offence. In practical reality, the perpetrator should be sought, prosecuted and imprisoned. As to why there is much space for disagreement, a minimal consensus lies in the need to signal concern by action and to protect other children from any repetition of his dangerousness.
- At the same time, we should not be complacent about the problematics inherent in our current system of justice and punishment. We must 'worry' the assumption that it is an effective way of deterring such crimes, or functional in rehabilitating offenders.
- Indeed, we must specifically worry about the consequences of locking up perpetrators of sexual assaults on children together, because of the potential this provides for these men to actively reinforce and consolidate the narratives which enable and endorse such conduct.
- At the same time, we must not be lulled into thinking that merely indoctrinating offenders with an alternative set of more acceptable, conduct-prohibitive discourses will result in changed conduct when they re-enter a largely unchanged society.

In terms of protecting children in general from such crimes:

- We must be prepared to challenge those legitimated, orthodox, narratives pervading through everyday, ordinary discourse, which may warrant predatory seductive conduct towards children.
- This includes a long-term project of troubling of the whole way our society

construes, constructs and consumes sexuality, not just adult–child sex. In this, while being alert to the power of received narratives, sexuality must not be taken as given or fixed but negotiated and negotiable.

- Similarly, we must be willing to trouble the ways we construe children, and the authority of the adult world over them. This includes acknowledging the way we deny children full access to the discursive-practices whereby we constitute our world, and the place of children within it.
- We must not be ingenuous over: the potential costs (particulary unexpected, down-side costs) of such an endeavour; the lure of singularizing accounts (including singularizing own own); the resistances we are likely to face; and, the immense difficulty of the task.

Beryl: To which I'd like to add . . .

   Interrupter: So you shall.

Discursive Health Warning

The Narrator General has determined that such cultural tectonic endeavours are not to be entered into lightly, whether we are talking at the general cultural level or of work with perpetrators or those who feel at risk of such conduct. Although discursive interventions (in the sense of seeking to change the interplay between texts) may seem the most innocuous mode of social intervention, something that is inevitably in play in culture anyway, it is not risk-free, whether we are talking about the moral, political or consequential domains.

Our point is that, as critical polytextualist, once we accept engagement in any such a venture, we cannot avoid being morally located. To do so, is not, of course, to resist access to the constructed, local and contingent form of such engagement, but to accept critical movement between that and location at point-positions in debates about social policy and individually-focused action.

Operating without any possibility of absolute faith, seeing all moral and ideological 'anchors' as hooked into what can only be, at best, a relative and discursively maintained 'sea bed' of shifting practical reality, acceptance of engagement means to have reflectively entered into the flux of enabling, disabling, deconstructive and reconstructive textuality – along with all others who, 'for good or ill', enter into a struggle for the past, the present and the future. Whether that future contains an increasingly polytextualized condition, a shift into a new meta-Orthodoxy, a run-down into entropy or something else is unknowable. So too is the impact of any engagement (and indeed disengagement). If minimalists are allowed dreams they sound rather like this:

> at each historical moment, in each local situation, however trivial, actuality is changed a little. It is changed everywhere at every instant

by which possibilities among hosts of others become actual . . . by which choice is made, which words are spoken, which acts are performed in which situation and in relation to whom, by each of us. This will not impress those who dream of remaking all of actuality in their image, and it rather lacks mastery and pazzazz. (Bannet 1993: 123)

In this section we have explored a possible response to a hypothetical call to involvement. Every such call raises the same dilemma: should we attempt to enable it into conduct?

> *Interrupter: I still think you ask a great deal of the reader, but I now accept that you can, in your terms, cover issues of conduct. But isn't there a sting in the tail? Aren't you saying that 'an analysis of action cannot fully encompass the means for authorizing or otherwise re-action'?*

Beryl: A sort of discursive *Gödel's Theorem* you mean? Yes, I am. But remember all that stuff about twitching togas at the start of Chapter 5? I'm into circles, remember.

To boldly go

Finally, and this feels like a good place to finally come to an end, the climate of problematization is often metaphorized as a journey, one made possible by the troublesome but moving possibilities of language. Under minimalism, what must be recognized is that what matters is travelling, not arriving – there is no destination, only the 'disturbing pleasure' of the journey itself.

It is worth remembering back to some of our earliest such travels in childhood (ours and, of course, our Modern culture's) via Lewis Carroll, both down the rabbit hole and through the looking glass. Beryl knows what it is to be Alice: 'when she thinks she knows what a word means, it turns out to mean something else' (Auden 1974: 36). It is worth returning to the sentences that come just before that quotation:

> In both worlds [wonderland and looking-glass land], one of the most important and powerful characters is not a person but the English language. Alice, who had hitherto supposed that words were passive objects, discovers that they have a life and a will of their own.

A prime traveller in these language games was Wittgenstein, arguing in his *Preface* to the *Philosophical Investigations* how his task of investigating modes of life in language 'compels us to travel across a wide field of thought crisscross in every direction' (1978: vii). Which in turn produced a text that he characterized by means of an informative metaphor: 'The philosophical remarks in this book are, as it were, a number of sketches of landscapes which are made in the course of these long and involved journeys' (ibid.).

The odyssey of the text, under minimalism, is an exciting project precisely because it is so open, so much an enterprise upon which 'to boldly go'. That much is clear from its advertisement [even in such early exemplars as Eco's *The Open Work* (1989)] and we are happy to admit to having been affected by that advertising, to having studied the copy and copied the study. A minimalistic journey is an 'opportunity' to 'explore', to 'unsettle'. It is 'about transformations'; in short, an invitation to emigrate beyond return promulgated in a Zeitgeist short on frontiers (final or otherwise). Of course in a climate of *caveat emptor*, a leap into the unknown can translate into going over Niagara Falls in a barrel! However, for once, the advertisers were straightforward with us, the unknown is also unknowable:

> ... to constitute 'objects' as texts is to break with a distinction between fact and fiction. Metaphor is real and the real is metaphor ... There is no deep real ... below the surface; there is no extra-textual ground for social analysis to cling to. We, like writers of 'fiction', are at sea. (Game 1991: xii)

Writers inevitably draw on their cultural archive, and the archetype of 'The Journey' well cloaks the emerging emigrant narratives. Or so, at any rate, it seems now, re-reading the germinal texts of our own odyssey. *Changing the Subject* (Henriques, Hollway, Urwin, Venn and Walkerdine 1984), for example, begins with *The point of departure* and, having outlined the itinerary, concludes: 'At this point, we have taken the reader as far as we have travelled. Our history is not finite, our search is unfinished' (p. 9). Needless to say, *Changing the Subject*, the readerly book, does end. It is as a writerly text that it is infinite. Even so, this quotation allows us to mark that our minimalist ambitions for our book, *Textuality and Tectonics*, have been rather different. Our operating archetype was not journey as quest but journey as episodic transformations. Hence, there is a passing completion to the narrative, even if we leave open the reading that the (E)nterprise may pass through infinite episodes: that endings are also beginnings. Our episodes thus re-narrate the collective development of analytics of the textual and the practice of that analytic. However, in having an end (because we have ends) it also cannot avoid being back-written – in other words, to have been informed by where it was going.

Hence, we have no reason not to be 'up front' about our ends. This book has been a telling of an episode in our lives: how a group of social scientists (by biography) encountered the climate of problematization and the polytextual product (the writings of Beryl Curt) that resulted. Beryl was a forum, a location in which we wrote and read, voiced and re-voiced, until we had discoursed into plausibility 'all the world's a text', practised it until it passed for real (which does not mean it was the only reality for us, but an additional reality). Now we have nearly completed passing it on and the book is Beryl. We can have an interesting inter-textuality with Mulkay (1985: 2) when he says (as 'reader'):

> You make it sound as if the book is another person; whereas, in fact, it is no more than a collection of diverse and, in many ways, discrepant and socially generated discourses. Well, on second thoughts, that's a pretty good definition of a 'person' as well.

Interrupter: Well I can see that fades away your personhood but I have to say I see no sign of textual fading. Quite the reverse, we seem to have got, very late, into yet more 'thick description' of the textual turn.

Beryl: Not at all, I think it neatly dissolves the difference between us.

Senior editor [entering, dressed as a Textual Tern]: Which is just as well, as you have now reached your word limit, I'm afraid.

THE END

Glossary: the bluff guide to Beryl

-ing: as in 'knowledging' – re-writing and reading a noun as actively constituted (in this case, to construct-into-knowledge). See Box 1.2.

-ness: As in 'tableness' – having the qualities of (a table).

abduction: Stephenson took the term from the philosopher, Charles Peirce, who viewed it as covering 'all the operations by which theories and conceptions are engendered' (Peirce 1934: 414). Stephenson viewed it as 'inference, like induction, but concerned with explanation, whereas induction was descriptive – one proceeded from the sample to the whole in induction, but from the whole to an explanation or interpretation in abduction' (Stephenson 1961: 11). We use it to denotate the craft of interrogating and scrutinizing texts. Unlike traditional notions of deduction or induction, abduction does not assume that knowledge can be derived canonically, but re-constructively via understandings, interpretations and explanations. Abduction, as we use it, is neither a scientific nor a philosophical technique. It is a practical craft, which can only be conducted by persons-in-culture (immanent with culture-in-persons).

Academy (The): A term used by Foucault (1970) to describe the locus of secret and exclusive – and thus prized – scholarly knowledge, which, even when those outside the Academy get hold of it, cannot be fully deciphered. It is the site of 'discourse with a veil drawn over it' (p. 88). Today it is used generally as a disdainful term to describe the ivory tower of the academic hegemony.

attitude: Variously, a kind of cool chutzpah or something that psychologists measure, that does not exist outside of 'attitude scales'. See, however, the much more cool (q.v.) term, NATURAL ATTITUDE (q.v.).

beryline: Pertaining to Beryl. Beryl is better known as aquamarine and emerald (hexagonal beryllium aluminium silicate), used as a moderator in nuclear reactors and to harden alloys. This mineral identity seems fitting for a cultural tectonicist, especially one having a role in 'going critical'. Beryl also likes being a gem!

chreod: An imminent pathway or track (cf. Waddington 1977).

complementarity: A term borrowed from relativity physics to describe the condition between two incommensurable states or two incommensurable theory languages brought to a phenomenon. The common example of a state of complementarity is that of light considered as a waveform and light considered as made up of particles. By extension, as here, the condition between two manifesting expressions of one presenting 'social object' or two expressed knowledgings of a given 'social issue' where these form separate factors in a Q-methodological study.

concourse: Stephenson defined a concourse as 'a collection of self-referable statements spoken by participants' in relation to an issue, topic or even a particular event, such as a widow escaping from a burning house, worried about her dog still inside (Stephenson 1989: 7). (See, for example, Stephenson 1986, for a fuller exposition of his Concourse Theory of Communication.) We use it somewhat more generally to describe the universe of possible elements (such as propositions) from which discourses can be configured in relation to something, be that a 'social problem', an issue, a cast of characters or whatever. A concourse is a *bounded* universe (albeit, usually, a large one) because discourses are always located in place and time, and constrained by that which is locally and contingently available as text at any historical moment. See Chapter 4 for a fuller theoretical treatment, and Chapter 5 for its place in Q-methodological research.

constructionism (often called 'Social Constructionism'): An approach to psychological and social science which stresses the extent to which our realities are humanly built or socially constructed (cf. Berger and Luckman 1967; Coulter 1979; Harré 1986; Kitzinger 1987). Constructionist approaches are often and most easily contrasted with essentialist approaches (q.v.). Instead of viewing concepts such as 'mind', 'emotion' and 'lesbianism' as timeless essential 'things' which are merely reflected or represented (more or less accurately) in language, constructionism emphasizes that these are constructed categories which gain currency through social usage in context. However, constructionism should also be distinguished from phenomenological approaches which tend to stress the importance of the individual's 'interpretation of reality' (Kelly's 'personal construct theory' for example, see Kelly 1955) and to underestimate the importance of the social. To say that something is 'socially constructed' is not to say that it is not real (e.g. that it is the product of an individual's imaginings). It is to make a point about the nature of that reality.

cool: A term used to describe things of which we approve – not-boring, quite nice really.

critical polytextualism: This approach treats all forms of social 'reality' as textualized – that is, multiply 'written' and 'read', 're-written' and 're-presented'. It is about exploring this multiplicity of texts in terms of the discursive practices and representational labour by which they are 'knowledged into being', mongered, muted, rhetorically pitted one against the other, and so on. It does this 'critically' – i.e. in ways which are always alert to notions like power/knowledge synarchy. See Chapter 2 for a fuller treatment.

critical polytexturism: A condition created when the counterpoint between tectonic activity and Ar-text has 'gone critical'. Beryl's resulted from an exploding bottle of red wine (Wittenham 1989; see Hicks 1993) on the occasion of Steve and Casey Brown coming to dinner.

curt: Blunt and concise to the point of rudeness. (Ironic)

deconstruction: A term most often attributed to the French philosopher Jacques Derrida (see, for example, 1990). To deconstruct a text, issue or argument is not to destroy it but to affirm its limitations and to display its constructed nature. Texts which claim to refer to 'the truth' (an article in a psychology journal, for example) are favoured targets for deconstruction. A deconstruction would follow the argument of the text very closely and draw attention to exclusions, avoidances and absences (the things that are significantly missing); the avenues which could have been taken, but were not; and the usage of taken-for-granted concepts, dualisms and rhetoric to create the effect of truth.

determinism: 'The doctrine that all events, including human action, are determined by causes regarded as external to [and inaccessible to] the will' (*Concise Oxford Dictionary*). Often, this term is used critically to describe social theory or psychology which over-emphasizes a single primary cause or mechanism in explaining a state of affairs. Recent work suggests that the problem with such causal explanations is not simply their over-emphasis of one causal factor, but that they limit discussion and inquiry to causal analysis. The word 'deterministic' can therefore be used broadly to criticize the view that theory must describe human life in terms of the cause-and-effect vocabulary of the physical sciences, regardless of how complex and multifactorial the view may be.

differance: That which makes every instance of the word differance 'different', not just from all other words but also from every other instance of the word 'differance'; while at the same time 'defferring' indefinitely any final attribution as to why this is (see ITERABILITY).

discorporation: To become removed or released from bodily form – an ironizing of any transcendent reading of shaking off the mortal coil (*Source:* R. Heinlein, *Stranger in a Strange Land*).

discourse: An increasingly popular term which, although drawn from the lexicon of linguistics, has acquired in the social sciences a wider range of usage than simply to describe 'chunks' of speech or writing. The word tends to be used by researchers concerned with the constructive, productive and pragmatic aspects of language use, rather than the descriptive or representational aspects. This shift of focus has come about through a recognition that language can never neutrally describe the world, because language itself is an active part of the world. A 'discourse analysis', for instance, is not a search 'behind' the word or sentence for the 'cognitions', 'motivations' or other psychological entities, which from a positivistic perspective would be seen as underlying language. Rather, talk and other texts are seen as social practices which are productive of experience and which construct the realities in which we live. For this reason, some researchers talk of 'a discourse' (such as Wendy Hollway's 'male sexual drive discourse'). In this sense the 'male sexual drive discourse' consists of all kinds of statements (whether professional, technical or lay) which re-produce the idea (and re-construct the reality) that men have a powerful and all consuming need for sexual release.

discursive practice: The activities by which text is 'knowledged into being' through discursive activities such as 'writing', re-presentation and 'reading' (e.g. to warrant action or promote ideology); discursive practice operates tectonically (i.e. by the action of text upon text).

disturbing pleasure: A term we have re-written from Game (1991) where she defines it as 'that which disrupts the givenness of the social world in a positive form of pleasure – as opposed to fear which produces negation and closure' (p. 191). For example, in suggesting that twenty years ago it might have been called 'The Joy of Deconstruction', we get 'disturbing pleasure'. Did the earth move tectonically for you?

doxa: Denotes simultaneously the glory that we bestow upon or attribute to God, and the glory that is God: we glorify Him because He is glorious. Orthē doxa (orthodoxy) is straight or true doxa (i.e. when our glorification is appropriate to His glory). Doxa, as a 'climate of problematization' concept refers to any tacit or background knowledge which is taken-for-granted. Bourdieu (1992) distinguishes beliefs which are doxatic from those which are orthodox or heterodox (multiple and contested) on the grounds that doxatic beliefs, in appearing to correspond perfectly with the world-as-it-is, appear self-evident and hence are not directly discursively articulated. Doxa 'goes without saying because it comes without saying' (Bourdieu 1992: 167). When doxa is challenged, if it is to maintain its power, it must be articulated in the form of an orthodoxy.

empiricism: Despite having been subject to much criticism, most of psychology today is still empiricist. An empiricist epistemology holds that we gain knowledge of reality only through the exercise of our senses (albeit aided by various methods and techniques). The form of experience most valued by positivists is that gained under experimental conditions, for it is believed that such methods yield objective data (data which tell of the world as it really is). Thus empiricists tend to adhere to a realist ontology and to dismiss ungrounded 'theory' (as metaphysics). For strict empiricists, it is thought that true understanding can be derived directly from behavioural observation and that all theory must be generated and assessed only through rules of evidence.

endism: The condition of being awash with Millennial fancies and feelings (usually terminal).

epistemology: Epistemological questions are questions concerned with knowledge and with the relationship between the knower and the known (subject and object). An epistemology is thus a theory of knowledge (including deciding upon preferred methods and means of validation – how can we know, and how do we know that we know?).

essentialism: Plato held that for each type of earthly thing, animal or object in the physical world, there exists an ideal extra-earthly form. For example, a table gains its 'tableness' by virtue of its relationship to the 'essence of tableness', i.e. by virtue of its relationship to the 'ideal form' of table. Similarly, each member of the category 'knife' derives its knifely properties (sharpness, hardness, ability to cut) from its relationship to the ideal form or essence of the knife. Although the full implications of the 'doctrine of forms' are rarely adopted by modern scientists, certain positivistic approaches can be described as essentialist in this way. For example, intelligence testing in psychology rests upon the assumption that actions or responses to questions are a manifestation of, and hence can be a measure of, some underlying essence of 'intelligence' ('g'). Likewise, Eysenck's measure 'extraversion' reads behind selected actions for a deep, biologically grounded essence to that behaviour. When people settle arguments by referencing 'human nature', the broadest of essentialist pseudo-explanation is at work.

fragmentation paradox: According to Graham (1992) this relates to the argument that postmodernism does not actually represent anything new, but is no more than what has happened as modernism begins to lose direction and to fall apart. Applied to social science, it focuses on things like its increasing disciplinary specialism, its small-scale and local 'crises' and squabbles, its ever increasing muddle and lack of direction, and argues that far from there being a 'paradigm shift' (q.v.) all that can be seen is fragmentation.

french theory: A portmanteau term used by Ann Game in her book *Undoing the Social*, 1991, to cover recent critical writings by Francophone writers.

gaze: The activity of seeing, in the Foucaultian sense. In talking of 'a gaze', both the seeing-subject and the seen-object are treated as constructed rather than pre-given or taken-for-granted. Hence, 'seeing' can change and specific gazes (e.g. clinical, feminist) come into being (at least in a genealogical gaze!).

genealogy: Although ordinarily used to denote the tracing of a line of descent (perhaps the lineage of a family or a species of plant), genealogy has been developed as a powerful social science method by Michel Foucault. In simple terms, a Foucaultian genealogy is a form of deconstruction which uses history. It deconstructs the 'solidity' and 'realness' of categories like 'criminality' and 'femininity' by drawing attention to the ensemble of historical and cultural conditions which together provide the conditions of existence for that category.

glamour: Beryl's forte. But apart from that, a power of the effect of enchantment (q.v.). A Scottish variant on 'gramarye' reminding us that magic comes from book-learning.

gloss: Literally, a short explanatory or elucidatory note. Here, any brief reading shifting the previous or conventional meaning.

god games: According to John Fowles (1977), *The Godgame* was his alternative title for *The Magus*. He says:

I did intend Conchis to exhibit a series of masks representing human notions of God from the super-natural to the jargon-ridden scientist; that is, a series of illusions about something that does not exist in fact, absolute knowledge and absolute power. (p. 10)

Haraway (1991) has, in some ways, a parallel project over totalizing projects in science 'being nowhere while claiming to see comprehensively' (p. 191). We need to be 'on to the god-trick and all its dazzling – and therefore, blinding – illuminations' (ibid.). See also her discussion of G.O.D. the Generator of Diversity. Hence, for a critical *poly*textualist – God Games.

governmentality: For Foucault, 'Governmentality' represents the principal way in which 'power' operates in modern Western societies. He sees the modern era to be characterized by the growing importance of knowledges and techniques for the disciplining and organization of the population. Governmentality emerged coevally with, and is inseparable from, the development of new 'social' institutions and organizations such as prisons, schools, mental hospitals, factories and, importantly, the human sciences. The concept of governmentality embodies a move away from understanding power either as an abstract, universal essence, or simply as a force wielded by some 'powerful' agency which constrains freedom (a view which Foucault 1979a called the 'repressive hypothesis'). Instead, power is understood as, in part, a productive force (comprising a complex set of strategies, objectives, knowledges, institutionalized ways of realizing aims, etc.) which shape, guide, manage and structure (govern) the possible field of action of others.

grand narrative paradox: Graham (1992) sees this as the paradox arising from postmodernism rejecting the imperialist pretensions of the modernist quest for explain-all 'grand theories', but yet it has, itself, come to be treated as a 'grand theory'. We seek to avoid this paradox by adopting a more minimal agenda, that of working under a 'climate of problematization'.

hermeneutics (see also Box 2.1): Hermes was a winged messenger for Ancient Greek Gods. Hermeneutics is a form of enquiry concerned with the interpretation of meaning. It began as a quest to adjudicate between competing versions of the Bible. It was thought possible, through hermeneutics, to rediscover the original meaning of the Bible, i.e. the word of God. The term has more recently been appropriated by philosophers and researchers interested in the construction and re-production of meaning (Dilthey, Heidegger, Gadamer and Ricoeur are perhaps the most influential). As such, hermeneutics represents a powerful alternative approach to positive empiricism (which tends to dispense with meaning altogether).

heterogeny: We have adopted this term to describe diversity, in preference to the more 'dodgy' notion of 'pluralism', which has become encumbered by unwanted ideological connotations with *un*critical relativism, in which 'anything goes'. See, however, Chapter 9's examination of 'critical pluralism'.

intertextual: Pertaining to links between texts, either (relatively) specific ones or the infinite iterations of relatedness that feature in some dialects of poststructuralism (q.v.).

issuance: What (and how) an 'issue' is 'at'. We use the formation to point out that issues, such as 'juvenile crime', do not arise of their own accord, do not force themselves into view as if they were acne on the face of 'social nature'. However, we are not content to swap the realism of the campaigner for the sociological relativism of the media mediated 'moral panic' thesis. 'Issuance' points to the textuality and tectonics of the circumstances as much as 'talk' surrounding them. While facts and opinions are conventionally thought of as separate, for us they are inextricably entangled with one another.

iterability: Derrida argues that language is defined by the fact that it permits something to be 'repeated over time' in another context. This potential for repetition-of-the-same is, he argues, more fundamental to language than any question of a speaker's intent. Indeed, he uses this feature of language – iterability – to undercut any claim that the meaning of an utterance is solely determined by the speaker's intent. Iterability denotes, then, not only repetition, but also change or alteration. Iteration is *repetition with a difference*. This difference is *essential* to the repetition, because the whole point of repetition is to join or articulate different contexts (both temporal and spatial). As Derrida himself puts it 'Iterability alters . . . it leaves us no choice but to mean (to say) something that is (always, already, also) other than we mean (to say)' (Derrida 1987: 200). The concept of iteration is also used in the statistics of factor analysis. Here the product of a mathematical formula is used repeatedly in a calculation to alter the data set. This feedback loop is followed, over and over again, until the 'best solution' is reached – in this case, the 'best solution' for a factor estimate. Here 'best' is conventionally defined, with a set limit placed on the number of iterations. Q-method is iterative, in this sense, but all research methods are, in a Derridean sense, iterative.

life-world: English rendering of the German *Lebenswelt* (sometimes left untranslated). The taken-for-granted universe of ordinary experience, the ordinary realities – as opposed, say, to the world as represented by physics. Both terms (in their respective languages) are widely used in phenomenological writings. (*Origin*: Husserl).

lithosphere: The formal name for the Earth's crust, its rigid outer layer.

methodolatory: The worship of method to the point of credulous adulation.

minimalism: The craft of producing texts that achieve their effects from basic, reduced or sampled resources – often by way of iteration (q.v.). For example, the music of Steve Reich. Here we have expanded its meaning, to describe that aspect of work under a 'climate of problematization' which strives to avoid such traps as grand narrative. See Chapter 9 for a fuller treatment.

narrative: Narrative is closely related to story. When we tell a story or a narrative, we offer a symbolized account of some event or sequence of actions (or whatever). A narrative thus serves to organize and shape meaning according to a temporal structure (it has a beginning, a middle and an end). The concept of narrative is becoming increasingly popular among researchers of constructionist persuasion (see Chapter 1). Not only can psychological accounts (such as Freud's discussion of infant sexuality or Piaget's theory of cognitive development) be reconceptualized as, primarily, narratives or stories (and hence deconstructed), but also we can all be said to live stories. Our hopes, ambitions, fears, dreams, and so on are narrative in form (we tell ourselves and other people stories about who we are, who we have been, who we will be, and so on). It is hence through the medium of narrative that we relate to others and construct ourselves as meaningful, knowable subjects. As with the terms 'discourse' and 'construction', then, narrative/story should not be understood in terms of a fact/fiction, real/unreal dualism. In a sense, we are made real by stories.

natural attitude: A stance of unquestioning acceptance of the Life-World (q.v.). Major tasks of phenomenology are its examination and its critical suspension. (*Origin:* Husserl).

ontology: Usually, before epistemological questions are asked (how can we know questions), it is deemed necessary in the language game of philosophy to clarify and to ask ontological questions. These in general have the form 'what is there to be known?' 'Of what categories of thing does the world consist?' When constructionists (q.v.) criticize essentialists (q.v.), for instance, they are calling into question the validity of essentialist ontology. Conversely, when a positivist criticizes constructionism, the focus is principally epistemological ('your methods are not rigorous') (see *tritunic*).

orthogonal: At right-angles to one another. In mathematics, orthogonal variables are independent of one another, they do not co-vary. Applied to factors in a Q-study, it means that as they co-vary they are in complementarity with each other.

ouroboros: The alchemic symbol of the snake or serpent swallowing its own tail to form a complete circle (cf. Eddison, *The Worm Ouroboros*, 1926).

panchreston: A term, theory or observation which 'explains all' in the same way that a panacea is supposed to 'cure all'. (*orig.* Hardin 1950)

pandects: Over-narratives that singularize their accounts into totalizing treatises.

pangaea: The name given in geophysics to the hypothetical original landmass of Palaeozoic times. By the end of the Palaeozoic, it is said to have divided into Godwanaland and Laurasia.

panopticon: An architectual model for a prison, designed by Jeremy Bentham, consisting of a central watchtower surrounded by a circular building divided into cells. Each cell extends the width of the building and has windows on each side. By the effect of backlighting, the occupants of the cells are always visible from the watchtower, but the prisoners cannot see the observer. This arrangement 'ensures that the surveillance is permanent in its effects' and therefore the Panopticon induces 'a state of conscious and permanent visibility that assures the automatic functioning of power' (Foucault 1979b: 201). Thus panopticon is used as a metaphoric term to show how certain people can be regulated and normalized through the operation of disciplinary power.

paradigm shift: A phrase coined by Kuhn (1970) and much over-used by others ever since. The word 'paradigm' here refers to the 'world-view' of the scientific community at a period in place and time. Rather like a revolution as it relates to a dominant political 'world-view', in science also we can find the (relatively) rapid replacement of one paradigm (say, Newtonian science) with another (say, Einsteinian science). Kuhn is often called a relativist because the notion of a 'paradigm shift' as a collective re-orientation challenges ideas of science being dictated by 'the way things are' by a 'mirroring of nature'.

periodization paradox: The third of Graham's (1992) paradoxes of postmodernism, this she sees as arising out of the reading that for a movement to be 'post-' something (be it modernism, structuralism or whatever) implies that what is going on is a sequential process. This is 'dodgy' because it smacks of 'grand theory' and in particular because it elides all too easily into a triumphant story of progress – a story totally inimical to postmodernist thought (hence the paradox). It is thus important to recognize that the 'post-' suffix is not intended to imply a time slot when something 'happened', but contrapuntal force, such as being a reaction against something else.

perturbated/perturbating: A back-formation from perturbation, following the model of masturbation/masturbated/masturbating. The words are intended to carry a similar active implication. To be read as more operative and dynamic than perturbed/perturbing. (Neologism)

phenomenology: A philosophy developed principally by Husserl which has proved influential in the social sciences. Phenomenological approaches are critical of reductionist and mechanistic explanations of human life and behaviour. For phenomenologists, lived phenomenological experience is placed at the centre of enquiry. In order to understand human action and Being, it is thought necessary to gain access, not to what an object or action 'really is' (an impossible quest which the phenomenologist chooses to 'bracket off' as unanswerable), but to how that object is experienced and interpreted by the individual in question. In concentrating on phenomenal reality, and not the supposed 'brute' reality we believe we have access to when we adopt what Husserl, and later Schutz called the 'natural attitude' (q.v.), phenomenologists employ concepts such as intentionality (which refers to the directedness of consciousness), noema (that which is experienced as experienced) and noesis (a 'mode' of experiencing). Phenomenology tends to be divided into two brands: 'transcendental' (which follows Husserl's doctrine) and 'existential' (which shades into Heideggerian hermeneutics).

polysemy: The (ambiguity) and multiple meaning of words.

pomo: The familiar, diminutive of postmodern.

positioning: A concept developed by post-structuralist writers to emphasize and expand upon the active nature of discourse and narrative. Narratives and discourses do not merely transmit 'information' from one person to another, they actively situate the people involved according to a meaningful relationship. In telling a story, we position ourselves and others. Depending on our position in a narrative we have different rights, obligations, expectancies, privileges, and so on. To an extent, our identities are constructed according to the subject positions available to us in the narratives which make up our everyday lives. Even everyday, mundane conversation can be analysed to show the operation of different positionings which are variously accepted, resisted, ignored or whatever by the people involved.

positivism: Approaches can be said to be positivistic when they are based upon a strong belief in the powers of rigorous scientific method to answer and solve the problems of human existence. The approach is usually held to originate with Auguste Comte in the early nineteenth century. It is often used as a term of abuse to criticize highly dogmatic rationalist and reductionist forms of enquiry.

post-structuralism: A term sometimes identified with deconstruction (q.v.) or, more broadly, French Theory (q.v.). We have the same kinds of worries with this term as we do over postmodernism (q.v.). When you read what sort of a paddy Foucault got into about being called a 'structuralist', you will see our caution is well-founded. He says, in his Preface to *The Order of Things* 'In France certain half-witted "commentators" persist in labelling me a "structuralist". I have never been able to get it into their tiny minds that I have used none of the methods, concepts or key terms that characterize structural methods' (1970: xiv).

postie: A postmodernist (q.v.).

postmodernism: That which results from the presencing practices of self-identified or other-identified postmodernists. Rosenau (1992) – who almost uniquely calls it post-modernism – covers 184 pages 'explaining it' from the position of a 'modern' author. We have gained from Rosenau's efforts a strong motivation not to try to gloss (q.v.) it ourselves!

presencing: The positioning (q.v.) of (generally) non-human objectivities into available discursive locations and practices. A contrasted reading to the notion that objectivities have inner essences (q.v. essentialism).

pro-text: A proposition designed to tease and puzzle, intended to open up possibilities of re-writing, as in 'Make up your minds' or, one of our favourites (found in the subway in Vienna), 'You never know'. Pro-texts can be promoted by the slogan 'Pro-text and survive'. (Neologism)

problematic: [as noun] Any specified field of contention. Anything which has been problematized (presenced as a problem) has thereby been discursively transformed into a new object: a problematic.

psychology: The science of measuring (mental) things that do not exist.

rXe-presentation: An analytic used in describing pattern in the presentation of imaged or concretized understandings. A 'showing', a 'manifestation'. This term, and its choice over 'representation' is dealt with in detail in Chapter 6.

re-vista: Literally 'revista' is Castilian for both re-viewing, and a vantage point from which terrain can be observed. Beryl has taken it from the name of a villa where she once stayed in Formentera, which overlooked a strangely beautiful landscape of lagoons and salt-pans (Thank you Thomson's Holidays!). In Catalan it is even more wonderfully polysemic; it means: the action of examining something to see that everything is in order; a military inspection; a periodical publication concerned with critical matters; or the theatrical representation of a frivolous character (Elies i Busqueta 1983).

reductionism: Reductionism refers to the attempt to reduce or 'boil down' any complex phenomenon into the simple elements which are thought to constitute it or cause it. Reductionism has proved useful in sciences such as chemistry (where, for example, water can be reduced to oxygen and hydrogen), but it is more contentious when applied to psychological or social science issues. To reduce 'waving at someone' to the various muscular movements this entails, for example, is to miss the usual point of waving. Likewise, it is uselessly reductionist to reduce a piece of music to the notes which comprise it (if, that is, one wants to appreciate or understand the music). In such cases, as stated by members of the Gestalt school of psychology, the 'whole is greater than the sum of the parts'. Reductionism is therefore often used as a critical term along with essentialism and positivism (the three often go together). Not to be confused with minimalism (q.v.) which is really quite cool (q.v.).

reification: To reify an issue or term is to thingify it. That is, reification involves treating a non-material concept as if it were a material thing. A good deal of constructionist work attempts to show that many of the entities and processes that psychologists strive to discover and measure are reifications (and hence undiscoverable). Humanly made concepts such as 'cognition' and 'emotion' may no more refer to 'things' than do phlogiston (a substance formerly believed to exist in all burnable objects) and unicorn. In this sense, deconstruction and genealogy are forms of de-reification. Has links to A.N. Whitehead's 'fallacy of misplaced concreteness'.

representational labour: The *work* of reality-making (e.g. as goes on in a literal or metaphorical laboratory). Notions of a tension between this and the *play* of *disturbing pleasure* (q.v.) are part of the modernistic *homo faber/homo ludens* duality.

scientized: Turned into a scientific sounding concept [insult].

scopophilia: Pleasure in looking – particularly male sexual pleasure in positioning women in an erotic gaze (general location of use is Psychoanalysis, particularly as used in Feminist Art Theory).

seeded thematics: A method of scrutiny by which representational labour (q.v.) is encouraged by 'seeding' a story.

simulacrum: According to Baudrillard, the following are the sucessive stages through which representation (q.v.) and images have historically passed: '1/It is the reflection of a basic reality. 2/It masks and perverts a basic reality. 3/It marks the absence of a basic reality. 4/It bears no relation to any reality whatever: it is its own pure simulacrum' (Baudrillard 1983).

singularizing: A 'singularizing' discourse is one which promotes a single, exclusive knowledging of what is at issue, denying all others as either 'untrue' or mere opinion. Young (1980), for example, writes of the biomedical discourse, that 'these beliefs appear to the people who use them . . . to merely reflect "empirically observed" facts of nature . . . taken for granted, commonsensical, and admitted without argument: they attract no epistemological scrutiny and receive no formal codification' (p. 36). Our concern with singularization is that, by so totalizing knowledge, and by its active denial of alternatives, it promotes hegemonic power and warrants conduct which would, otherwise, come under scrutiny.

social constructionism: See *constructionism.*

story: See *narrative.*

structuralism: A concern with structures-as-expressed and/or with the inference from expression of underlying and generative form. Thus Piaget exemplifies structuralism in psychology. Otherwise, everything a post-structuralist (q.v.) desires into deconstruction! Note we are not calling Foucault a structuralist.

sympatricity: Originally the competing yet synergistic condition between diverse species in an ecosystem. This term was appropriated from biology by Press (1980) in order to describe the way different discourses may co-exist and compete within a local and contingent cultural ecology of discourses. See Chapter 1 for more detail.

tecton: A technical device describing an aggregate of textuality within and upon which tectonic processes operates, which allows us to 'freeze' textuality in order to concentrate on tectonics. See Chapter 3.

Textuality and Tectonics: You really haven't been paying attention, have you!

thematic decomposition: The alleged *representational labour* (q.v.) of dead authors (as in 'What is Beethoven doing sitting in his grave tearing up manuscripts? Decomposing!'). In T 'n' T, it is a way of doing discourse analysis without admitting it until the Glossary.

tritunic: A confusingly polysemic word, though highly localized in its application. In one meaning it pertains to a form of harmless, guileless, badinage and bonhomie, sometimes alcoholically mediated. In another it has a distinctly more negative tone, as a form of scoffing discourse antagonistic to critical polytextualism. Whether or not it *matters*, of course, is another thing altogether.

trope: Conventionally, an explicit figure of speech, or interpolation. Foucault (1970: 80) defines it as 'the different relations that words may have with the same representative content'. In PoMo-speak, tropes are tropic possibilities, pathways through a text that a reader could re-write themselves (and the text) into following (as with Textuality and Tectonics). Much deconstructive reading depends upon paying very close attention to tropes and highlighting their adherent ambiguity. The oppositional reading style of deconstruction (q.v.) uses these ambiguities to 'wrong foot' the text under consideration taking the reader along a less travelled path through the text, usually to a quite unexpected destination (see XANADU).

truth game: The kind of 'strategy-game' played in social policy with people's lives, where the goal is governmentality (q.v.) and the rules are defined by scientized (q.v.) ad-equations to the truth of human nature. In a very simple sense, for example, the conditions of possibility for being a thief include the existence of a concept of private property. In a more complex and thorough way, it is possible to show how less obvious constructions (such as the 'homosexual' or the 'nymphomaniac') gain currency, usage and reality in a particular discursive and institutional context.

voice: Ideology pervades discourse, particularly that concerned with understanding and conduct, sometimes only subtly, sometimes acting more explicitly as a conceptual frame by which ideas are understood and positioned and actions warranted. For example, heterosexuality is constituted differently under liberal-humanism and feminism, and hence a liberal-humanistic discourse on this topic will take not only a different stance on heterosexuality from that of feminism, but what is salient – indeed what is considered relevant at all – will differ. We have used the term 'voice' to refer to the way ideology is expressed within discourse. See Chapter 4 for a fuller treatment of this notion. In particular we have argued that it is the 'voicing' of ideology (and not causality or the operation of 'natural laws') which provides linkage between, say, understandings of a topic and the prescription or warranting of conduct. This argument is developed more fully in Chapter 9. This concept is also used and discussed extensively in Gleeson 1991.

xanadu: A quite unexpected destination (or a load of Porlocks!).

References

Aakster, C.W. (1986) Concepts in Alternative Medicine, *Social Science and Medicine*, 22(2), 265–73.

Ajzen, I. and Fishbein, M. (1973) Attitudes and normative beliefs as factors influencing behavioural intentions, *Journal of Personality and Social Psychology*, 21(1), 401–15.

Antaki, C. (ed.) (1981) *The Psychology of Ordinary Explanations of Social Behaviour*. Academic Press: London.

Ardries, T. (1975) *The Doomsday Germ*. Panther: St. Albans.

Armon-Jones, C. (1985) Prescription, explication and the social construction of emotion, *Journal for the Theory of Social Behaviour*, 15(1), 1–21.

Ashmore, M. (1985) A question of reflexivity: Writing sociology of scientific knowledge. Unpublished DPhil Thesis, University of York.

Asimov, I. (1960 orig. 1951) *Foundation*. Grafton: London.

Auden, W.H. (1974) Today's 'wonder-world' needs Alice, in R. Phillips (ed.) *Aspects of Alice*. Penguin: Harmondsworth.

Baddeley, A.D. (1992) Is memory all talk? *The Psychologist*, October, 447–8.

Banks, I. (1985) *The Wasp Factory*. Futura: London.

Bannet, E.T. (1993) *Postcultural Theory*. Macmillan: Basingstoke.

Bannister, D. and Fransella, F. (1971) *Inquiring Man: The Theory of Personal Constructs*. Penguin: Harmonsworth.

Barthes, R. (1968) *Elements of Semiology*. Hill and Wang: New York.

Barthes, R. (1972) *Mythologies* (trans. A. Lavers). Jonathan Cape: London.

Barthes, R. (1975) *Roland Barthes by Roland Barthes*. Macmillan: Basingstoke.

Barthes, R. (1979) *A Lover's Discourse: Fragments*. Pan: London.

Barthes, R. (1981) The death of the author (from Image-Music-Text 1977), in J. Caughie (ed.) *Theories of Authorship*. Routledge: London.

Bartlett, F.C. (1932) *Remembering*. Cambridge University Press: Cambridge.

Baruch, D. (1949) *New Ways in Discipline*. New York.

Bass, E. and Davis, L. (1988) *The Courage to Heal: A Guide to Women Survivors of Child Sexual Abuse*. Harper Perennial: New York.

Baudrillard, J. (1983) *Simulations*. Semiotext[e]: New York.

Baumgart, H. (1990) *Jealousy: Experiences and Solutions*. University of Chicago Press: Chicago.

Becker, H.S. (1963) *Outsiders: Studies in the Sociology of Deviance*. Free Press of Glencoe: London.

Berger, P.L. (1966) Identity as a problem in the sociology of knowledge, *European Journal of Sociology*, 7 (Spring), 105.

Berger, P.L. (1982) Secular branches, religious roots, *Society*, 20(1), 64.

Berger, P.L. and Luckmann, T. (1967 orig. 1966) *The Social Construction of Reality*. Penguin: Harmondsworth.

Bhaskar, R. (1978 orig. 1970) *A Realist Theory of Science*. Harvester Wheatsheaf: Hemel Hempstead.

Bhaskar, R. (1979) *The Possibility of Naturalism*. Harvester Wheatsheaf: Hemel Hempstead.

Billig, M., Condor, S., Edwards, D., Gane, M., Middleton, D. and Radley, A. (1988) *Ideological Dilemmas*. Sage: London.

Bourdieu, P. (1992 orig. 1977) *Outline of a Theory of Practice*. Cambridge University Press: Cambridge.

Boyne, R. and Rattansi, A. (eds) (1990) *Postmodernism and Society*. Macmillan: Basingstoke.

Brown, S.R. (1980) *Political Subjectivity: Applications of Q Methodology in Political Science*. Yale University Press: New Haven.

Brown, S.R. (1993) RXe-presenting dysphoria, paper presented to the General Meeting of the European Association of Experimental Social Psychology, Lisbon.

Browne, K., Davies, C. and Stratton, P. (1988) *Early Prediction and Prevention of Child Abuse*. Wiley: London.

Bulwer-Lytton, E.G.E. (1830) Paul Clifford. [see Rice 1984]

Burgoyne, J., Omrod, R. and Richards, M. (1987) *Divorce Matters*. Penguin: Harmondsworth.

Burman, E. (1990) Differing with deconstruction: a feminist critique, in I. Parker and J. Shotter (eds) *Deconstructing Social Psychology*. Routledge: London.

Burman, E. (1992) Developmental psychology and the postmodern child, in J. Doherty, E. Graham and M. Malek (eds) *Postmodernism and the Social Sciences*. Macmillan, Basingstoke.

Buss, A.R. (1979) *A Dialectical Psychology*. Invington: New York.

Butler-Sloss, E. (1988) *Report of the Inquiry into Child Abuse in Cleveland*. HMSO: London.

Cancian, F.M. (1987) *Love in America: Gender and Self-development*. Cambridge University Press: Cambridge.

Carlson, R. (1972) Understanding women: implications for personality theory and research, *Journal of Social Issues*, 28(2), 17–32.

Chesler, P. (1972) *Women and Madness*. Avon: New York.

Child Study Association of America (1926) *Guidance of Childhood and Youth*. CSAA: New York.

Christie, J.R.R. and Orton, F. (1988) Writing a text on the life, *Art History*, 11(4), 545–63.

Cixous, H. (1986) *Entre l'Ecriture*. Editions des Femmes: Paris.

Clanton, G. and Smith, L.G. (eds) (1977) *Jealousy*. Prentice-Hall: Englewood Cliffs, NJ.

Clark, D. and Haldane, D. (1990) *Wedlocked? Intervention and Research in Marriage*. Polity Press: Cambridge.

Cleckley, H. (1964) *The Mask of Insanity*. Mosby: St Louis.

Collin, F. (1985) *Theory and Understanding: A Critique of Interpretive Social Science*. Blackwell: Oxford.

Cosminski, S. (1977) The impact of methods of analysis on illness concepts in a Guatemalian community, *Social Science and Medicine*, 11, 325–32.

Coulter, J. (1979) *The Social Construction of Mind*. Macmillan: London.

Coulthard, M. (1977) *An Introduction to Discourse Analysis*. Longman: London.

Cousins, M. and Hussain, A. (1984) *Michel Foucault*. Macmillan: Basingstoke.

Crawford, R. (1984) A cultural account of 'health': control, release, and the social body, in J.B. McKinlay (ed.) *Issues in the Political Economy of Health Care*. Tavistock: London.

Dale, P., Davies, M., Morrison, T. and Waters, J. (1986) *Dangerous Families*. Tavistock: London.

Daly, M., Wilson, M. and Weghorst, S.G. (1982) Male sexual jealousy, *Ethology and Sociobiology*, 3, 11–27.

Danzinger, K. (1990) *Constructing the Subject*. Cambridge University Press: Cambridge.

Darmon, P. (1985) *Trial by Impotence: Virility and Marriage in Pre-revolutionary France* (trans. P. Keegan). Chatto and Windus: London.

Davies, C. (1975) *Permissive Britain: Social Change in the Sixties and Seventies*. Pitman: London.

Department of Health (1992) *The Health of the Nation: A Strategy for Health in England*. HMSO: London.

De Rosa, A. (1987) The social representation of mental illness in children and adults, in W. Doise and S. Moscovici (eds) *Current Issues in European Social Psychology: Volume Two*. Cambridge University Press: Cambridge.

Deleuze, G. (1986) *The Field: Leibniz and the Baroque*. Les Editions Minuit: Paris.

Deleuze, G. (1990) *Foucault*. University of Minnesota Press: Minneapolis.

deMause, L. (1974) *The History of Childhood*. Psychohistory Press: New York.

Denzin, N.K. (1977) *Childhood Socialisation*. Jossey-Bass: San Francisco.

Denzin, N.K. (1988) Blue Velvet: postmodern contradictions, in M. Featherstone (ed.) *Theory, Culture and Society, Special Issue on Postmodernism*, 5(2&3).

Denzin, N.K. (1989) *Interpretative Interactionism*. Sage: London.

Department of Health (1990) *The Health of the Nation*. HMSO: London.

Derrida, J. (1974) *Of Grammatology*. Johns Hopkins University Press: Baltimore.

Derrida, J. (1974/1986) *Glas* (trans. J.P. Leavey and R. Rand). University of Nebraska Press: Lincoln.

Derrida, J. (1978/1990) *Writing and Difference* (trans. A. Bass). Routledge: London.

Derrida, J. (1982) *Margins of Philosophy*. Harvester: Brighton.

Derrida, J. (1987) *The Post-card: From Socrates to Freud and Beyond*. University of Chicago Press: Chicago.

Derrida, J. (1991 orig. 1987) Ulysses gramophone: hear say yes in Joyce, in P. Kamuf (ed.) *A Derrida Reader: Between the Blinds*. Harvester: Brighton.

Doherty, J., Graham, E. and Malek, M. (eds) (1992) *Postmodernism and the Social Sciences*. Macmillan, Basingstoke.

Dominelli, L. (1989) Betrayal of trust: a feminist analysis of power relationships in incest abuse and its relevance for social work practice, *British Journal of Social Work*, 19(4), 291–308.

Douglas, J.D. and Johnson, J.M. (1977) *Existential Psychology*. Cambridge University Press: New York.

Dunn, N. (1967) *Poor Cow*. MacGibbon and Kee: London.

Eccleston, C. (1993) On the possibility of attentional psychoanalgesia. Unpublished PhD Dissertation, University of Reading.

Eco, U. (1989 orig. 1962) *The Open Work* (trans. A. Cancogni). Hutchinson Radius: London.

Eco, U. (with others) (1992) *Interpretation and Overinterpretation*. Cambridge University Press: Cambridge.

Eddison, E.R. (1926 repr. 1970) *The Worm Ouroboros*. Ballantine: New York.

Edwards, D. and Potter, J. (1992) *Discursive Psychology*. Sage: London.

Ehrenreich, J. (ed.) (1978) *The Cultural Crisis of Medicine*. Monthly Review Press: New York.

Elies i Busqueta, P. (1983) *Nostre Diccionari: Diccionari Il. Lustrat Sopena de la Llengua Catalana*. Editorial Ramon Sopena: Barcelona.

Elliott, M. (1985) *Preventing Child Sexual Assault: A Practical Guide to Talking with Children*. Bedford Square Press: London.

Fairclough, N. (1992) *Discourse and Social Change*. Polity: Cambridge.

Finkelhor, D. (1984) *Child Sexual Abuse: New Theory and Research*. Free Press: New York.

Finkelhor, D., Araji, S., Baron, A., Doyle Peters, S. and Doyle Peters, G.E. (1986) *A Sourcebook on Child Sexual Abuse*. Sage: Beverly Hills, CA.

Fitzgerald, Z. (1932) *Save Me The Waltz*. Charles Scribner's Sons: New York.

Foucault, M. (1969) What is an author? In J.V. Harari (ed.) *Textual Strategies*. Cornell University Press: Ithaca.

Foucault, M. (1970) *The Order of Things*. Tavistock: London.

Foucault, M. (1972) *The Archeology of Knowledge*. Tavistock: London.

Foucault, M. (1979a) *The History of Sexuality, Vol. 1: An Introduction*. Allan Lane: London.

Foucault, M. (1979b) *Discipline and Punish: The Birth of the Prison*. Penguin: Harmondsworth.

Foucault, M. (1979c) Interview with Lucette Finas, in M. Morris. and P. Patton (eds) *Michel Foucault: Power, Truth, Strategy*. Feral: Sydney.

Foucault, M. (1982) The subject and power, in H. Dreyfus and P. Rabinow (eds) *Michel Foucault: Beyond Structuralism and Hermeneutics*. University of Chicago Press: Chicago.

Foucault, M. (1984) What is enlightenment? In P. Rabinow (ed.) *The Foucault Reader*. Penguin: Harmondsworth.

Foucault, M. (1988) Technologies of the self, in L.H. Martin, H. Gutman and P.H. Hutton (eds) *Technologies of the Self*. Tavistock: London.

Fowles, J. (1963) *The Collector*. Jonathan Cape: London.

Fowles, J. (1977) *The Magus* (a revised version). Triad: St Albans.

Frege, G. (1960) *Translations from the Philosophical Writings of Gottlob Frege* (eds P. Geach and M. Black). Blackwell: Oxford.

French, M. (1978) *The Women's Room*. Sphere Books: London.

Freud, A. (1958) Adolescence, *Psychoanalytic Study of the Child*, 13, 255–78.

Gadamer, H.G. (1975) *Truth and Method*. Sheed and Ward: London.

Game, A. (1991) *Undoing the Social: Towards a Deconstructive Sociology*. Open University Press: Milton Keynes.

Garfinkel, H. (1967) *Studies in Ethnomethodology*. Prentice-Hall: Englewood Cliffs, NJ.

Gavey, N. (1992) Technologies and effects of heterosexual coercion, *Feminism and Psychology*, 2(3), 325–52.

Geleerd, E.R. (1961) Some aspects of ego-vicissitudes in adolescents, *Journal of the American Psychoanalytical Association*, 9, 394–405.

Gergen, K.J. (1991) Emerging challenges for theory and psychology, *Theory and Psychology*, (1)1, 13–36.

Gergen, K.J. and Gergen, M.M. (1988) Narrative form and the construction of psychological theory, in T.R. Sarbun (ed.) *The Narrative Perspective in Psychology*. Praeger: New York.

Giami, A. (1986) Les representations du handicap, in G. Bellelli (ed.) *La Representation Sociale de la Maladie Mentale*. EAESP and University of Naples: Naples.

Gilbert, G.N. and Mulkay, M. (1982) Warranting scientific belief, *Social Studies of Science*, 12, 38–48.

Gillis, J.R. (1988) From ritual to romance: towards an alternative history of love, in C.Z. Stearns and P.N. Stearns (eds) *Emotion and Social Change: Toward a New Psychohistory*. Holmes and Meier: New York.

Gilman, S.L. (1982) *Seeing the Insane*. Wiley: New York.

Gilmartin, B. (1977) Jealousy among the swingers, in G. Clanton and L.G. Smith (eds) *Jealousy*. Prentice-Hall: Englewood Cliffs, NJ.

Gilroy, P. (1993) *The Promised Land*. Harvard University Press: Cambridge, MA.

Gleeson, K. (1991) Out of our minds – the deconstruction and reconstruction of madness. Unpublished PhD Thesis, University of Reading.

Gonzalez-Crussi, M. (1988) *On the Nature of Things Erotic*. Picador: London.

Graham, E. (1992) Postmodernism and paradox, in J. Doherty, E. Graham and M. Malek (eds) *Postmodernism and the Social Sciences*. Macmillan: Basingstoke.

Greenwood, J.D. (1992) Realism, empiricism and social constructionism: psychological theory and the social dimensions of mind and action, *Theory and Psychology*, 2(2), 131–53.

Grossberg, L., Nelson, C. and Treichler, P. (eds) (1992) *Cultural Studies*. Routledge: London.

Hack Tuke, D. (1872) *The Influence of the Mind on the Body*. John Churchill: London.

Hale, G. (1993) Deconstructing grief. Postgraduate work in progress, University of Reading.

Haraway, D.J. (1984) Primatology is politics by other means, in R. Bleier (ed.) *Feminist Approaches to Science*. Pergamon: London.

Haraway, D.J. (1991) *Simians, Cyborgs, and Women: The Reinvention of Nature*. Free Association Press: London.

Hardin, G. (1950) The meaninglessness of the word protoplasm, *Scientific Monthly*, 82, 112–20.

Harré, R. (1979) *Social Being: A Theory for Social Psychology*. Blackwell: Oxford.

Harré, R. (1983) *Personal Being*. Blackwell: Oxford.

Harré, R. (ed.) (1986) *The Social Construction of Emotion*. Blackwell: Oxford.

Harré, R. (1992) What is real in psychology: a plea for persons, *Theory and Psychology*, 2(2), 153–9.

Harré, R. and Secord, P.F. (1972) *The Explanation of Social Behaviour*. Blackwell: Oxford.

Harris, T. (1989) *The Silence of the Lambs*. Mandarin: London.

Harvey, D. (1989) *The Condition of Postmodernity*. Blackwell: Oxford.

Hassan, I. (1987) *The Postmodern Turn: Essays in Postmodern Theory and Culture*. Ohio State University Press: Ohio.

Hauck, P. (1981) *Jealousy: Why it Happens and How to Overcome It*. The Westminster Press: Philadelphia.

Heidegger, M. (1962 orig. 1927) *Being and Time*. Blackwell: Oxford.

Heidegger, M. (1971) *Poetry, Language, Thought*. Harper and Row: New York.

Heidegger, M. (1977) The age of the world picture, in *The Question Concerning Technology and Other Essays*. Harper and Row: New York.

Heider, F. (1944) Social perception and phenomenal causality, *Psychological Review*, 51, 358–74.

Henriques, J., Hollway, W., Urwin, C., Venn, C. and Walkerdine, V. (1984) *Changing the Subject: Psychology, Social Regulation and Subjectivity*. Methuen: London.

Herzlich, C. (1973) *Health and Illness*. Academic Press: New York.

Hicks, F. (1993) *How to Avoid Being Sued: The Key to Practical Ethics*. Mount Effort Press: Long Wittenham.

Hochschild, A.R. (1983) *The Managed Heart: Commercialization of Human Feeling*. University of California Press: Berkeley.

Hollway, W. (1989) *Subjectivity and Method in Psychology*. Sage: London.

Hoyles, M. (1979) *Changing Childhood*. Writers and Readers Press: London.

Ibañez (Gracia), T. (1990) *Approximaciones a la Psicologia Social*. Sendai: Barce-lona.

Ibañez, T. (1991) Social psychology and the rhetoric of truth, *Theory and Psychology*, (1)2, 187–202.

Ibañez, T. (1993) Constructing a Representation or Representing a Construction, mimeograph, Universitat Autonoma de Bellaterra: Barcelona.

Ingleby, D. (1985) Professionals as socialisers: the 'psy complex', in A. Scull and S. Spitzer (eds) *Research in Law, Deviance and Social Control: 7*. Jai Press: New York.

Irigaray, L. (1985) *That Sex which is not One*. Cornell University Press: New York.

James, W. (1955) *Pragmatism*. Meridian Books: New York.

Jameson, F. (1984) Post-modernism, or the cultural logic of late-capitalism, *New Left Review*, 146, 79–146.

Jenkins, P. (1992) *Intimate Enemies: Moral Panics in Contemporary Great Britain*. Aldine de Gruyter: New York.

Jervis, M. (1993) First confess to sexual abuse: a man accused of child abuse turned to a private clinic for assessment and to prove his innocence, *Guardian*, 3 February.

Jordanova, L. (1989) Children in history: concepts of nature and society, in G. Scarre (ed.) *Children, Parents and Politics*. Cambridge University Press: Cambridge.

Kamuf, P. (ed.) (1991) *A Derrida Reader: Between the Blinds*. Harvester Wheatsheaf: Hemel Hempstead.

Keller, E.F. (1985) *Reflections on Gender and Science*. Yale University Press: New Haven.

Kelly, G.A. (1955) *The Psychology of Personal Constructs*. Norton: New York.

Kempe, C.H., Silverman, F., Steele, B., Droegmueller, W. and Silver, H.K. (1962) The battered child syndrome, *Journal of the American Medical Association*, 181, 17–24.

Kemper, T.D. (1988) A Manichaean approach to the social construction of emotions, *Cognition and Emotion*, 2(2), 353–65.

Kesey, K. (1962) *One Flew Over the Cuckoo's Nest*. Picador: London.

Kitzinger, C. (1987) *The Social Construction of Lesbianism*. Sage: London.

Kitzinger, J. (1990) Who are you kidding? Children, power and the struggle against sexual abuse, in A. James and A. Prout (eds) *Constructing and Reconstructing Childhood: Contemporary Issues in the Sociological Study of Childhood*. Falmer: London.

Kitzinger, J. (1992) Sexual violence and compulsory sexuality, *Feminism and Psychology*, 2(3), 399–418.

Kitzinger, C., Wilkinson, S. and Perkins, R. (1992) Theorizing heterosexuality, *Feminism and Psychology*, 2(3), 293–324.

Klein, P. (1988) *Psychology Exposed: Or the Emperor's New Clothes*. Routledge: London.

Knorr-Cetina, K. (1991) *The Manufacture of Knowledge*. Pergamon: Oxford.

Kolb, D. (1986) *The Critique of Pre-Modernity: Hegel, Heidegger and After*. University of Chicago Press: Chicago.

Kristeva, J. (1980) *Desire in Language*. Blackwell: Oxford.

Kuhn, T.S. (1970) *The Structure of Scientific Revolutions* (2nd edn). Tavistock: London.

Kvale, S. (1990) Postmodern psychology: a contradictio in adjecto? *The Humanist Psychologist*, 18, 35–55.

Labov, W. (1972) *Sociolinguistic Patterns*. University of Pennsylvania Press: Philadelphia.

Lacan, J. (1977) *Ecrits: A Selection* (trans. A. Sherridan). Tavistock: London.

Lather, P. (1990) Postmodernism and the human sciences, *The Humanistic Psychologist*, 18, 64–81.

Lawson, A. (1988) *Adultery: An Analysis of Love and Betrayal*. Blackwell: Oxford.

Leventhal, H. and Hirshman, R.S. (1982) Social psychology and prevention, in G.S. Sanders and J. Suls (eds) *Social Psychology of Health and Illness*. Earlbaum: Hillside, NJ.

Levi-Strauss, C. (1966) *The Savage Mind*. Weidenfeld and Nicolson: London.

Lewis, C.T. (1923) *An Elementary Latin Dictionary*. Oxford University Press: Oxford.

Litton, I. and Potter, J. (1985) Social representations in the ordinary explanation of a riot, *European Journal of Social Psychology*, 15, 371–88.

Lobsenz, N.M. (1977) Taming the green-eyed monster, in G. Clanton and L.G. Smith (eds) *Jealousy*. Prentice-Hall: Englewood Cliffs, NJ.

Lowe, I. (1991) The search for the engine of change, in F. Gale and I. Lowe, *Changing Australia*. Australian Broadcasting Corporation: Sidney, Australia.

Martinez, W. (1992) Who constructs anthropological knowledge? Towards a theory of ethnographic film spectatorship, in P.I. Crawford and D. Turton (eds) *Film as Ethnography*. Manchester University Press: Manchester.

Marx, K. (1978) Speech at the anniversary of the 'People's Paper', in R.C. Tucker (ed.) *The Marx–Engels Reader*, 2nd edn. Norton: New Jersey.

Mazur, R. (1977) Beyond jealousy and possessiveness, in G. Clanton and L.G. Smith (eds) *Jealousy*. Prentice-Hall: Englewood Cliffs, NJ.

McGuire, W.J. (1986) The vicissitudes of attitudes and similar representational constructs in twentieth century psychology, *European Journal of Social Psychology*, 16, 89–130.

McKinlay, A. and Potter, J. (1987) Social representations: a conceptual critique, *Journal for the Theory of Social Behaviour*, 17, 471–88.

McNamee, S. and Gergen, K.J. (eds) (1992) *Therapy as Social Construction*. Sage: London.

Miller, A. (1986) *Thou Shalt Not be Aware*. Virago: London.

Miller, A. (1987a) *For Your Own Good*. Virago: London.

Miller, A. (1987b) *The Drama of Being a Child*. Virago: London.

Modleski, T. (1982) *Loving with a Vengeance: Mass-produced Fantasies for Women*. Archon: Hamden, CO.

Morss, J.R. (1990) *The Biologising of Childhood*. Lawrence Erlbaum: Brighton.

Mortimer, P. (1962) *The Pumpkin Eater*. Hutchinson: London.

Moscovici, S. (1988) Notes towards a description of social representation, *European Journal of Social Psychology*, 18, 211–50.

Moscovici, S. and Hewstone, M. (1983) Social representations and social explanations: from the 'naive' to the 'amateur' scientist', in M. Hewstone (ed.) *Attribution Theory: Social and Functional Extensions*. Blackwell: Oxford.

Mulkay, M. (1985) *The Word and the World: Explorations in the Form of Sociological Analysis*. George Allen and Unwin: London.

Mulkay, M. (1991) *Sociology of Science: A Sociological Pilgrimage*. Open University Press: Milton Keynes.

Neisser, U. (1992) The psychology of memory and the sociolinguistics of remembering, *The Psychologist*, 5(10), 451–2.

Nelson, S. (1987) *Incest, Fact and Myth*. Stradmullion: Edinburgh.

Nettleton, S. (1992) *Power, Pain and Dentistry*. Open University Press: Buckingham.

Newell, P. (1989) *Children are People Too: The Case Against Physical Punishment*. Bedford Square Press: London.

O'Dell, L. (1993) *The Harm Warrant*. Paper presented to the European Association of Experimental Social Psychology General Meeting, Lisbon.

Open University (1989) *Child Abuse and Neglect: An Introduction*, Course Unit P554. The Open University: Milton Keynes.

Opie, I. and Opie, P. (1955) *The Oxford Nursery Rhyme Book*. Oxford University Press: Oxford.

Orwell, G. (1949) *Nineteen Eighty-Four*. Secker and Warburg: London.

Owens, C. (1993) *Discoursing the self: singlehood and couplehood*. Paper presented to the European Association of Experimental Social Psychology General Meeting, Lisbon.

Papineau, D. (1987) *Reality and Representation*. Blackwell: Oxford.

Parker, I. (1989) *The Crisis in Modern Social Psychology, and How to End It*. Routledge: London.

Parker, I. (1990) The abstraction and representation of social psychology, in I. Parker and J. Shotter (eds) *Deconstructing Social Psychology*. Routledge: London.

Parker, I. (1992a) *Discourse Dynamics*. Routledge: London.

Parker, I. (1992b) Discoursing discourse: social psychology and postmodernity, in J. Doherty, E. Graham and M. Malek (eds) *Postmodernism and the Social Sciences*. Macmillan: Basingstoke.

Parton, N. (1985) *The Politics of Child Abuse*. Macmillan: London.
Parton, N. (1992) *Governing the Family: Child Care, Child Protection and the State*. Macmillan: Basingstoke.
Peirce, C.S. (1934) On selecting hypotheses, in C. Hartsgorn and P. Weiss (eds) *Collected Papers of Charles Sanders Peirce, Volume 5, Pragmatism and Pragmaticism*. Harvard University Press: Cambridge, MA.
Peter, L. (1980) *Quotations for Our Time*. Methuen: London.
Pines, A. and Aronson, E. (1981) Polyfidelity: an alternative lifestyle without jealousy? *Alternative Lifestyles*, 4(3), 373–91.
Potter, J. and Litton, I. (1985) Some problems underlying the theory of social representation, *British Journal of Social Psychology*, 24, 81–90.
Potter, J. and Wetherell, M. (1987) *Discourse and Social Psychology: Beyond Attitudes and Behaviour*. Sage: London.
Potter, J., Wetherell, M., Gill, R. and Edwards, D. (1990) Discourse and noun, verb or social practice? *Philosophical Psychology*, 3, 205–17.
Press, I. (1980) Problems in the definition and classification of medical systems, *Social Science and Medicine*, 14b, 45–57.
Randall, M. (1979) *Journey*. Hamlyn: Feltham.
Reicher, S. (1993) *What is Critical in Critical Psychology?* Paper presented to the European Association of Experimental Social Psychology Small Group Meeting on Critical Social Psychology, Barcelona.
Rhinehart, L. (1972) *The Diceman*. Granada: London.
Rice, S. (1986) *It was a Dark and Stormy Night: The Best (?) from the Bulwer-Lytton Contest*. Abacus: London.
Righton, P. (1980) The adult, in B. Taylor (ed.) *Perspectives on Paedophilia*. Batsford: London.
Rogers, R.S. (R. Stainton Rogers) (1974) A normative approach to attitudes and cognitive consistency. Unpublished PhD Thesis, University of London.
Rorty, R. (1989) *Contingency, Irony and Solidarity*. Cambridge University Press: Cambridge.
Rorty, R. (1992) The pragmatist's progress, in U. Eco (with others), *Interpretation and Overinterpretation*. Cambridge University Press: Cambridge.
Rose, N. (1985) *The Psychological Complex*. Routledge: London.
Rose, N. (1990) *Governing the Soul: The Shaping of the Private Self*. Routledge: London.
Rosen, R.D. (1978) *Psychobabble: Fast Talk and Quick Cure in the Era of Feeling*. Wildwood House: London.
Rosenau, P.M. (1992) *Postmodernism and the Social Sciences: Insights, Inroads and Intrusions*. Princeton University Press: Princeton, NJ.
Ryle, G. (1973 orig. 1949) *The Concept of Mind*. Penguin University Books: Harmondsworth.
Sampson, E.E. (1989) The deconstruction of the self, in J. Shotter and K. Gergen (eds) *Texts of Identity*. Sage: London.
Saraga, E. and Macleod, M. (1991) A feminist reading of recent literature on child sexual abuse, in P. Carter, T. Jeffs and M.K. Smith (eds) *Social Work and Social Welfare Yearbook: 3*. Open University Press: Milton Keynes.
Sarbin, T. (ed.) (1986) *Narrative Psychology: The Storied Nature of Human Conduct*. Praeger: New York.
Sawicki, J. (1991) *Disciplining Foucault: Feminism; Power and the Body*. Routledge: London.
Schofield, M. (1965) *The Sexual Behaviour of Young People*. Longman: London.

Schwichtenberg, C. (1993) *The Madonna Connection: Representational Politics, Subcultural Identities and Cultural Theory*. Westview Press: Colorado.

Semin, G.R. and Rogers, R.S. (Stainton Rogers, R.) (1973) The generation of descriptive-evaluative responses in scale answering behaviour: a model, *European Journal of Social Psychology*, 3(3), 311–28.

Shotter, J. (1984) *Social Accountability and Selfhood*. Blackwell: Oxford.

Shotter, J. (1992) Social constructionism and realism: adequacy or accuracy? *Theory and Psychology*, (2)2, 175–82.

Shotter, J. (1993) *Cultural Politics of Everyday Life*. Buckingham: Open University Press.

Shotter, J. and Gergen, K.J. (eds) (1989) *Texts of Identity*. Sage: London.

Shotter, J. and Parker, I. (1990) (eds) *Deconstructing Social Psychology*. Routledge: London.

Showatter, E. (1985) *The Female Malady: Women, Madness and English Culture, 1830–1880*. Virago: London.

Showatter, E. (1991) *Sexual Anarchy: Gender and Culture at the Fin de Siecle*. Bloomsbury: London.

Shulman, A.K. (ed.) (1979) *Red Emma speaks: The Selected Speeches and Writings of the Anarchist and Feminist Emma Goldman*. The Guildford Press: London.

Silverman, D. (1985) *Qualitative Methodology & Sociology: Describing the Social World*. Gower: Brookfield, VT.

Sokoloff, B. (1948) *Jealousy: A Psychological Study*. Staples Press: London.

Stainton Rogers, W. (1986) *Cultural Representations of 'Addiction': Links and Disjunctions between Perspectives*. Paper given to the Special Theme Meeting of the European Association of Experimental Social Psychology, Lisbon, Portugal.

Stainton Rogers, W. (1987) Accounting for health and illness: a social psychological investigation. Unpublished Doctoral Thesis, The Open University.

Stainton Rogers, W. (1991) *Explaining Health and Illness: An Exploration of Diversity*. Harvester Wheatsheaf: Hemel Hempstead.

Stainton Rogers, W. and Stainton Rogers, R. (1986) *Social Issues and Participant Democracy*. Paper presented to the Second Annual Conference for the Scientific Study of Subjectivity, Missouri, USA.

Stainton Rogers, W. and Stainton Rogers, R. (1989) Taking the child abuse debate apart, in W. Stainton Rogers, D. Hevey and E. Ash (eds) *Child Abuse and Neglect: Facing the Challenge*. Batsford: London.

Stainton Rogers, R. and Stainton Rogers, W. (1990a) What the Brits got out of the Q: and why their work may not line up with the US way of getting into it! *Electronic Journal of Communication/ La revue Electronique de Communication*, Troy: New York. Computer file, access via EMail 'Send ROGERS VIN190' COMSERVE@RPIECS.

Stainton Rogers, R. and Stainton Rogers, W. (1990b) *Radical Social Constructionism: Q-methodology and the Postmodernist Treatment of Beliefs, Values and Ideologies as Cultural Texts*. Paper presented to the Third Europe-Israel Conference on Beliefs, Values and Ideology, The Jacob Blaustein Institute for Desert Research, Mitzpe Ramon, Israel.

Stainton Rogers, R. and Stainton Rogers, W. (1990c) *Social Constructionists as Raconteurs: Reflections on the Telling of Stories*. Paper given to the General Meeting of the European Association of Experimental Social Psychology, Budapest, Hungary.

Stainton Rogers, R. and Stainton Rogers, W. (1992a) *Stories of Childhood: Shifting Agendas of Child Concern*. Harvester Wheatsheaf: Hemel Hempstead.

Stainton Rogers, R. and Stainton Rogers, W. (1992b) *Textuality and Tectonics: Social Psychology, the Millenium and Construction of homo narrans narratur*. Paper presented to the Czecho-Slovak Medium Size meeting of the European Association of Experimental Social Psychology, Smolenice, Slovakia.

Stainton Rogers, W., Stainton Rogers, R., Lowe, I. and Kitzinger, C. (1986) *When Social Issues are Multiplexly Represented: Q-methodology, Social Policy and Participant Democracy*. Paper given to the Special Theme Meeting of the European Association of Experimental Social Psychology, Lisbon, Portugal.

Stearns, C.Z. and Stearns, P.N. (1986) *Anger: The Struggle for Emotional Control in America's History*. University of Chicago Press: Chicago.

Stearns, C.Z. and Stearns, P.N. (1988) *Emotion and Social Change: Toward a New Psychohistory*. Holmes and Meier: New York.

Stearns, P.N. (1989) *Jealousy: The Evolution of an Emotion in American History*. New York University Press: New York.

Stenner, P. (1992) Feeling deconstructed? With particular reference to jealousy. Unpublished PhD Thesis, University of Reading.

Stenner, P. (1993) Discoursing jealousy, in E. Burman and I. Parker (eds) *Discourse Analytic Research: Repertoires and Readings of Texts in Action*. Routledge: London.

Stenner, P. and Eccleston, C. (in press) On the textuality of being: towards an invigorated social constructionism, *Theory and Psychology*.

Stephenson, W. (1935) Technique of factor analysis, *Nature*, 136, 279.

Stephenson, W. (1953) *The Study of Behaviour: Q-technique and its Methodology*. University of Chicago Press: Chicago.

Stephenson, W. (1961) Scientific creed: 1961, *Psychological Record*, 11, 1–26.

Stephenson, W. (1979) Q-methodology and Newton's Fifth Rule, *American Psychologist*, April, 354–7.

Stephenson, W. (1982) Newton's Fifth Rule and Q-methodology: application to self psychology, *Operant Subjectivity*, 5(1), 37–57.

Stephenson, W. (1983) Quantum theory and Q-methodology: fictionalistic and probabilistic theories conjoined, *Psychological Record*, 35, 41–8.

Stephenson, W. (1986) Protoconcursus: the concourse theory of communication, *Operant Subjectivity*, 9(2), 30–72.

Stephenson, W. (1987a) Measurement of self perception: some reflections on the article by Knight, Fredrickson and Martin, *Operant Subjectivity*, 10(4), 125–35.

Stephenson, W. (1987b) William James, Niels Bohr, and complimentarity: IV: Schrodinger's cat, *Psychological Record*, 38, 523–44.

Stephenson, W. (1989) The Quantumization of Psychological Events, *Operant Subjectivity*, 12(1/2), 1–24.

Stevenson, R.L. (1990 orig. 1886) The strange case of Dr Jekyll and Mr Hyde, in J. Calder (ed.) *Doctor Jekyll and Mr Hyde and Other Stories*. Penguin: Harmondsworth.

Taussig, M. (1986) *The Nervous System*. Paper presented to the British Medical Anthropology Society Conference, Cambridge, England.

Thomas, A. (1987) Cultural representations and personal meanings in the social construction of gender: a psychological study. Unpublished PhD Thesis, University of Reading.

Townsend, P. (1969) Foreword, in P. Morris (ed.) *Put Away: A Sociological Study of Institutions for the Mentally Retarded*. Routledge and Kegan Paul: London.

Trivers, R.L. (1972) Parental investment and sexual selection, in B. Campbell (ed.) *Sexual Selection and the Descent of Man: 1871–1971*. Aldine: Chicago.

Vizard, E. and Tranter, M. (1988) Recognition and assessment of child sexual abuse, in A. Bentovim, A. Elton, J. Hildebrand, M. Tranter and E. Vizard (eds) *Child Sexual Abuse within the Family*. Wright: London.

Vollmer, H. (1977) Jealousy in children, in G. Clanton and L.G. Smith (eds) *Jealousy*. Prentice-Hall: Englewood Cliffs, NJ.

Vygotsky, L.S. (1962) *Thought and Language*. MIT Press: Cambridge, MA.

Waddington, C.H. (1977) *Tools for Thought*. Paladin: St Albans.

Walkerdine, V. (1990) *Schoolgirl Fictions*. Verso: London.

Walling, W.H. (1909) *Sexology*. Puritan(sic): Philadephia.

Wallston, K.A. and Wallston, B.S. (1981) Health locus of control scales, in H.M. Lefcourt (ed.) *Research with the Locus of Control Scale, Vol. 1: Assessment Methods*. Academic Press: New York.

Warner, N. (1992) *Choosing with Care*. HMSO: London.

Warren, C.A.B. (1987) *Madwives – Schizophrenic Women in the 1950's*. Rutgers University Press: New York and London.

Weldon, F. (1971) *Down Among the Women*. Penguin: Harmondsworth.

Wetherell, M. (1991) *Romantic Discourse: Analysing Investment, Power and Desire*. Paper presented at the Fourth International Conference on Language and Social Psychology, University of California, Santa Barbara, CA.

Wetherell, M. and Potter, J. (1992) *Mapping the Language of Racism*. Harvester Wheatsheaf: Hemel Hempstead.

White, G.L. and Mullen, P.E. (1989) *Jealousy: Theory, Research and Clinical Strategies*. The Guildford Press: London.

Wilkinson, S. (ed.) (1986) *Feminist Social Psychology: Developing Theory and Practice*. Open University Press: Milton Keynes.

Wilson, E.O. (1975) *Sociobiology*. Harvard University Press: Cambridge, MA.

Wittgenstein, L. (1953) *Philosophical Investigations*. Blackwell: Oxford.

Wittgenstein, L. (1958) *Philosophical Investigations*, 2nd edn (ed. G.E.M. Anscombe and trans. G.E.M. Anscombe and R. Rhees). Blackwell: Oxford.

Wittgenstein, L. (1961) *Tractatus Logico-philosophicus*. Routledge: London.

Wittgenstein, L. (1965) *The Blue and Brown Books*. Harper and Row: New York.

Wittgenstein, L. (1980) *Remarks on the Philosophy of Psychology, Vol. 1* (eds G.E.M. Anscombe and G.H. Von Wright and trans. G.E.M. Anscombe). Blackwell: Oxford.

Wittgenstein, L. (1981) *Zettel*, 2nd edn (ed. G.E.M. Anscombe and trans. G.E.M. Anscombe and G.H. Von Wright). Blackwell: Oxford.

Woolgar, S. (1988a) *Science: The Very Idea*. Ellis Horwood: Chichester.

Woolgar, S. (ed.) (1988b) *Knowledge and Reflexivity: New Frontiers in the Sociology of Knowledge*. Sage: London.

Worrell, M. and Stainton Rogers, W. (1992) *Child Concern: Discourse of Predation, Protection and Paternalism*. Proceedings of the International Excellence in Training Conference, University of Dundee.

Young, A. (1980) The discourse on stress and the reproduction of conventional knowledge, *Social Science and Medicine*, 14b, 133–46.

Zola, I. (1972) Medicine and an institution of social control, *Sociological Review*, 20, 487–504.

Index